IN THE
ENEMY'S
HOUSE

Also by Howard Blum

902821415 1

Please return/renew this item by the last date shown.
Items may also be renewed by the internet*

https://library.eastriding.gov.uk

* Please note a PIN will be required to access this service
- this can be obtained from your library

IN THE
ENEMY'S
HOUSE

*The Greatest Secret
of the Cold War*

HOWARD
BLUM

AMBERLEY

First published 2018

Amberley Publishing
The Hill, Stroud
Gloucestershire, GL5 4EP

www.amberley-books.com

Copyright © Howard Blum, 2018

The right of Howard Blum to be identified as
the Authors of this work has been asserted in
accordance with the Copyrights, Designs and
Patents Act 1988.

ISBN 978 1 4456 8382 9 (hardback)
ISBN 978 1 4456 8383 6 (ebook)

British Library Cataloguing in Publication Data.
A catalogue record for this book is available
from the British Library.

Designed by Fritz Metsch.
Printed in the UK.

I stood in the vestibule of the enemy's house, having entered by stealth. . . . I had no idea where the corridors in the KGB's edifice would take us, or what we would find when we reached the end of the search—but the keys were ours, and we were determined to use them.

—FBI Counterintelligence Supervisor Bob Lamphere

Naught's had, all's spent,
Where our desire is got without content.
'Tis safer to be that which we destroy
Than by destruction dwell in doubtful joy.
—William Shakespeare, *Macbeth*

Contents

A Note to the Reader

The main foreign intelligence arm of the Russian state has been reorganized and renamed several times throughout its history. For the sake of clarity and convenience, it is called the KGB in this account. That was the organization's final name before the collapse of the Soviet Union in 1991.

PROLOGUE:

"The Storks Fly Away"

BOB LAMPHERE STARED AT THE phone, waiting, willing it to ring. It was the tail end of the afternoon on a perfect late spring day—June 19, 1953—in Washington, D.C., the time of day when Bob liked to have a restorative scotch and soda. Instead, Bob, usually so rock steady, calm even in crisis to the point of detachment, found himself in the fifth-floor office of his boss, the assistant director of the FBI, anxiously staring at the phone. Waiting.

If there was one thing Bob should have learned in his twelve years as an FBI agent, in all the long days and longer nights he'd spent on espionage cases, it was how to wait. He had sat in parked cars until his legs grew stiff, stood with stolid discipline under leaky awnings in the teeming rain, huddled down low in his seat in the back of movie theaters. "Physical surveillance," the Bureau manual insisted, was an essential skill for fieldwork. Any agent, especially one like Bob who had risen to the rank of supervisor in the Intelligence Division, either learned patience or went looking for another job. But there had never been a wait like this.

Bob tried telling himself he had done what he could. He had written—damn the consequences!—a blunt memo to J. Edgar Hoover stating that the facts of the case were clear: at the very least the wife did not deserve her sentence. She should not be executed. And the director, in a response that filled Bob with both surprise and a measure of respect, swiftly put this argument into a letter that he signed with his looping schoolboy cursive and had hand-delivered to the judge.

The judge, however, would not be persuaded. He was adamant. If the prisoners did not cooperate, the sentence would be enforced just before nightfall.

Now all Bob could do was stare at the phone. It was a direct line to the death house in Sing Sing prison. Al Belmont, the hard-edged, by-the-book assistant director of the FBI's Domestic Intelligence Division, whom Bob had known since their quarrelsome days years ago working in the New York field office, was in charge of the command post. In Belmont's suit jacket pocket he had a typed list of questions that Bob, in a wishful burst of optimism, had helped prepare; two stenographers were on call in an adjacent room. And farther down a long, dimly lit prison corridor, behind a steel door with the word "Silence" above the lintel, was the electric chair.

There would be two reasons for the phone to ring in the fifth-floor office in the Justice Department Building in Washington. Either the two prisoners had finally agreed to provide "pertinent information." Or they would have received three jolts of electricity—2,000 volts for three seconds, dropping to 500 volts for fifty-seven seconds so as not to cook the flesh; another 2,000 volts, steadying to 500 volts; and a final 2,000-volt surge—and were now dead.

The office grew crowded, and Bob knew all the newcomers; he had done some things, been in some difficult places, with a few of them. But Bob was in no mood for reminiscing. He remained quiet, aloof, locked in his own tight circle of dread.

After a while, Bob's eyes wandered absently about the room. Heavy blue curtains framed a double window, and when he looked out he saw that long, gray shadows were starting to stretch across the courtyard below: the sun was setting. And all at once his blood ran cold.

———

AT ABOUT THE SAME TIME, a half-hour's drive into suburban Virginia from downtown Washington, Meredith Gardner, Bob's unlikely collaborator and, no less improbably, good friend, was suffering his own pangs of guilt.

The evening in the modest one-story ranch that sat in the cul-de-sac off Old Dominion Drive had been, at least at first, routine. Meredith had been determined to push from his mind the grim events unfolding in Sing Sing prison—and the role he had covertly played in this drama. Restraint was natural to his demeanor, just as it was a necessity in his secret life.

And so, as usual on Friday night, there had been a family dinner; Blanche, a Phi Beta Kappa graduate of Mount Holyoke who had done her own hush-hush government work during the war, cooked for her husband and the two children. After the table was cleared and the children had gone off to play, Meredith, his tie still knotted tightly, a glass of sweet sherry within reach on the end table, sat in the living room with his wife. They were at opposite corners of the room, each in identical wing chairs covered in an identical floral print, each with a book in their hands. What were they reading? It could have been—almost literally—anything. The family library was both obscure and eclectic. A Slovak grammar primer, a Spanish-language history of Turkey, an analysis of slavery in the Bible, a Chinese–Russian dictionary—all were well thumbed. Books crowded the small house like wild, entangling vines. Volumes spilled out from a pair of tall, mahogany-stained bookshelves, cluttered tabletops, and were stacked in knee-high piles on the floor so that walking from one room to the next was as difficult as navigating a maze. Meredith relished this evening ritual, this period of quiet community with his wife; and tonight it was a refuge that was deeply needed.

Then suddenly the lights in the house went out. And in that same moment, their eight-year-old son, Arthur, let out a hair-raising howl.

Meredith hurried into the children's room. He found his frightened son with his thumb wedged into the wall socket, and Ann, their four-year-old daughter, sitting complacently in the electric chair. Or that was how a teary Arthur, after his finger, albeit without most of the nail, was carefully extricated from the socket, identified the contraption in which he had placed his little sister.

A good deal of planning had clearly gone into building the device. Arthur had taken the child's car seat from the family Studebaker, wrapped the frame with a pair of wires connected to the transmitter that powered his electric trains, and then attempted to complete the electrical circuit by inserting the wires into the socket. He'd imagined a burst of electricity surging up through the car seat and giving his sister a mean tickle. Instead, he'd managed to short all the fuses in the basement fuse box, and given himself the shock of his life.

Once he'd gotten the lights back on, and was certain that neither of his children was seriously injured, Meredith confronted his son.

"What in heaven's name were you thinking?" he demanded. "Why of all things would you want to build an electric chair?" Meredith's voice was, as always, soft, measured, precise. Yet there was a telltale clue to his mood: when he was angry, a Southern twang, the vestige of a childhood in Mississippi and Texas, would become more pronounced. At this moment, the lilt was unmistakable.

"Poppa, I heard you and Momma talking. I wanted to see what it was," the boy said. He went on hurriedly, desperate to be exonerated: "I was playing. It was a game. I didn't want to hurt Ann."

Meredith stared at Arthur, but did not respond. It was as if his mind had abruptly wandered off, and now his distracted silence filled the room. At last he kissed his son gently on the top of the head and walked off.

Only years later would he explain to his son a bit about what he'd been thinking then. That he, too, had been caught up in what had started as a game. An intellectual challenge, a rigorous test of wits even more daunting than any of the *London Times* crossword puzzles he so relished. He had never considered the consequences. He had never imagined his actions, the deductions that had previously filled him with pride, the long chase, that any of this could result in two gruesome deaths, could leave two young boys orphaned.

After Arthur was in his pajamas, when it was time to say good night, the boy went looking for his father. He found him sitting on the wooden picnic bench in the backyard, alone, apparently lost in thought, with the darkness of the late-June evening closing in.

FAR OFF, ACROSS THE WORLD, it was a predawn morning in the weathered yellow-brick building on Lubyanka Square in Moscow. Inside the KGB headquarters—or Moscow Center, as the spy fortress was known—Alexander Feklisov sat in the First Directorate staff office. He had arrived after midnight. Sleep had proved impossible; he could not push what was happening in America from his mind. He had tried to leave the apartment on Pestschanaya Street without awakening his wife, but it was difficult to move about in the cramped space and not make noise. Still, Zina did not ask him where he was going, or why. She was used to the eccentric hours of his profession.

Now he sat in the large room with its pale-green walls, a space corridors away from his own small office in the British Section, waiting for the clock to strike three a.m., the shortwave radio already tuned for the hourly update broadcast by the BBC World News Service. Like the two Americans, men he had never met but whose files he'd carefully read, he continued to hope against all reason that there would be a last-minute reprieve.

As the top of the hour relentlessly approached, as he, too, struggled to come to terms with a somber, looming fear, the tense events gave a dangerous edge to his memory. A long-forgotten evening intruded. And he found himself recalling the last time he had seen his agent, the friend he called "Libi."

It had been in a Hungarian restaurant, the Golden Fiddle, on the

West Side of Manhattan. Feklisov—Sasha to his comrades in the spy trade—had chosen the restaurant after considerable deliberation. It was a comfortable place with white tablecloths and heavy flatware, and served a hearty, spicy goulash they could wash down with carafes of an inexpensive yet pleasant Portuguese red; and, good *konspiratsya*, a small orchestra played gypsy music so they'd be able to talk freely without fear of being overheard. It would be, he'd decided, the perfect setting.

Sasha waited until the meal was done and the waiter had removed the empty dinner plates. "I have to give you some news," he said softly, leaning across the table. "I'm about to leave New York in a very short time. I'm going back home."

Libi seemed unnerved by the announcement. "What do you mean?" he asked after a moment. "You're leaving me? Why?"

"You know the normal stay abroad is three to four years. I have been here for five and a half years."

"So?"

"So, if I stay too much longer *you-know-who* might start getting suspicious."

"You're sure you can't stay longer?"

"It's not my call," Sasha said, as if making an apology.

Handlers are taught to instill confidence in their agents, to be father, mentor, confessor all in one; how else can they persuade them to take such chances, to put themselves in such danger? But that evening, Sasha couldn't help feeling that Libi, now that the news had been shared, was trying to reassure *him*. That was why when the orchestra had stopped playing, Libi had risen from the table, approached the bald violinist with the gaunt, chiseled cheekbones, and, after pressing some cash into his hand, told him what he wanted to hear.

The musician came to the table and fell into a slow, melancholic tune.

"You know what that song was?" Libi had asked when he'd finished. "A Hungarian song called 'The Storks Fly Away.'"

At the time, Sasha had been touched. He thought his agent was telling him that change is inevitable, yet life goes on. The ring of spies, these heroes of Mother Russia, will continue, will endure, just as one season inevitably follows another, just as the storks fly away, only to return.

But sitting safely in Moscow Center, Sasha could not help but be branded by his own self-deception. He had not understood at all what Libi, full of stoic resignation, had been telling him. Only now he did. At this unsettled hour, there was no disguising the reality. He had flown away, and he, and the Center, had left Libi, had left all of them, on their own, with no chance of escape. And all he could offer in return for their courage and sacrifice was his remorse.

THEY WAITED. AND AS THEY continued their solitary vigils, as the announcement from Sing Sing prison pushed closer and closer, the three men shared a common predicament. They had all served as soldiers in a secret war that had done nothing less than change world history. They had all believed in the righteousness of their cause, in the excesses of their enemy. They had all paid high prices, but never considered it a sacrifice. Yet at this moment, with every tick of the clock pounding in their heads like a hammer on an anvil, each of them could not help feeling he had done something unforgivable, something that had deeply violated his own sense of honor.

How had it come to this?

Part I

The Blue Problem

1

THE INCIDENT IN CHINATOWN CHANGED everything for Bob Lamphere. Without warning, it had come down in an instant to this: gun drawn, an angry crowd pressing in on him, and his target fixed in his sights. A volley of enraged, keening voices rose up behind him, but Bob pushed all the noise out of his mind. His focus narrowed. And his finger increased its pressure on the steel trigger. He was ready—his mind set—to fire.

Until that moment in the winter of 1944, Bob had been convinced that the FBI didn't offer him what he wanted from the world. Its sensibility grated, with all those rigid regulations (a towrope missing from a government tugboat generated as much paperwork as a murder investigation, he complained), with the powerful insistence on an even more intrusive personal conformity (the required snap-brim hats and starched white shirts, the regulation Bureau briefcase). This wasn't for him. He'd put in another year or two, he thought, until the war ended, and then there'd be plenty of opportunities for an ambitious young man with a law degree. And as he knew only too well, the Bureau, for that matter, was disenchanted with him. Hoover favored "straight arrows," and Bob was having a hard time playing that role. There'd be no protests when he moved on. His departure would be dismissed, if anything was said at all, as part of the normal attrition.

IT HADN'T ALWAYS BEEN LIKE that. When Bob, just twenty-three, had joined the FBI back in September 1941, he'd been gung ho, energized by the wistful notion that once his probationary period was over he'd be in the front line of an elite group of derring-do lawmen, continuing in the great tradition of the tommy gun–toting G-men who'd relentlessly chased down John Dillinger. Fawning newspaper reports regularly proclaimed that the FBI were the best that law enforcement had to offer, and Bob, who had no small sense of pride, was certain that was where he belonged.

And, another vanity, he was confident he looked the part: square-jawed, broad-shouldered, thick black hair with a precise part, and, not least, deep brown eyes that would routinely hold a person with a gaze as steady as a marksman's. He wasn't a big man, maybe a tad over five-foot-ten if he made an effort to stand erect, a trim welterweight, but he had a presence. Handsome in an even-featured all-American way, a man's man, someone you just knew at a glance had grown up fishing in mountain streams and hunting deer in deep woods.

Yet while that was true, Bob nevertheless hadn't had much of a childhood. He'd been raised in Mullan, Idaho, a small hardscrabble mining town plunked down in a high canyon overshadowed by the formidable Coeur d'Alene Mountains. His father, a no-nonsense disciplinarian with a quick temper, was what people in those parts knew as a "leaser." The way Joe Lamphere had it figured, it made more sense to lease a mine and hire hands to work for him than to have to answer to some know-it-all mine owner. Besides, each time he'd signed on for work in one of the big silver mines, it was never long before he went off on a tear about one thing or another to the shift boss. The man in charge would respond by muttering something dismissive and often crude, Joe would let loose with an angry punch, and the next thing Joe knew, he'd be given his walking papers. Running things himself, then, made a lot more sense, although the economics of it were often precarious.

In contrast to her husband's fitful rages, Lilly Lamphere was a preternaturally calm, almost taciturn presence, as seemingly bland and unassuming as the flat Minnesota country near the banks of

the Leaf River where she'd been raised. Or, perhaps, as some relatives speculated, her seeming withdrawal from family life, if not the
world, was simply a defense against Joe's pugnacious bluster. When
she wasn't cooking, she'd be deep into some book; she had run the
post office in quiet Trout Lake, Minnesota (there were more fish in
the lake than people in the town, the locals were fond of saying),
for several years when they'd first been married, and had taken to
spending the vacant hours escaping into whatever book she could
find. Lilly had a fondness for Jane Austen, but the Bible was her
favorite; you could turn to any page and learn something, she liked
to say.

With his two incompatible parents locked into their own disparate worlds, Bob grew up as the overlooked middle child. The way
he remembered it, he was pretty much always on his own. Which
suited him fine. There was nothing he liked better than heading up
into the hills, wandering about on the ridgeline with his .22 rifle
and his mongrel hunting dog, "out of sight of people from dawn to
dusk."

Still, Bob was both of his parents' son. He had his dad's temper, all
right. He got into his share of fights at school; the immigrant Finnish
miners' sons in Mullan saw him as an outsider, and even though he
was outnumbered he wouldn't take their guff. It was rough going for
a while. But after he took some boxing lessons, putting in strenuous
hours on the heavy bag and sparring nearly to the point of utter ex-
haustion day after day in the ring, he was able to give as good as he
got.

It was a rough-and-tumble skill that came in handy when he was
older and worked summers in his father's mine. His father made it a
point that Bob should pull the worst jobs, sticking him deep in the
hole so nobody could say that Joe Lamphere was playing favorites.
Nevertheless, there were always a few ornery miners who'd try to
give the boss's son a hard time, and Bob would invariably only take so
much before he'd call them on it. Fists would fly, and at the end, more
often than not, he'd be the one left standing.

From his mother, Bob had inherited a love of reading. History, particularly books about the Civil War, kept him occupied as he lay in bed before falling off to sleep. And the more he read, the more Bob came to realize that books, an education, could be his path out of a life in the mines. He'd spent too many summers twisting the sweat out of his socks each night after climbing up from the dark, suffocatingly hot hole not to want something else for himself. So he set his sights on getting into college—Bob liked to challenge himself—and he did well enough in high school to be accepted into the University of Idaho's accelerated law program: in five years, he'd earn both his law and his bachelor's degree.

But then in 1940, out of the blue, his mother took sick and, as if in an instant, she was gone. And now Bob could see no reason for sticking around in Idaho. The way he rationalized things, his father, who had grown sickly over the last few years, wouldn't last long without his wife; it would be a kindness if Bob spared his old man the burden of financing his final year of law school. Bob would enroll somewhere else, find himself a job, and pay his own tuition. Yet even bolstered by all this comforting, altruistic logic, part of him knew he was just ready to get out of Idaho. He was eager to put some distance between all he'd endured while growing up and his future.

Bob wound up in Washington, D.C., a quaintly genteel Southern city in the early 1940s that nevertheless seemed a cosmopolitan world away from the isolated northern Idaho hill country. He found a clerk's job in the Treasury Department, a menial, entry-level bit of paper pushing. But it paid him enough to cover the tuition for night classes at National Law School, and while his nine-to-five workday was set in stone, the job was undemanding, so he could find time to study, too.

His days and nights were full. Bob, in fact, was too busy to return to Mullan for his father's funeral—and, anyway, his father, knowing his time was running out, had written to tell his son not to interrupt his studies for his sake when the time inevitably came. In 1941, Bob not only got his degree, but, without the help of a cram course, passed the D.C. bar on his first try.

And now Bob began to think seriously about what he'd do next. He set off brimming with confidence; the world of government, as he envisioned it, was his oyster. After all, the New Deal had lavishly expanded the federal bureaucracy; there had to be plenty of jobs available for a young lawyer. Yet once he began knocking on doors throughout official Washington, Bob quickly began to understand that a law degree was one thing, and connections—political, school, and family—were another. And a lot more valuable.

But as fate would have it, just as he was wondering if it might make sense to return to Idaho, where people at least knew the Lampheres, one of his professors happened to mention that the FBI had sent word to the law schools in the district: the Bureau was looking for candidates.

"THIS APPLICANT PRESENTS A FAIR appearance and during the interview he was chewing about four sticks of gum. He is timid in approach and his personality is leaning toward the negative side. . . . The recommendation is unfavorable."

That was how the Bureau's initial interviewer sized Bob up. But from Bob's perspective (or so he'd suggest years later, when all his subsequent success went a long way toward invalidating this dismal appraisal), Mr. Wilcox, with typical Bureau rigidity, had just been trying to shove him into a box where he'd never fit. Where the FBI saw timidity, Bob saw a quiet confidence; he didn't feel any need to bang any drums on his own behalf. As for his "negative personality," Bob put that down to his tendency to weigh both sides of any proposition. And as for his chewing gum, well, Bob would concede, with a mature embarrassment, that you could take the boy out of Idaho, but you couldn't take Idaho out of the boy. Yes, he'd later acknowledge, at twenty-three he still had to get used to big city ways.

Yet someone in the Bureau must have had some appreciation of Bob's qualities, because, despite the interviewer's grumpy evaluation, on September 16, 1941, he received a letter signed by J. Edgar Hoover: "You are hereby offered an appointment as a Special Agent in the Federal Bureau of Investigation, United States Department of Justice, in grade CAF 9, with salary at the rate of $3200 per annum."

THERE WERE FIFTY FLEDGLING G-MEN in Bob's class at Quantico, the Marine base in Virginia where the FBI had its training center. He was the youngest, and yet he was, he'd acknowledge with a contrarian's pride, "more than a bit brash" when thrown into the competitive instructional exercises. It was, as he recalled, a group cut pretty much from the same calico cloth: small-town boys mostly from the Midwest, white, Protestant, and, like their revered Director Hoover, staunch patriots and no less staunch political conservatives.

And their timing in joining the Bureau, they congratulated one another, pumped with their newfound camaraderie, was propitious. They had signed on at a great moment in history, the winds of war and unrest blowing across the globe. Nazism, fascism, communism—these hostile "isms" were the new enemies that would replace the John Dillingers. Heroes-in-the-making, they were, to a man, eager to join the fight against the insidious forces determined to infiltrate and subvert America.

But before they could be dispatched into this seething, complicated new world, they had to be trained for the task. It was a demanding process. Classes were from nine a.m. to nine p.m., Monday through Saturday, with just a half-day on Sunday as a grudging concession to the Sabbath. They shot .38 pistols and tommy guns until they could routinely cluster their shots in the center of the target, flipped their opponents onto gym mats with exotic jujitsu moves, lifted fingerprints off the most unpromising surfaces, learned how to testify in a clear, concise English in the courtroom, and made sure to say "Yes sir" and "No sir" to practically everyone they encountered.

And throughout the whole grueling process, two articles of faith, two inviolable tenets, were constantly drummed in. One: you'd better not screw up. If you displeased a superior, or, heaven help you, Mr. Hoover, your career would be over in an ignominious instant. (There was no civil service protection, and, as a consequence, there were no second chances. There was only the director's iron prerogative.) And, two: the FBI was the best of the best, and you were expected to be better than all other lawmen, in every category. Nothing less would be tolerated.

Yet all the training, all the indoctrination, only made the waiting all the harder. When the sixteen weeks were finally over, after Bob had passed the final exam and had been given his credentials, his gold badge, and his .38, he rejoiced. At last, his great, new, important adventure was about to begin.

2

BOB, THE STERN-JAWED NEOPHYTE AGENT, was sent in the early days of the anxious wartime winter of 1942 to the Washington field office. It was a time when the home front remained on edge, still unnerved by the surprise attack on Pearl Harbor and wondering what might come next. While across the Atlantic, the war in Europe was shaping up to be a long, no-holds-barred brawl, with the prospects for victory seeming more and more beyond the Allies' grasp. Bob was eager to do his part.

Straight off, he was apprenticed, as he was promisingly informed, to "an experienced agent." Yet what were his mentor's experiences? As far as Bob could tell, he had measured out his years in the Bureau filling out forms and obeying countless regulations, and now he'd been designated to pass on this dull knowledge to his protégé.

It was a grim apprenticeship. Bob learned how to sign in and out of the office each day with an automaton's precision, to make sure there was always a Number 3 card on file to show what case he was working on at the moment, to fill out the 302s detailing his daily progress on any investigation, to update each month the serial numbers of any firearms he owned, and on and bureaucratically on.

Worse, the constant monitoring, the lack of independence, let alone the lack of trust, were not just gnawing but, Bob felt, offensive. Coffee breaks—a telling example—were prohibited; in this draconian world, they were viewed as nothing less than fraud, the theft of government time. If you had knowledge that one of your fellow field agents was breaking even the most minor of rules, you were duty bound to report him (yet those who did were branded with the epithet of "submarine"—i.e., they attacked with stealth—by their more laissez-faire colleagues). If you were not at home and reachable at the phone number on file, the Bureau required you to call in every two hours. Even the unexpected good fortune of spending a night at a girlfriend's house was no excuse; you still had better call to leave the number with the office before settling in. And don't even think you could get away with an evening off the leash: the Bureau would randomly telephone an agent's home, checking to see if he was in—and woe be it the next day to the man who had been negligent enough to go off without leaving a contact number.

Bob loathed all these stringent rules, and the more he felt squeezed by them, the more he wanted to rebel. Taking orders was one thing, but this was tedious and demeaning. The Bureau, he felt, was constantly looking over his shoulder, monitoring his every move. By both instinct and disposition, he was still the free spirit whose greatest pleasure was wandering off into the hills. He didn't need a watchdog. He was beginning to wonder if he had made a disastrous mistake.

BOB WAS QUIETLY SUFFERING THROUGH this raw, uneasy mood when his first field assignment came in. He was ordered to Birmingham, Alabama; the Bureau deliberately threw novice agents into waters far from where they'd been raised and then observed with cool detachment if they sank or swam.

Bob swam. Away from headquarters and Hoover's looming tyrannical presence, life as an FBI agent was a lot closer, he happily discovered, to what he had once imagined it might be. There were still the petty regulations, the daunting mountains of paperwork, and the puritanical restrictions on personal conduct and dress, but there was also the chance to be a cop working for the best team in the country.

The special agent in charge (SAC) of the office took careful measure of Bob, apparently liked what he saw in this gruff, strapping, quietly confident young man, and then turned him loose to work on an eclectic slew of wartime cases. There was Bob, joining in a raid on a series of brothels adjacent to an army base in Tennessee, checking into whether a death at a defense plant in Huntsville might be a murder (it wasn't), and looking into suspected sabotage at coastal dockyards.

While in the process, going around the South, flashing his gold badge and Bureau credentials, he experienced something that was as gratifying as it was unexpected: despite his youth, people instinctively respected him. It was a time, he would recall, when "the FBI agent was a king." And Bob, although new to the throne, quickly took to all its trappings. He enjoyed the prestige his Bureau employment conferred.

For Bob, the South was a friendly, hospitable place. People were always going out of their way to invite a new agent to dinner, buy him a beer, or simply introduce themselves and ask if there was anything they could do to make his time in Birmingham more comfortable.

Not least of the perks, Bob, who always had a mischievous eye for the ladies, encountered a bevy of agreeable young women as he traveled across the South. But he couldn't help finding their manner too restrained, too genteel. He liked a woman "who knew how to laugh," he'd say with a sly grin.

For Bob, this was no casual metaphor. Rather, it was a very specific desire. One woman's throaty, naughty laugh had captured Bob's heart and continued to echo evocatively in his memory. He had met Geraldine Elder—everyone called her Geri—at a frat party back when he had been attending the University of Idaho. But Geri was not your typical coed. She had been raised largely by her maternal grandmother, a beaver trapper, on a remote Wyoming ranch. When her grandmother died, her father, an itinerant barber, took over her upbringing, and she traveled with him across the Pacific Northwest. Yet despite this vagabond childhood, a life where making ends meet was always a tense challenge, Geri had managed not only to go to school but to excel. Her elementary school teachers, who skipped her one grade, and then, still impressed by her abilities, another for good measure, judged her the smartest girl in the class. And with a pert, aquiline nose, fierce blue eyes, and a smile as wide, bright, and fresh as the great outdoors of her childhood, she was, it was generally conceded, darn near the prettiest, too.

By the time Bob first saw her across the room at the frat party, Geri had already made up her mind to quit college. She was determined to learn how to fly, and soon took a bookkeeping job to pay for the lessons. She was a natural pilot, with a steady hand on the stick and a soul full of daring. Nearly three years later, when Bob, after a deluge of ardent letters and long-distance phone calls, had convinced her to marry him and move across the country to live in Alabama, Geri had established a reputation as one of the few pilots in Idaho who'd ferry smoke jumpers into the very heart of a blazing forest.

The wedding took place in March 1942, in Birmingham, just the two of them and a preacher, and it wasn't long before both newlyweds realized they'd made a colossal mistake. What they admired in each other—the certitude, the determination, the uncompromising ambition—were rock-hard qualities that collided time after time in the petty course of married life. They were, it was growing painfully clear, too alike to be comfortable sharing a future together.

Then, three rocky months after the wedding, the Bureau intervened to make an already deteriorating situation much worse. Bob was transferred to New York.

THE BIG CITY WAS A world away from the Big Sky Country where they'd been raised. Nothing was familiar, nothing offered a sense of peace or safety. Thirty years later, Bob still fiercely held "a small town person's distaste" for the "raucous, frantic, ultramodern" tempo of

New York. For Geri, who in her previous life had literally piloted her small plane into the eye of an inferno, "to step off a curb and into traffic was an adventure." They found a claustrophobic three-room apartment in Jackson Heights, Queens, and no sooner had they moved in than they both were looking for a way out.

Thanks to the war, Geri found it first. She volunteered for the Women's Flying Training Detachment and was quickly accepted into the first class of women aviators. In November, she eagerly hightailed it to Houston for training. She never came back to New York, or, for that matter, to Bob. (In fact, after her much-decorated service in the war, Geri, along with her new husband, ran, for decades, a bush pilot service that crisscrossed Alaska.)

Bob, fearful of portraying himself as rash, waited what he hoped was a sufficiently decorous four months before informing the Bureau of the change in his marital status. In March 1943, he wrote Inspector Acers, his superior in the New York field office: "An agreement has been reached between the writer and his wife that they are to remain separated, and a divorce is contemplated. . . . Both the writer and his wife believe this is desirable in view of the fact that the marriage has not been happy or successful." But he took care to reassure the inspector that "the marital difficulty is not the outgrowth of any quarrel, and there has been no infidelity, or anything of that nature."

Inspector Acers, however, was not placated. He dashed off a censorious note to the director, insisting that Bob's glib explanation of his impending divorce was "illogical." And Hoover, now also chagrined, in turn notified the SAC of the New York office to "closely observe the work of Agent Lamphere and submit a special efficiency rating on him."

Although there were raised eyebrows in the Bureau, for Bob, being a bachelor again was liberating. He got out of the stifling Queens apartment, found a room for forty-five dollars a month in a hotel off Gramercy Park in Manhattan, and, as he happily recalled, "footloose, I began to enjoy the city's distractions." He discovered the smoked-filled, late-night glamour of nightclubs: Café Society and the Astor Roof were his frequent haunts. And in wartime New York, a city whose young men had gone off in droves to fight the Nazis, Bob encountered armies of abandoned women. He felt, he'd concede, a bit of guilt that he was still on the home front while their boyfriends were off in distant places waging war, but with a pragmatic shrug and a wry smile, he came to terms with the situation. A handsome fox turned loose in the chicken coop, he did his best to console the many lonely women he met.

To his surprise, Bob was now having a wonderful time in New York. There was only one drawback—his job.

THE NEW YORK FIELD OFFICE has always been the Bureau's largest and busiest; in the 1940s, it employed more than a thousand of the FBI's approximately seven thousand agents. Bob felt diminished, painfully insignificant, in this sea of white shirts and snap-brim hats. And while in Alabama Bob had been given the latitude to run his cases as he saw fit, in New York he was just one small voice in a large chorus. The bosses set the tune, and he was expected to sing along.

Still, he was kept busy. In three and a half years, he made more than four hundred arrests. Nearly all involved Selective Service cases, Bob doggedly traipsing through the streets of New York to track down draft dodgers. It was an assignment that reinforced Bob's growing misgivings about "missing the war." The city's sidewalks were a long way from the front lines, and he couldn't help feeling he was shirking his duty, especially since his brother Art was in the thick of things in the Pacific. He was giving serious thought to quitting the FBI and volunteering for the army; with his experience he'd get assigned to G-2, the intelligence division, he expected.

But that was before the incident in Chinatown.

NEW YORK LOCAL SELECTIVE SERVICE Board Number 1 had more delinquent cases than any local board in the country. This statistic, however, was deceiving. Since the Lower Manhattan board's authority extended to both the flophouses of the Bowery and the immigrant tenements of Chinatown, not every man who failed to report for service was trying to shirk his patriotic duty. The young men living a troubled, down-and-out life on the Bowery rarely got around to checking their mail. And many of the recent arrivals from China had offered up an invented name to the immigration authorities when they entered America, and then immediately reverted to their old family name once they were living and working in New York; draft board notices, as a consequence, often went undelivered.

FBI agents, though, didn't want to hear any stories. They routinely insisted ignorance was no excuse: you break the law, you get hauled off to jail. Bob, however, was sympathetic. His treatment of these nuanced cases was more understanding, more shaped by a sagacious diplomacy than the strict a-law-is-a-law arrests carried out routinely by other G-men assigned to Board 1.

And his demeanor was noticed. His tact was appreciated. He developed a growing reputation for evenhandedness among the family groups who ruled Chinatown. He was often a guest at elaborate dinners where exotic delicacies were served, foods that Bob could not have even begun to imagine in his Idaho boyhood. The On Leong Tong, the Hip Sing Tong, and the Chinese Merchants Association all saw this young broad-shouldered, round-eyed FBI agent as someone they could trust.

It was these elders who told Bob about Thomas John Whelan. Whelan, as Bob observed firsthand when he checked out the story he'd been told, was a U.S. Treasury agent who was running a lucrative shakedown racket in the back rooms of Chinatown.

Flashing his badge, Whelan would charge into businesses, demanding to inspect the books. "I want to see the records of the Social Security payments you've been making for your employees," he'd order. When these records could not be produced (because, almost invariably, the required payments to the government had not been made), Whelan would huff and puff with indignant authority that he had no choice but to cart the merchant immediately off to jail. You're facing five years, he'd growl. You'll be deported. Then having brandished the stick, he'd offer the carrot. Of course, he'd go on conspiratorially, he would be willing to forget about the whole thing in exchange for a cash payment of five hundred dollars, or a thousand if he thought the merchant could afford it.

Whelan had successfully pulled this routine about a dozen times before Bob was alerted. And the next time Whelan tried it, Bob was hiding in an adjacent room, listening to it all go down. As had been previously agreed, the merchant paid his money, and Bob, now a witness to the crime, waited until Whelan was back out on the street to make his arrest.

Bob announced, "FBI. You're under arrest!" And then Whelan drew his service revolver.

Bob pulled out his .38.

It was a standoff. Two government agents, guns drawn, facing each other on a busy Chinatown street.

Only now, Whelan, with a shrewdness born out of desperation, began to appeal to the gathering crowd. I'm a Treasury agent. You know me. This man is trying to rob me. He's not with the FBI. And the gathering multitudes took one look at the two armed men and quickly decided that age trumped youth: the Treasury agent had to be the one telling the truth.

All at once Bob could feel the crowd closing in on him. Later, he would say, it was fortunate that he was too scared to think. Instead, he tightened his pull on the trigger of his gun and declared in what he hoped was a clear, steady voice, "Whelan, you have two choices: either you lower your gun or I'm gonna shoot you straight through the heart."

Whelan lowered his gun.

In the aftermath of Bob's gutsy showdown, the Bureau, as the now laudatory appraisal in his new fitness report indicated, began to realize that maybe they had been wrong about Lamphere. Perhaps he *was* the sort of agent who embodied the staunch virtues of fortitude and commitment that Hoover had decreed. And Bob, exhilarated by the moment's sudden challenge and proud of his finding the instincts to live up to its demands, began once again to believe that he had a meaningful future in the FBI.

Only the Bureau, wanting to reward him for both his ingenuity and courage, assigned Bob to the Soviet Espionage (SE) squad. And Bob at once felt betrayed. His suddenly promising career had just as suddenly been channeled into a very dead end. He was being relegated to an obscure and inconsequential Bureau outpost. The Russians, after all, were our wartime allies. They weren't cooking up any nefarious plots. Getting assigned to SE, he was bitterly certain, was like being "shipped off to Siberia."

3

S BOB, GRUDGING AND UNCERTAIN, was beginning his new job, a stone's throw across the Potomac River from Washington, D.C., in a former junior college for fashionable young women that had been hastily transformed into a top-secret government facility, Meredith Gardner was moving into his own new battle—the Blue Problem. But unlike Bob, Meredith was excited by the prospect of throwing himself into the midst of this baffling challenge. The truth was, in so many ways Meredith was the personification of everything that the gun-toting, good-time-loving, nightclub-hopping FBI agent was not.

Just a quick glance revealed the deep, fundamental differences. Meredith was long, lanky, and ascetic, a man whose very thinness seemed to suggest that all the fun had been long ago squeezed out of him. He had a fondness for tweed sport coats, rep striped ties, and button-down white Oxford shirts—a deliberately donnish attire. Dark horn-rim glasses and a shock of unruly black hair that fell across his forehead as if blown by a sudden gust of wind further helped to evoke the image of a grad student perpetually heading to his next seminar.

Proudly, Meredith was a thinker, a man who took refuge in ideas. He collected them with an indiscriminate passion. Yet always orderly, whenever he found something that caught his interest—a curious fact about beetle morphology, the past-tense conjugation of a Japanese verb, a tasty brand of biscuit—he'd jot down these little treasures on index cards, and then when he could find the time, transcribe them into one of his many gray-covered schoolboy notebooks. It was his habit to quote Lucretius's prescription for a life well lived: "He knows what it is to know." Meredith, too, strived to reach a similar state of grace. He infused his own life with a deep, constant, joyful pursuit of knowledge. And like the pensive Lucretius, he found beauty in abstractions: he enjoyed thinking about thought.

And while Bob seemed to come to life in a crowded, smoke-filled barroom with a glass of scotch in his hand, Meredith's demeanor, even after a drink or two, was private to the point of being totally self-absorbed. This shyness was both a natural reticence and a well-developed defense against any boor who might try to penetrate his decidedly inward existence. People, especially those who didn't know him well, had a tendency to dismiss his detachment as arrogance, but that was too rash and too shallow an appraisal. More often than not, it was simply that he wasn't interested in what anyone else had to say; what was going on in his mind was enough for him.

Still, he could be judgmental, even haughty. Meredith insisted on precision in thought and in expression. Let someone offhandedly complain that "it was a million degrees outside," and he couldn't help but point out that "if that were indeed the case, we'd all evaporate." Similarly, he'd pounce when "decimate" was used imprecisely. And all he had to do was hear "at this point in time" and he'd explode with a grouchy lecture about the annoying and unnecessary redundancy in the phrase. "Meredithisms," his coworkers, more often with indulgent shrugs than not, called these frequent corrections.

Given his stiff, on occasion even hostile, demeanor, it's perhaps understandable that Meredith didn't make friends easily. But that never concerned him. He could not see the need. And as for conversation, he made do by talking to himself. (One of his colleagues waggishly passed this small joke around: "A gardner's best friend is his mutter"—the punch line, such as it was, predicated on *Mutter* being the German for "mother.") His was a circumspect life: he liked ideas, words, genealogy, crossword puzzles, a glass of sweet sherry, his pipe or, if that wasn't handy, an unfiltered Camel, and solving unsolvable problems. And because Meredith knew he was very good at what he did, he was, in his solitary, undemonstrative way, quite content.

But most strikingly, of all the polar differences between these two young men, between the gregarious plow horse and the solitary deep thinker, when Meredith arrived at the former girls' college, Arlington Hall, he was, at just thirty, already a legend.

EVERY GENIUS, IT HAS BEEN said, needs the spark that will ignite his unique mind, and for Meredith this catalytic moment occurred when he was eight. The year was 1920, and he was living in a down-at-the-heels clapboard rooming house in Austin, Texas, that his mother, Corrine, ran because it was the only way she could think of making ends meet. Just a year earlier, the Gardners, a family that could proudly trace their roots back to Queen Margaret of Scotland, had been settled happily in the Deep South cotton belt town of Okolona, Mississippi. But then Daniel Gardner suddenly died, leaving his widow and their two boys nearly penniless. Corrine made her way to Austin, somehow scratched together the money to buy a rickety home that desperately needed a fresh coat of paint, and put out a sign announcing "Rooms to Let."

In the years after World War I, Austin was beginning to flex its muscles as a city: businesses were opening and newcomers kept arriving, and the rooms were quickly taken. And Meredith, though enrolled in grade school, was expected to help out. One of his responsibilities was to deliver the mail to their boarders. That was how he saw the newspaper.

It was a Yiddish-language paper that was received by a tenant whose name and occupation have long been forgotten. But what was remembered, and decades later Meredith shared the memory

with his son with a genuine trace of bewilderment, was how the exotic Hebrew letters and the strange words had fascinated the young
boy. It was all a perplexing puzzle, and so he set out to solve it. He
had no plan of attack, but nevertheless it all—a sudden presto!—soon
fell into place. It was like when he first learned to read as a precocious three-year-old; it just sort of happened. And so it wasn't long
before the nimble-minded eight-year-old taught himself Yiddish
and even Hebrew, and now confident of his newfound talent, went
on to teach himself German. Next he got his hands on a Spanish
textbook, and he quickly mastered that, too. He just had the knack;
languages never remained foreign to him for long.

By the time he was twenty-three, Meredith was fluent in at least
a dozen languages, including Sanskrit. At the University of Texas,
he breezed through his undergraduate degree and then went on,
without pause, to pick up his master's. His professors considered him
a scholar of uncommon promise; there was a good deal of talk that
it wouldn't take much more work to prepare his master's thesis for
publication. But years later, what remains, arguably, most striking
about the essay—"A Semasiological History of High German"—is
its epigraph. Meredith chose a well-known bit of Horace, and its
opening words, if one bothered to translate the Latin, seemed to
sum up the young, defiant outsider quite well: "I hate and spurn
the profane crowd." Yet it was the quotation's final lines that, years
later, after all Meredith had accomplished, would prove prescient:
"I, the priest of the muses, sing the songs not having been heard
before." And indeed he would.

But in preparation for that still unimagined calling, in 1938 Meredith went off to the University of Wisconsin to earn his doctorate in
German. It was, apparently, a troubled period for the young scholar.
Was he having doubts about his calling? Was he, at last, beginning
to sow his long-dormant wild oats? Meredith kept his own counsel,
and so any answers can only be speculation. But what is known is that
often enough to be remembered, and often enough to draw concern,
Meredith would sit in seminars with his head cradled in his hands, a

man sullenly nursing a massive hangover. And what would his professors say about this unscholarly behavior? A distinguished member of the faculty one morning turned to the room full of students, gestured toward Meredith, who sat hunched in an almost fetal position, and explained to the class with benevolent understanding, "Mr. Gardner is our genius—but a genius with a bit of spice."

Meredith's intellectual journey next took him in 1940 to the University of Ohio in Akron. He taught German to the undergraduates and was universally feared as a demanding and uncompromising taskmaster; don't sign up for Gardner's course unless you are prepared to work harder than you've ever worked before, was the warning passed around campus. And when he was not terrorizing undergraduates, he was putting the finishing touches on his dissertation, a long, deep journey into the fundamental meanings of words in High German.

But as much as Meredith enjoyed being locked away in the groves of academe, after the attack on Pearl Harbor he knew he'd soon have to enter a more dangerous world. And, not least, he was a patriot; he wanted to do his duty. So in a way Meredith was already prepared when the head of the department suggested to him, with a transparent vagueness, that he knew some people in Washington. They're doing some things with codes. Someone who knows German might come in handy. Would you be interested?

"Yes, I think I'd like that very much," Meredith answered. He would always tell people it was a decision he made without hesitation.

In the winter of 1942, Meredith reported to Arlington Hall.

4

EREDITH, TO HIS SURPRISE AND discomfort, entered
a world of women. The nation's premier code-breaking
facility, the Signal Security Agency, was nearly entirely
staffed by female civilians. (It would be renamed in 1945, with proprietary pride, the Army Security Agency—ASA—but the intelligence
mandarins before and after referred to it simply as Arlington Hall.)
Row after row of young women sat hunched over desks performing the painstaking task of cataloguing the mountains of intercepted
enemy messages; or, after some rudimentary training, worked as linguists; or simply buzzed about doing clerical chores. At the height
of the war, the ASA would employ over five thousand women. But
while the handful of men like Meredith—mathematicians, foreign-
language specialists, anthropologists, even a few undergraduates with
impressive scores on IQ tests or simply a fondness for puzzles—who
had signed on for the top-secret work knew what they were getting
into, the brigade of women, although volunteers, had been pretty
much shanghaied.

One typical recruiting center, for example, had been set up in the
midst of the daily bustle of the fortress-like Lynchburg, Virginia, Post
Office building on Church Street. Comfortably nestled between the
Blue Ridge Mountains and the James River, Lynchburg was considered a friendly, all-American sort of town by the Army brass and so
Lieutenant Pasvo Carlson, a young Signal Corps officer, had been
dispatched to troll for civilian female volunteers. He was armed with

Nordic good looks, a bright smile, and a largely vague and often spe-
cious bill of goods.

The job, he'd begin truthfully enough, was with the Army in the
Washington area. And the pay would be attractive; you'd enter at
the grade of SP-5 and earn $1,800 a year, plus a bonus for Saturday
work, and for most of the women, many of them schoolteachers, this
would be a considerable raise. But in response to the eventual question
of what the job would entail, the lieutenant's lips were tightly sealed.
Under orders from his superiors, he'd explain with a terseness made
even weightier by the drama of wartime, he could not reveal any details. The specifics were top secret.

Yet before any potential recruit's imagination could fill this
void with a bleak vision of work in a subterranean bunker, Carlson
jumped in with a cheerier prospect. Like a carnival barker zeroing
in on his mark, he'd produce impressive brochures and picture postcards of a workplace that seemed more like a Virginia hunt-country
resort than a secure Army outpost. There was a shimmering out-
door swimming pool, stables filled with sleek-coated horses, a pil-
lared yellow-brick colonial mansion as large and impressive as any
they had seen in *Gone With the Wind*, and all these goodies were
scattered about, as one brochure boasted, "a 100-acre campus offering . . . interesting variety with its open lawns, landscaped gardens,
and wooded sections."

Nudged on by the enticing promise of a sojourn at a well-groomed
country estate and attractive pay, not to mention their own earnest
desire to have a chance to help the Allied cause, hundreds of women
signed on for this unexplained, hush-hush Army work. Then, after a
brief indoctrination in Army offices in downtown Washington—a few
maddeningly nonspecific hours at most—the new recruits would make
their own way, quite often by taxi, to the address on Glebe Road in
Virginia that had finally been revealed. And as soon as they arrived at
the front gate, they'd feel betrayed. What they saw was nothing like
what had been dangled in front of them.

In its heyday Arlington Hall had indeed been the manicured junior college for pampered young ladies pictured in the postcards and the brochures. But the school had already lost much of its gloss (as well as a sizable chunk of its enrollment) when the Army, brandishing the War Powers Act, purchased the property in 1942 for the court-ordered price of $650,000. Soon the pool was drained and the stables emptied. Rows of dingy barracks now lined the unkempt lawns. The interior of the mansion building had been subdivided into a maze of cramped, closet-like rooms separated by plywood walls, or simply by rows of filing cabinets. And a steel-mesh fence topped with curling circles of razor-sharp barbed wire encircled the grounds. By the time Meredith, as well as the hundreds of new female recruits, arrived, the Army had firmly imposed its brutal aesthetic on Arlington Hall.

But while there were grumblings from many of the arrivals that they had been seduced with false promises—a guilty Lieutenant Carlson made it a point to hurry off whenever accusatory stares were shot his way—once the top-secret work was revealed, its undeniable wartime urgency put a damper on their complaints. The Army wranglers—as the teams of cryptanalysts were known—were doing nothing less than breaking both the German and Japanese ciphers. The ability to read the enemy's encoded messages would undoubtedly save lives, shorten the war, and, if exploited with ingenuity and blessed by luck, help pave the way toward an Allied victory on both fronts. An empty swimming pool no longer seemed like a hardship when measured against the opportunity to play a supporting role in this grand effort.

As for Meredith, he threw himself with his customary focus and insight into every problem that was thrown his way. The British had already made extraordinary headway on the Wehrmacht codes before he came onboard, but his fluency in German helped to smooth a few lingering rough edges. Impressed, his superiors decided to turn him loose on the Japanese cables.

The code breakers here, too, had already worked wonders. First, they had untangled the new, sophisticated Japanese cipher, code-named "Purple," and then they went on to build a replica of the Purple encoding machine that employed a complex electrical rotor system along with a twenty-five-character alphabetic switchboard without, miracle of ingenious miracles, ever having seen the actual Japanese device; their inspired deductions were all intuitive suppositions. But they still needed readers who could make sense of the unlocked text. Of course, the ability to translate Japanese with effortless fluency was a prerequisite for the team, and Meredith, while he could claim expertise in Lithuanian, Sanskrit, and Old Church Slavonic, as well as the more mundane European languages of German and Spanish, did not know a single word of Japanese. So, to the amazement of his superiors, while he was also busily laboring away on the German messages, in his spare time, hunched day and night over his monastic desk in the main building, in three months he taught himself Japanese. As if in an instant, he was fluent. He became a key member of the unit deciphering the cables traveling in and out of the Imperial War Command in Tokyo.

And while Meredith's accomplishments were soon attracting curious attention from the Army Signal Corps brass who ran Arlington Hall, they were no surprise to one of the new recruits. From the moment Blanche Hatfield learned that he was working with the wranglers, she had been keeping a curious but discreet eye on him. After all, it wasn't every day that you got to observe a legend.

BLANCHE WAS NOT THE TYPICAL Arlington Hall female recruit. She not only knew before volunteering—"fully cognizant" was how it read in her file—what the Army was up to, but she had ample reason to believe she could lend a hand. It was as if, as she'd confidently informed the examiner when she'd applied, the job had been conceived with her nimble talents in mind.

Not that anyone would know it to look at her. While Meredith had the brooding, rumpled mien of quirky genius, a quick glance at Blanche suggested nothing so eccentric. A precocious twenty-three-year-old, she might have been dismissively categorized as another of those pearls and twin-setted coeds who had populated the corridors of Arlington Hall in its previous gilded life. Hazel-eyed, and with bobbed hair that, when the light hit it full force, had a bold reddish sheen, she embodied a mix of breeding and material comfort that animates women of a certain background. A well-mannered smile, yet full of a jaunty charm, completed the pretty picture.

But while Blanche had indeed grown up in a big Victorian house in Evanston, Illinois, and her pedigree included well-heeled generations of prominent church and university officials, she also had a wonderful mind. Her father was chairman of the German Department at Northwestern University (the "Keep Off the Grass" signs that surrounded his acres of lawn were posted in a pedantic variety of languages); her brother would go on to become chairman of the German Department at Harvard; and Blanche had also begun to make her way in the family business. At Mount Holyoke College she had majored in German, getting elected to Phi Beta Kappa in the process. Then she went on to earn her M.A. at the University of Wisconsin, again in German.

It was while she was working on her master's that, as she would one day tell her children, her professors had regaled the students with heady tales about one of their predecessors in the department. How he had the sort of mind that appears once in a generation. How he could grasp impossibly difficult concepts in a flash, make connections that had eluded other linguists, offer insights that were nothing less than stunning in their uniqueness and clarity. The way they talked about this grad student, he might as well have been a god; and in time he would become a sort of deity in Blanche's feverish imagination. And now here was Meredith Gardner in the (ghostly pale) flesh, laboring in the same top-secret code-breaking facility as she was.

Blanche knew she had to meet him. She spent considerable time mulling over her approach. And even then, when she had worked out what she thought would be an appropriate introduction—flirtatious, while also making clear that she was a woman of accomplishment—she still hesitated. It was not so much that Meredith seemed intimidating. Rather, gazing at him bent over his desk, deep in some arcane yet no doubt vital puzzle, she wondered if he would even hear her voice. He appeared totally self-contained, completely detached from all that was going on around him. An intrusion into his very private world could be doomed from the start.

For days she made excuses to put off the encounter. Finally, with a sudden burst of courage, she pounced.

"Ich dachte, Sie wären eine Legende!" she announced. (And she knew there was no need to offer a translation: "I thought you were just a legend!")

When Meredith finally looked up, as Blanche would always tell the tale, he did not speak for what seemed ages. She waited, all the time fearing that by barging into his isolation she had committed an unpardonable sin. He must think me the silliest of young women, she decided. But then he smiled, and a conversation, small and trivial, followed. It was only after Blanche returned to her own desk that she realized they had spoken to each other entirely in German.

Fraternization at Arlington Hall was not specifically prohibited, but it was frowned on; it was a military facility, after all. And so their courtship remained one more closely guarded secret among all the many others that they protected.

BUT IT WAS THE NATURE of that covert world that there was always at least one more bit of hush-hush activity swirling around in the shadows than was guessed at. And so it was at Arlington Hall. While Blanche and Meredith did their best to make sure no one knew about their blossoming relationship, in one of the few private offices in the main building, a two-member team had secretly begun to examine the Blue Problem.

5

COLONEL CARTER W. CLARKE WAS, depending on the way one looked at the world, either a realist or a deeply suspicious fellow. But since he was the deputy chief of the Military Intelligence Service this was a caution that had its practical advantages.

And so it was that even as the war in Europe continued, the colonel found himself thinking that Arlington Hall shouldn't be focused on just the German and Japanese codes. America needed to read Russia's mail, too. It was crucial, all his professional and personal instincts rose up to warn him, that the nation knew precisely what the Russians were up to.

THE UNITED STATES ALREADY HAD filing cabinets bursting with Soviet message traffic gathering dust. With intermittent assiduousness, the government had been collecting copies of Russian cables—diplomatic and trade—sent to and from Moscow for years. The program had begun modestly in the more languid prewar days when a half-dozen or so undermanned Signal Corps monitoring stations spread from Fort Monmouth (in New Jersey) to Fort McKinley (in the Philippines) began pulling Russian cable traffic in sporadic bursts from the airwaves. Then in 1940, in a clandestine arrangement made possible by David Sarnoff, who, conveniently, was both the chief executive of RCA (then the nation's major commercial telegram cable company) and a reserve Signal Corps officer, Russian cables sent from and received in RCA offices in New York, Washington, and San Francisco were routinely photographed. Working in the back rooms of RCA offices, supplied with flimsy cover stories, the Army photo technicians were, unlike the monitoring station staff, able to get perfect copies of every message. After the attack on Pearl Harbor, a wartime America quickly instituted rules for the censorship of all international mail and communications; telegraph companies were now required to turn over copies of every foreign communication. By 1942, the file cabinets at Arlington Hall were bulging with a nearly complete inventory of all recent message traffic sent to and from Moscow.

Not that it did the spymasters any good. There was never much thought or energy put into reading these cables. Early on, when the array of monitoring stations first began gathering the Russian messages, the head of the Signal Intelligence Service, Major D. M. Crawford, threw up his hands in defeat after only a half-hearted fight: "Judging by what is known of Russian cryptographic methods," he as good as moaned to his superiors, "the Russians are employing complicated, scientifically constructed systems designed to resist the organized efforts of expert cryptanalysis."

Besides, in those halcyon prewar years, knowing what the Russians were up to struck the deep thinkers in military intelligence as an abstract, largely irrelevant, exercise; the national interest in the late 1930s was defined in defiantly parochial terms. Later, in the wake of the German army's blitzkrieg across Europe, Congress, with America on the sidelines and largely hoping they could keep it that way, passed the Lend-Lease Act in 1941. A staggering fortune of armaments and supplies—over $11 billion worth by the war's end—was sent under the terms of the act to the assailed Soviet fighters, matériel that was to be repaid in kind after the war. In this arm's-length way, the U.S. government tacitly cheered the Soviet army on, all but formally acknowledging they were fighting the nation's battles, too. And once the country entered the war, it found itself locked in common cause with the Russians. Both U.S. and

Soviet soldiers shed blood in the shared battle to defeat Hitler. The two nations, if not friends, were allies.

But Colonel Clarke's apprehensive mind was, even as the war was still being fought, focusing on the inevitable peace conferences. A Friday-night poker player, the colonel had a metaphor handy: the sessions would be high-stakes contests. It was imperative that America walk away from the table with its fair share—or better—of the pot. And past experience had taught him that the odds of coming out ahead certainly increased if one knew what cards the other player was holding. He confided this game-winning strategy in a carefully oblique memo to a G-2 colleague in May 1942:

"The end purpose [is] enabling an American peace delegation to confront the problems of the peace table with the fullest intimate knowledge possible . . . to secure the purposes and attitudes, overt and covert, of those who sit opposite them."

Eight months after this hope of obtaining "the fullest intimate knowledge possible" had started gnawing at him, in January 1943, a small kernel of intelligence crossed his desk. It was a memo churned out by the code breakers toiling on the Japanese problem at Arlington Hall, a minor revelation they had stumbled upon; in other circumstances it might have gone unnoticed in the constant flow of more valuable tactical information. But at this moment it held the prospect of just the sort of game-winning advantage the cagey colonel was seeking.

It was a message from the General Staff in Tokyo to the attachés in Berlin and Helsinki. It began: "We have commenced the study of Russian diplomatic codes and obtained the following results. . . ." The results, as outlined, were at best modest. The Japanese had not broken the Russian codes. However, with the help of the Finns, who had been exchanging cryptographic material they had recovered after the Red Army's 1939 invasion with Tokyo's code breakers, they had made some progress. The Japanese had, as one impressed Army code breaker acknowledged, "uncovered clues."

That was all the encouragement Colonel Clarke needed. In the first months of 1943, it was becoming possible to envision the long endgame that would lead to the defeat of Hitler. With an expedient practicality, he now looked toward a more complicated future. And he began to ponder how Signals Intelligence—"sigint," to use the professionals' word—might help.

On Monday, February 1, 1943, just one day before the official surrender of the besieged German Sixth Army at Stalingrad, the colonel ordered the Army Signals Intelligence command to start work on "the Russian problem." A special "compartment" was established at Arlington Hall.

THE PROGRAM WAS TOP SECRET. And the staff was minimal—just two recent arrivals at Arlington Hall. Second Lieutenant Leonard Zubko had an engineering degree and had just completed Infantry School at Fort Benning. His only qualification for this assignment, as best he could surmise, was that he spoke Russian (both his parents were born in the Ukraine). Gene Grabeel, his coworker, had even less apparent skills. A graduate of Longwood College in Farmwood, Virginia, she had been an unhappy high school teacher when the affable Lieutenant Carlson approached her in the Lynchburg Post Office. She had listened to his pitch, discussed it with her father, who agreed that it might make sense to go to Washington "and shuffle papers," and as soon as a replacement teacher was found, she reported to the duty officer at Arlington Hall. Four weeks later she was sitting at a wooden table across from a bewildered Lieutenant Zubko in the corner of a tiny room in the main building. And lining an entire wall of this claustrophobic space were eight shoulder-high filing cabinets crammed with years of Russian cable traffic.

They couldn't make sense of a single one.

6

WHICH WAS PRECISELY WHAT THE Russians had intended. The messages had been encoded in an unbreakable code. It was by shrewd design, much more sophisticated, much more ingenious than either the German or Japanese systems. The Soviet cryptologists had, in effect, locked the door once; then they locked it again; and, finally, just to be sure no one could get in, they threw away the key.

The system worked, in its plodding, laborious, and seemingly foolproof way, basically (and hypothetically) like this:

A Russian spy, call him Paul Revere, came in from the cold to the New York *rezidentura* (as the Soviet diplomatic missions were known) with an important message that needed to reach Moscow without delay: "The British are coming."

The cipher clerk grabbed the message from the secret agent and jumped into action. Like a diligent copy editor, he smoothed Paul Revere's unpolished prose, taking care that it conformed to all the elements of style that had been drummed into him in cipher school. He must, he knew straight off, disguise the source. The security-conscious KGB prohibited the mention of an agent's actual name in a cable; only aliases could be transmitted. So the dutiful clerk checked a top-secret list for Revere's code name. He found it: Silversmith.

The rest of the brief message needed some sprucing up, too. There is no "the" in Russian; the article is a notion alien to the language. Also, verbs were often deleted in cables, the logic being that they were implicit and only slowed down the recipient's unbuttoning of an urgent message. Finally, per another stylistic convention, certain nouns with Western national and ideological affinities, such as "British" (or, say, "CIA" or "FBI"), were replaced with an insider's jargon, a practice rooted more in a jaunty spy fellowship than any security concerns. Thus, "British" became "Islanders."

The edited message the clerk transcribed on his work sheet—the verbs deemed necessary—now read: "Silversmith reports Islanders coming." (Of course, KGB-trained clerks wrote in Russian, using Cyrillic characters; this example, for clarity's sake, is playing out in English.)

With the editing of the plaintext—i.e., the original message—completed, the clerk was ready to take the codebook out of the safe. The codebook was a secret dictionary that allowed the members of the club—in this case, KGB officers—to communicate with fellow clubmen without outsiders being able to understand. It was employed to translate the information into the secret language—to encode it.

The club's shared covert language was numerical. Words, as well as symbols and punctuation, and often entire phrases, were reduced to four digits. If a word was not in the KGB's dictionary—an American family name or some abstruse scientific term, for example—then there was a prearranged way to handle that, too: a specific four-digit number was employed to announce to anyone in the club receiving the message, "Here's where we're going to begin spelling an untranslatable word." Next, the word would be spelled out in Roman letters, with two-digit designations for each letter taken from a "spell table" that was an appendix to the secret dictionary. And, finally, to indicate that this strange (at least to a Russian reader) word was completed, there'd be another specific two-digit number—the "end spell" code.

Working carefully, checking and rechecking each word in the codebook, the code clerk would soon have come up with a translation:

Silversmith	reports	Islanders	coming
8522	7349	0763	6729

Next was another small but crucial security measure. The four-digit dictionary words were transformed into unique five-digit numbers by a simple bit of hocus-pocus: the initial digit of the second four-digit group was tacked on to the end of the first group, and so on, the immediately subsequent digits moving forward until each group was now five numbers. However, for the final unit, the remaining digit would become the first number of the original last word. The clerk's work sheet would now read like this:

Silversmith	reports	Islanders	coming
85227	34907	63672	96729

And with this, the first lock on the door had been turned: the message had been encoded.

But the turning of the second lock—the enciphering—was the precaution that ensured the door would be impossible for a thief to open. The clerk now consulted another secret codebook stored in his safe—the "one-time pad." It was about the size of a pocket diary, and each dense page was lined with columns of sixty-five-digit numbers. The numbers had been randomly spewed out by a primitive computer at KGB headquarters. And—this was the sly tradecraft that rendered the final encoded and enciphered message unbreakable—only two copies of each one-time pad existed; one in Moscow Center, as the warren of offices belonging to the KGB's espionage and foreign counterintelligence sections were uniformly known, and the other in the cipher clerk's safe.

Swiftly, he went to work to put his encoded message into the protective shell of this new cipher. The procedure was quirky, but not very complex. The numbers on his work sheet would be combined with the random numbers on a specific page of his one-time pad (and in this example, the one-time pad numbers are as imagined as the hypothetical message). However, there was one catch. The rules for addition were not as normally taught in grade school, but, rather, followed what mathematicians call the Fibonacci series, a nonadditive system; any number larger than nine was not carried forward. So, the clerk would go back to his work sheet and do the math:

Silversmith	reports	Islanders	coming
85227	34907	63672	96729
71148	36564	56340	32468
56365	60461	19912	28187

With the creation of these new five-digit numbers, the second lock would be firmly turned: the message had been enciphered.

But there still remained one more essential step. The clerk would copy the first five-digit group at the top left-hand corner of the page of the one-time pad he had used and stick it at the beginning of the cable. This would tell the recipient: Turn to this page in your one-time pad to unbutton this message. If, say, the group of numbers at the top corner of the page were 67832, the message would look like this:

(67832)   56365   60461   19912   28187

Then—and this was crucial—he'd burn the page from the pad he'd just used. And he would count on the recipient, after deciphering the message, to likewise destroy the corresponding page in his copy of the one-time pad. This would ensure that the random code numbers could never be repeated, and without repetition the opposition wranglers would never have the advantage they'd need to untangle the code. The key would, in effect, have been thrown away.

There was one further task necessary, more a routine business procedure than a security measure. Since the cable would be sent to

Moscow through the circuits of a commercial telegraphic concern, the companies, such as RCA, required numbers to be converted into letters for transmission by Morse code. There was a standard conversion table:

0=O, 1=I, 2=U, 3=Z, 4=T, 5=R, 6=E, 7=W, 8=A, 9=P

Once this simple transposition was completed, the message would be sent. Within hours the field agent's original breathless warning that "the British are coming" would arrive on a desk in the cipher room in Moscow. It would look like this:

REZER EOTEI IPPIU UAIAW

The Moscow Center clerk would immediately roll up his sleeves and begin to reverse the encoding process, diligently converting letters into numbers, cipher into code, and code into words.

When the plaintext message finally made its way down the long corridors of Moscow Center to the appropriate KGB desk officer, he could read it—and, more important, act on it—confident that the secret it contained had never been revealed.

CERTAINLY, THE SECRETS CONTAINED IN the rows of filing cabinets perused with daily frustration by Lieutenant Zubko and Gene Grabeel remained inviolable. They had no idea how to penetrate the code. The best they could do was follow one of the leads that the intercepted Japanese message had revealed. Looking at the cable addresses, a shorthand used by the commercial companies, they were able to divide the traffic into two distinct groups: commercial messages coming and going from the Russian Ministry of Trade, and diplomatic messages with the Foreign Ministry address.

Two piles—the stack of trade messages, though, decidedly higher—soon rose on the wooden table in their office. It was a start, and this activity offered a small sense that they were beginning to make some progress. Perhaps, they both wanted to believe, familiarity would in time result in deeper insights. And they received another burst of encouragement when Colonel Clarke promised he would provide more manpower. Further, in a world where code names were an imprimatur of institutional importance, the brass at Arlington Hall, taking their lead from an ongoing classified Navy investigation of Russian radio networks known as "Blue Caesar," now referred to the cracking of the Russian code with a cover name: "the Blue Problem."

But then, without either warning or explanation, two months after the Blue Problem had been launched, it was ended. Both Zubko and Grabeel were ordered to report to new assignments.

7

B OB LAMPHERE, MEANWHILE, WAS DEALING with his own Russian problem. And in his world the results were no less frustrating than at Arlington Hall. For reasons he couldn't understand—just trying to work out the Bureau's logic left him livid—he'd been, as he sourly put it, "shoved out to grass" in the Soviet Espionage squad. The work, he felt, was not merely dull, it was pointless.

There were just a handful of agents, about fifty men from the thousand or so in the New York office, assigned to SE, and their job was to keep track of an even smaller cadre of suspected Soviet spies, operatives working under dodgy diplomatic or trade covers. It was watcher's work, and the experience, day after miserable day, had left Bob with a list of ardent reasons why it wasn't for him. He'd reel them off like the counts in an indictment. One: physical surveillance work was the time-honored stomping ground of the unambitious, FBI agents who were eager to stay out of the office since out of sight meant out of the supervisors' demanding minds. Two: it was passive duty, long days and nights literally just sitting around. Three: the mission was a waste of good manpower. It didn't take long for the target to get an inkling that it was more than just coincidence that whenever he looked over his shoulder, there was a stolid hulk in a suit and fedora trailing behind. What secret agent who knows he's being followed, Bob wanted to shout at his un-imaginative bosses, will meet up with his contacts? And a resolute Number Four: there was nothing to uncover. The Soviets—and here his logic was shared by many, including several of the G-2 strategists working at Arlington Hall—were on our side. The Russian Bear and Uncle Sam were both fighting the good fight against the Nazis. Allies don't spy on each other.

Bob looked back with a precocious nostalgia at his days making criminal cases, when he was on the front lines in Chinatown doing consequential work. Each wasted day sitting interminably in a car, or standing with a contrived casualness in a doorway, his eyes all the time searching for a glimpse of some inconsequential Russian, grated against his ambition. "When you get rid of one spy, another would take his place," he reasoned, his trip-wire temper growing hot at the absurdity that had taken over his life. His days and nights of surveillance "just went on and on. Little was breaking." While, he might have added, his career was petering away.

But just as he was on the verge of surrendering, of giving up all hope of a meaningful future, a series of unexpected events began to rattle all his preconceived notions. They were seemingly unconnected, and, at least initially, in no apparent way related to his dull responsibilities. Further, Bob would later concede, as a newcomer to the SE section he was "only peripherally involved in the matters." Yet "they impinged on many of my later cases in so many ways." And even at the time, one after another, they woke up a vague, yet nagging, sense of alarm in his mind: he grew to realize that "the Russians were operating all around us."

IT BEGAN WITH A LETTER. It was delivered to the Bureau headquarters in August 1943, and it was the sort of communication that, in most circumstances, would be quickly filed away and just as quickly forgotten. It was anonymous, postmarked Washington, D.C., and addressed, with an annoying presumptuousness, to "Mr. Hoover." There was one characteristic, though, that distinguished it from the flood of crank letters that arrived regularly in the FBI post office box—it was in Russian, typed in Cyrillic letters.

When it was translated, it told a fascinating story. "Exceptional circumstances," the unnamed writer dove in without prelude, "impel us to inform you of the activities of the so-called director of the Soviet intelligence in this country." What followed was a compelling espionage story—a gossipy, insider's description of a ten-member Russian spy network operating in America headed by Vassily Zubilin. Working under the banal diplomatic cover of second secretary at the Soviet embassy, this short, stocky Tweedledum of a man was, the letter claimed, the crafty deputy head of the KGB Foreign Intelligence Directorate Service and the chief KGB officer in the United States. No less startling was the assertion that his wife, Elizabeth, an unsmiling harridan who by all accounts treated her husband with undisguised contempt, was also a KGB field agent who ran her own network of well-placed agents.

It was pure intelligence gold—unless it was fool's gold. Some SE bosses argued that the letter was a shrewd bit of disinformation by the Russians to divert attention from the real brains behind their operation; the attempt to put the spotlight on a most improbable spy (and his even more improbable shrew of a wife) was a joke that must have left them laughing in Moscow Center when they dreamed it up. Others at the Bureau suggested that poor Zubilin had probably slept with a colleague's wife or docked an assistant's pay and this letter was the angry man's mischievous payback.

It fell to Bill Harvey, the resident Bureau expert on counterintelligence, to make a final judgment on the letter. Bob had worked with him, and once he'd gotten over Harvey's disconcerting appearance, the pear-shaped body, the eyes that always seemed to be on the verge of popping out of their sockets, and, another oddity, his croaking, foghorn voice, he had come to realize that Harvey was damn smart. He had a way of looking at a situation, separating the facts from the speculations, and then doing the sort of intelligence arithmetic that made it all add up.

After much consideration, Harvey decided the letter was largely the real thing. It documented "personnel, who . . . had long been active in illegal, conspiratorial, and quasi-intelligence operations." The letter was short on operational details, but its implicit message was disturbingly clear: the KGB was up to something in America.

THE NEXT SHOE CRASHED DOWN with a more resounding thud. But perhaps that was to be expected when Russian thugs batter down an apartment door to get their hands on a defector running for his life.

The "Corby Affair"—the code name taken from the brand of rye whiskey that fueled the interrogators during the long weeks when they were hunkered down with the defector in a lonely safe house deep in the Canadian woods—had its roots in a small moment of carelessness. Igor Gouzenko, a twenty-five-year-old cipher clerk who toiled in the imposing redbrick Soviet embassy on Charlotte Street in Ottawa, Canada, had left a piece of paper on his desk.

Access to Cipher Room 12 was only attained after navigating a daunting gauntlet—a bell artfully concealed beneath the main banister must be pressed; a spy hole in a thick steel door would slide open; and then, if the bruiser standing guard approved, one door, and then another, the second as solid as the door on a bank vault, would swing free. Inside the cipher room, the stringent KGB insisted on a litany of security precautions, and Gouzenko had broken one of the most fundamental. Eager to get home to his pregnant wife, he had rushed off before storing a top-secret cable in the room's safe. It was still lying on his desktop the next morning when Gouzenko returned. Chagrined, the young clerk hurried to lock the evidence of his indiscretion away, but it was too late. A cleaning woman, who also doubled as a KGB informer, had already alerted the KGB *rezident* at the embassy. Within days, an icy cable from Moscow ordered Gouzenko home.

He didn't want to go. For the past fifteen months, Gouzenko, his pregnant wife, and their young daughter had been living in the nearly regal comfort of a centrally heated two-bedroom apartment on Som-

erset Street, shopping in stores stocked with an unimaginable bounty
of goods. The prospect of a diminished life in Moscow, of raising two
children in such deprivation, was too grim. Desperate, Gouzenko
came up with a plan.

Full of cunning, as well as no small measure of daring, he spent
weeks conscientiously assembling a wide-ranging inventory of state
secrets. He held back documents marked "Burn after reading." He
copied classified cables. He discreetly turned down the corners of top-
secret papers in the files so that he could grab them when the time
seemed right.

Then on the evening of September 5, 1945—just three days after
the end of the war—he made his move. He hastily stuffed his trove
into his pants pockets, and under his shirt. He looked, he fretted,
as bloated as the Michelin Man. The security thugs would certainly
notice. But when he signed out, Gouzev, the hulking KGB man at
the door, just gave him a perfunctory nod. Gouzenko walked down
the front steps waiting to hear his name shouted, ready to feel a heavy
hand on his shoulder, but he made it all the way to the street, and then
to the corner. A streetcar stopped, and he boarded, heading downtown.

Gouzenko returned to his apartment on Somerset Street. He
and his wife were huddled together, anxiously trying to determine
what to do next, when they heard an assertive pounding on the front
door. "*Gouzenko!*" an authoritarian voice bellowed. "*Otkroite dver!*"
("Open the door!")

The family quickly escaped out the back door, which opened
on to a rear balcony shared with another couple. These neighbors, a
Royal Canadian Air Force sergeant and his wife, quickly appraised
the frightened young couple, heard the repeated thumping on the
door across the hallway and the accompanying angry growls in an
incomprehensible language, and decided the Gouzenkos had better
take refuge with them until things were sorted out.

By the time the constables arrived, the door of the Gouzenkos'
apartment had been smashed open and a crowd of Soviet diplomats,

some in military uniform, others in civilian clothes, were in the midst of systematically tearing the place apart. There was a tense confrontation, but it ended with the Soviet intruders indignantly claiming diplomatic immunity, while the Gouzenkos were led off under the watchful protection of a half-dozen broad-shouldered Royal Canadian Mounted Police.

A day later, Gouzenko was hidden away in a cabin in Camp X, a wartime training base for special operatives located deep in the snowy Canadian woods. "Corby"—as he was now identified in the secret transcripts—had only just begun spilling all he knew when two inquisitors, buddies of Bob's from the FBI's SE squad, arrived to claim America's share of the spoils. They listened with stunned concern, and then hurried to send a flash cable to their superiors.

Gouzenko's cache of documents had revealed that Russia had, as one agent put it with shivery rage, "stabbed Canada in the back." Its secret agents were aggressively running networks of spies north of the U.S. border.

But Gouzenko's knowledge had its limits. He couldn't shed light on how the KGB's activities in Canada fit into Moscow Center's master plan. Still, his evidence, once unimaginable to many who had labored in the wartime U.S. intelligence community, now led Bob inescapably to another even more unsettling question: Was there any reason not to assume that Russia had done the same to another of its allies, the United States? Or worse?

THE ANSWER TO THAT QUESTION grew clearer to Bob a few weeks later when "the Red Queen," as the tabloids would ultimately coronate her, came out of the shadows.

Elizabeth Bentley was the daughter of solid New England stock, a graduate of Vassar with a pert smile, shy charm, an inquisitive nature, and a very impressionable mind. She fell into espionage in stages, drifting along as circumstances, rather than a hard-driving dialectical commitment, pulled her in deeper and deeper.

While doing graduate work at the University of Florence, she had a fling with fascism; Mussolini's strident right-wing rantings gave her, she'd gush, "goose bumps." But after she returned to the States and began studying for a master's in Italian at Columbia University, she did a complete about-face. Bentley joined the Communist Party, mostly attracted, she would later explain, by the convivial community and rigid structure it brought to her lonely graduate student life. And for several years, this new infatuation served her well. Bentley was, as she frankly described herself, an "average run-of-the-mill Communist," her previously empty social calendar now jammed with a hectic schedule of meetings, demonstrations, and working dinners with her tight circle of Party friends.

Looking to earn some money while she continued her studies, in 1938 she found a job as a secretary at the Italian Library of Information, just a short subway ride from her apartment near Columbia. She hadn't been working there long before she realized that the only information the library dished out was fascist propaganda. A loyal Party member, she approached the leaders of her cell, offering to get the goods; she'd give them the proof of what the library was really up to. They brusquely explained there were more important concerns. But Bentley, her indignation at being duped when she took the job fueling her persistence, wouldn't take no for an answer. And in time the harassed Party officials passed her plan on to Jacob Golos.

Golos was the real thing, a Russian-born and Moscow Center–trained KGB operative based in New York. And he always had his eye out for new talent. He saw something in Bentley's enthusiasm, her amateur's eagerness to play spy. So he let her run with her small-time operation against the Italian Library. Under his tutelage, she was listening at closed doors, furtively sorting through her boss's trash.

And as Bentley lurked in the shadows, as she discovered the thrill that came with her new covert life, something unexpected happened. Golos had first struck her as "rather colorless and shabby—a little man in a battered brown hat, non-descript suit and well-worn shoes." But their shared danger proved to be a powerful aphrodisiac. She no longer paid much attention to his scuffed shoes. In her revisionist history, Golos grew in stature. He was now "powerfully built with a large head, very broad shoulders and strong square hands. His eyes were startlingly blue, his hair bright red." And, as if to seal the deal, she decided "his mouth was very much like my mother's." With her eyes wide shut, Bentley fell in love with the KGB man.

Golos, who had a wife and a son back in Moscow and a mistress in Brooklyn, soon added Bentley to the queue. Only, in addition to being his lover, she also served as his courier. Golos ran a widespread network of diverse and valuable contacts, from a chemical engineer who was passing on blueprints of secret industrial processes to a Washington-based cell with high-placed assets in the Treasury Department and even the White House. And Bentley was Golos's indefatigable legman, to use the jargon of her new profession. In her knitting bag—an inspired bit of tradecraft that even the veteran KGB man admired—she brought back haul after haul of secret documents; after just a single trip to Washington, she'd brag, her bag was stuffed with forty undeveloped rolls of microfilm.

On Thanksgiving 1943, Golos, as he'd requested, devoured "a super special meal with all the trimmings." It turned out to be his last supper; he died that night of a heart attack. And Bentley inherited his networks.

But her new KGB handler soon grew uncomfortable with the double mystery she presented—as a woman and as a possible traitor. At first he was eager to play matchmaker. "She is a rather attractive person," the agent runner informed Moscow Center. "If [only]I could give her in marriage to one of our operatives," he nearly pleaded. "If there is no one [here], why not send someone from home?"

Then Bentley's behavior grew erratic. She showed up drunk at one debriefing. At another she reported that she had found a new lover, a man she met in a hotel lobby. At still another, she revealed she was considering "an intimate liaison" with a woman. The KGB handler, now in full panic, didn't need to wait for any more warning signs. He cabled Moscow: "Only one remedy is left—the most drastic one—to get rid of her."

Did Bentley know what Moscow Center was mulling? As she tells the story, she simply had, after long, thoughtful walks on a Connecticut beach, reached the conclusion that "Communism . . . had failed me. Far from answering the problem of suffering and injustice, it had only intensified it." And so with "shaking knees" she walked into the FBI field office in New Haven in late October 1945, and announced, "I'd like to see the agent in charge."

Bentley hadn't arrived at the FBI's doorstep lugging the sort of hard, incriminating evidence Gouzenko had stuffed under his shirt. She was asking simply to be taken at her word. Compounding the problem, her allegations were as incendiary as they were incredible. She named more than eighty Soviet sources and agents, and identified a dozen U.S. government agencies whose secrets had routinely been passed on to the KGB.

A shaken Hoover, even before her charges could be investigated and substantiated, felt he had no choice but to inform the White House. On November 8, 1945, a special messenger delivered the director's preliminary report. "Information has been recently developed from a highly confidential source indicating that a number of persons employed by the Government of the United States have been furnishing data and information . . . to espionage agents of the Soviet government."

FROM HIS DESK IN THE New York SE section, Bob read the classified transcripts of Bentley's interrogation by the Bureau. And as he did, his exasperation mounted. Why wasn't the FBI, he'd complain to his colleagues, "forcing things by moving in aggressively and interviewing everyone connected with her?" Why weren't warrants obtained to search the homes and offices of the Russian agents she'd identified? The time had come, he believed, for action.

Bob's outlook had changed. He had walked down a path that led from an anonymous letter written in Russian received at Bureau headquarters, to the defection of a Soviet cipher clerk in Canada, to Elizabeth Bentley's arrival at the New Haven field office. And with this journey all his prior complacency faded. He began to understand that he was in the midst of an "intense but nearly invisible combat." It was a war, he acknowledged with a newfound alertness, where "the Soviets had built up an early lead." The Bureau would be forced to "play catch-up ball." Most disturbing, he could only wonder where this path he was on would ultimately lead him. What, he asked himself with a suddenly tremulous sense of foreboding, would he find at the end?

8

LIKE BOB LAMPHERE, BUT FOR far different reasons, the man known throughout Moscow Center by the work name of "Viktor" was also following with mounting apprehension the events unfolding in America. The successive defections in the fall of 1945—this "chain of failures," as the official KGB finding would bluntly concede—had suddenly put all his networks in jeopardy. Viktor—who, as General Pavel Fitin, was the stony master spy who headed the Foreign Intelligence Division—knew he had to make a difficult operational decision.

For the time being, he could reassure himself, security had been maintained. The betrayals had been an embarrassment; the air of mourning wafting through the corridors of the First Directorate was nearly palpable. But the enemy had not shown the ingenuity, or, in crueler professional truth, the requisite savagery to translate the traitors' raw intelligence into action. The FBI had not rolled up a single network. His agents still remained in place. The purloined scientific, commercial, and diplomatic secrets could continue to flow.

Or could they? Was this an unreasonable expectation, grounded more in wishful thinking than in prudent *konspiratsya*? Could he trust the continued loyalty of his American assets after they'd been sweated by the FBI? Perhaps Hoover was biding his time, allowing the existing networks to putter along because he'd already turned them. It was conceivable that the FBI director was embarking on a long game, determined to play the Center's own agents back at him, to use the existing networks as channels of disinformation. That was, Viktor knew, the sort of patient strategy he himself would employ if he'd been handed a bounty of similar riches.

In the annals of Moscow Center, Viktor had become mythic, largely because, against brutal odds, he had managed to survive. He was only thirty-seven, but he'd bobbed and weaved his way through a perilous lifetime of Stalin's bloody purges (his prediction of a Nazi invasion had particularly riled the Central Committee; only the sighting of German tanks crossing into Russia, as the oft-told story had it, saved his life). And now Viktor understood he was at another Rubicon: the future of the First Directorate's operations in America hung in the balance, and, just as likely, also his own. A bullet in the head could be the cost of rashness.

In the end, though, according to the testimony in the KGB archives, Viktor's decision was motivated by a single argument: nothing could be allowed to jeopardize Operation Enormoz. Of all the Center's ongoing plots against America, Enormoz was the crown jewel. It had been moving forward slowly, but with increasing promise. And, remarkably, in total secrecy. But now the defectors' incriminating testimony, he conceded with a doleful resignation, would certainly shake the enemy's watchers out of their doldrums. Increased scrutiny of the New York *rezidentura* must be expected. And with the enemy on battle footing, the likelihood grew of their discovering, whether through doggedness or plain dumb luck, his agents' connection to Enormoz. The clue might be just a single loose thread, but give it a judicious yank and—the whole ball of yarn would unravel. That must not be allowed to happen. The future of the Soviet Union, he understood without an iota of drama or embellishment, depended on Enormoz's success.

So, his mind firmly set and his motives clear, Viktor issued his instructions. In December 1945, a cable marked "urgent" was delivered to a metal-shuttered third-floor office in the Soviet Consulate on East Sixty-First Street in Manhattan, a short stroll from Central Park. This was the headquarters of the entire New York KGB station, the handlers running the agents and assets on the front lines in the secret war against America.

It ordered: Shut down all your sources. All intelligence activities in the United States must come to a halt. For the next six months, all agents were to go to ground.

RECEIVING THIS NEWS, ALEXANDER FEKLISOV, a KGB captain working under diplomatic cover at the consulate, felt as bereft as if he had just been informed of a close relative's death, which in a way he had been. He was being told to dismantle the very networks—his proxy families—he had painstakingly put in place. The intensity of his anger and disappointment took him by surprise.

Yet, as he would concede with a soldier's steely logic, "an order is always an order." So he went to work, contacting his agents one by one, telling them to cease and desist. He made sure, though, that they understood that the war was not over. This was just a strategic pause in the long-running fight against capitalism. In six months, the trumpet would sound and the comrades would be called back to battle. Therefore, he also pointedly instructed, on the last Monday of the sixth month, each was to appear at a specific location. If Feklisov himself couldn't manage to be there—the demands on a KGB agent runner were, after all, unpredictable—he gave them their recognition signals: carry a copy of the prior day's *New York Times* and look for a man wearing shoes with two differently colored laces. When he bends to tie them, that means all's right with the world: the agent could approach.

During the course of a painful week, Feklisov—since childhood, Sasha to his friends—obediently buried all his networks. All the while, every professional instinct in him wanted to rebel; it seemed unnatural to be performing what should be the opposition's work. Still, even as his mind raged through its silent tirades, he also fully realized Viktor was right: long-term security must be the essential concern.

For he, too, shared the secret. He, too, was aware of what was at stake. When the order came to stand down, Sasha was running agents working in the very heart of Operation Enormoz. He knew Moscow Center was getting closer and closer to stealing America's greatest prize—the mystery of how to build an atom bomb.

INTELLIGENCE WORK IS, MOST FUNDAMENTALLY, the job of collecting information. In that way it has much in common with journalism. Perhaps, then, it is not surprising that the operational history of Moscow Center's quest to steal the atom bomb can be traced, in significant measure, to the KGB's paying shrewd attention to an insightful piece of reporting.

On Sunday, May 5, 1940, a dramatic headline was splashed across the front page of the *New York Times*: "Vast Power Source in Atomic Energy Opened for Science." William Laurence, the paper's diligent science correspondent, had been following Nazi Germany's groundbreaking research into uranium-235 and had come to realize what they were after. The German scientists' discoveries, he concluded, had "tremendous implications . . . on the possible outcome of the European war." "Every German scientist in this field, physicists, chemists, and engineers . . . have [*sic*] been ordered to drop all other research and devote themselves to this work alone." Yet Laurence, restrained by a journalistic prohibition on speculation, did not connect all the glaringly obvious dots. He did not articulate his belief that Germany must be working feverishly on an atomic weapon. Instead he wrote only what he could confirm, and then waited for the summons to Washington to share all he *really* knew with the generals and policy makers. To Laurence's great disappointment, it never came.

But across the globe, in the gloomy offices of the Lubyanka, the *Times* report was greeted with the sort of concern Laurence would no doubt have felt more appropriate from the U.S. government. For the Moscow Center decisionmakers, its implications were alarmingly clear.

Leonid Kvasnikov was a bull of a man, the ruddy-faced, hard-drinking son of a railroad worker from Tula. He had grown up not far from the bucolic estate where Tolstoy wrote *War and Peace*, although his scrappy, struggling childhood might just as well have been lived in another country. Nevertheless, the Bolshevik authorities, scouring the proletariat for a new breed of Soviet heroes, read the glowing reports extolling young Kvasnikov's first-rate mind and he was recruited for the prestigious Moscow Institute of Chemical-Machine Building. After graduating with honors, then flying through the even more rigorous postgraduate engineering courses, he attracted the ever watchful attention of Moscow Center.

Kvasnikov had just completed his KGB training course when Lavrenti Beria, the cold-blooded tyrant ("our Himmler," was how Stalin, without a trace of irony, praised him) who ran the secret organization, plucked him out of the troops for a special job. He was assigned to a three-member scientific intelligence unit. Its mission: keep a sharp eye on what the capitalist scientists were up to.

Proving himself surprisingly deft in the dark art of Moscow Center politics, Kvasnikov rose quickly to become deputy chief of the section. And with that appointment, he earned a bit of freedom; Kvasnikov could now define his duties as he thought best. On his own volition, as much out of curiosity as foresight, he began following the flurry of recent articles in Western scientific journals outlining the advances in uranium research. But it was the *Times* report, heavy with its implicit warning, that served to shape all his inchoate instincts into a firm intelligence priority. Not without genuine personal risk in the cutthroat corridors of the KGB, he lobbied for action, and late in 1940 Moscow Center had the sense to agree. A cable went out ordering the KGB station chiefs in America, Britain, and Germany to gather "evidence on possible work in those countries on the creation of atomic weapons."

In the race to comply, the London *rezidentura* won, as the jargon might have put it, by a mole. A member of the Kim Philby spy ring, a group of long-term British penetration agents the Soviets had recruited after their graduation from Cambridge University, and who had over the years burrowed their way deep into England's establishment, passed on a thick top-secret United Kingdom Cabinet document titled "On the Use of Uranium for a Bomb." The report, while laden with laborious scientific data, delivered its conclusion with a swift punch: an atomic bomb "is possible" and would be "a very powerful weapon of war." It could be built by Britain, the report announced with unsupported certainty, within two and a half years.

The New York station took its time finding its own kernel of intelligence, but in the end what it delivered was no less tantalizing. Franklin Zelman, a KGB spook working under student cover, had gone up to Columbia University with the hope of convincing Clarence Hiskey, a chemistry professor who, from time to time, had shown up at Communist Party meetings, to write him a recommendation for his postdoctoral research. Afterward, as the unsuspecting professor accompanied the secret agent back to the subway, Hiskey, as if just breezily ruminating, sketched a doomsday scenario. "Imagine," he began, according to the report Zelman subsequently sent off to Moscow in March 1942, "a bomb dropped in the center of this city which would destroy the entire city." Zelman listened, but had no time for such nonsense. By his own abashed admission, he "scoffed at that." But as it turned out, that was the perfect response. The professor, goaded, stated firmly, "There is such a bomb. I'm working on it."

Both the pilfered British report and the chance conversation on a New York street pushed Kvasnikov, who now had caught the scent, into further action. He drafted a long, comprehensive memo. One section offered a detailed historical perspective, describing the burgeoning state of atomic research in the United States, Britain, and France. Another offered a rudimentary primer on how the bomb might work; and, considering he was writing three years before the first atomic bomb was dropped on Hiroshima, his physics was impressively accurate: "In designing the bomb, its core should consist

of two halves, whose sum total should exceed the critical mass."
And the final section, articulated with a daring presumption, was
a call for action: the State Defense Committee should establish a
special scientific advisory group to coordinate atomic research in
the U.S.S.R.

Beria read the report, found nothing to take issue with, and,
once the imprimatur of his signature was added, it was sent off to
Stalin in April 1942. Stalin, in good bureaucratic turn, passed the
memo on for implementation to Vyacheslav Molotov, his foreign
minister, protégé, and, for all practical purposes, partner in a litany
of crimes. But with the heavy fog of war spreading across the Soviet Union, clouds made darker by the ongoing German sieges of
Leningrad and Stalingrad, the long-term development of a science-
fiction bomb seemed irrelevant. The Motherland was fighting for
its life—*now!* Running from crisis to crisis, Molotov let the memo
sit on his desk.

Yet as the fortunes of war began to turn, so did the foreign minister's vision. He looked increasingly toward the future. And when
he reconsidered the KGB memo, he discerned the significance in its
implied promise. Under his edict, in the spring of 1943, Laboratory
Number 2 was established. The name was purposefully banal, a bit
of cover designed to cause a snooping enemy to move on. The squat
building on Pyzhevskii Lane in the center of Moscow was the headquarters of the Soviet effort to build an atom bomb.

From its inception, the KGB had its long arms firmly tethered to
the program. Kvasnikov, now Molotov's eyes and ears on the state of
uranium research, drew up the short list of three candidates to run
the top-secret laboratory. Molotov interviewed them, and in the end
he judged by personality; any objective evaluation of scientific accomplishment, he conceded with a helpless shrug, was beyond his grasp.
He chose the youngest, Igor Kurchatov.

One of Kurchatov's first requests was a meeting with the KGB.
Kvasnikov showed up on Pyzhevskii Lane and listened as the physicist made an ardent plea: Russian science needed assistance. The West

was far ahead in its work to build a bomb. To keep pace with American atomic research, the KGB would need to help. And by "help," Kvasnikov knew, the young scientist meant steal.

The KGB man quickly dashed off a stern cable to the New York station chief. "We attach great importance to the problem of Uranium-235 (we call it Enormoz)," he began. But just in case the *rezidentura* had missed the warning in the sentence, the next was a certain threat: "Although we are having some rather good opportunities working on the problem in the U.S., we haven't yet begun such cultivation."

A response swiftly came—but it was not the sort Kvasnikov had anticipated. Molotov summoned him, and he went off to the meeting with considerable dread. In Stalin's autocratic Russia, one never knew if he was to receive a medal or a bullet, and either could be delivered with the same chilling smile.

The foreign minister, though, had something else in store. He announced that he agreed with Kvasnikov's assessment: the New York station was sitting on its hands. He had, however, found a solution. He paused dramatically, and then went on brimming with a confidence that the KGB man would in retrospect find totally unnerving. Comrade Kvasnikov was being shifted out of Moscow Center. He was to leave at once for America. His new title: Deputy Chief of the New York Rezidentura. His assignment: to pursue all leads and gather all information about America's top-secret efforts to build an atom bomb.

It was an impossible mission. And at that moment, who could have blamed the beleaguered KGB man if he'd have preferred the small mercy of a swift bullet rather than the long anticipation of the one waiting inevitably for him down the road?

IT TOOK, OR SO IT seemed to a weary Kvasnikov, an eternity to reach America. First there was the grueling trip across wartime Russia to the port of Vladivostok, and then on to Japan where his transit visa problems dragged on and on. But in March 1943—nearly three months after boarding a train in Moscow—he arrived in New York.

For cover, he was assigned to Amtorg, the Soviet trade group located in midtown Manhattan. Yet he didn't even bother with the pretense of establishing himself as another in the flock of wheeling-and-dealing commercial apparatchiks; apparently he feared Molotov more than the FBI. He went right to work solely on the atomic problem. "Like a vacuum cleaner," he would later explain, he began to gather all the information he could find.

He hadn't been at the job very long before Moscow Center realized it had a problem. Kvasnikov was a superb deskman, a visionary even. He could see difficulties looming on the horizon and then offer up cogent solutions. But he wasn't a fieldman. It wasn't just that he didn't speak English, although certainly that didn't help. It was that he lacked the ability, the mix of charm and natural friendliness that inspired devotion, that was necessary to recruit agents willing to put their lives on the line. He was a gruff, detached, and overbearing presence, while an agent living with constant danger required, from time to time, a reassuring pat on the back and a grateful smile. Kvasnikov needed help.

9

KVASNIKOV RECEIVED NOT ONE BUT two legmen. Yet even before they were put into the field to help run the Enormoz networks, the two spies were already best friends. Alexander Feklisov, just twenty-five, and Anatoly Yatskov, barely a year older, had met in June 1939, on the bus taking new recruits to the KGB training school in Balashikha.

The School of Special Assignment, as it was formally known, was about an hour's drive from Moscow, and the bus trudged east along the Vladimir Highway, the same route infamously traveled by those exiled to Siberia—"the road of the enthusiasts," as the Stalinists, with a rare stab at wit, smirked. All the while, the two young men couldn't help but have a nagging fear that they were about to be interned in another sort of Siberia. They imagined a grim military compound patrolled by armed sentries and growling attack dogs. Their expectations were reinforced as the bus drove deeper and deeper into a dense forest, and then passed through a gate in a high wooden fence. Yet when they finally arrived, both enjoyed a similar sense of relief mixed with nothing less than a total surprise: the school was a palace.

Or it might just as well have been when measured against their squalid childhood homes. Every recruit shared a room with only a single other trainee, and there were two large beds, thick blankets, and—an even rarer luxury—a shower with ample hot water just down the hall. Sasha took it all in, and then confided to Yatskov that at his home on Worker's Alley in Tula he'd slept during the winter curled up on a hard wooden chest behind the oven, and in the summer, on a pile of wood stored in a nearby shed. Yatskov playfully boasted that his life in the Ukraine was far more grand—he crowded into a narrow bed along with his two younger brothers. And with that, a shared feeling that they both were born under the same dark star, their friendship began.

It was, of course, no accident that the two men with such similar backgrounds had been thrown together. It was all part of Moscow Center's careful design. Viktor had set the guidelines for recruitment, and he favored boys from peasant and worker stock; if they had a college degree, it had better be from a technical university. He had no interest in the delicate children of intellectuals; they'd never muster up either the determination or the endurance required to survive the rough-and-tumble demands of the Great Game. And, not least, the spymaster shared a strong streak of Stalin's icy paranoia: intellectuals simply could not be trusted.

The training program lasted a year, and its intensity, as well as their own competitive streaks, brought the two new friends even closer. There were six grueling courses each day. They juggled academic subjects such as foreign languages, Communist Party indoctrination, and the history of foreign countries along with the nuts-and-bolts classes in tradecraft. They learned from wily handlers just returned from the front lines the subtle skills of recruiting and managing agents, working a meet, and breaking a tail. They became masters of the black arts: sabotage and silent killing. At the end of the long year, there were a series of written exams followed by an interview before an unforgiving commission headed by Pavel Sudoplatov, the cold-blooded hood who had directed the operation to assassinate Trotsky. And when the results were posted, the two friends beat out all the rest, each winning an assignment to the prestigious First Directorate's American Section, each promoted to the lofty rank of captain.

Yet for all they had in common, "in many ways," as Sasha would frankly admit, "Anatoly was the opposite of me." A quick glance confirmed that judgment. Feklisov was big and broad, a handsome man with a towering blond pompadour over a wide Slavic face. Yatskov had the dreary look of an apparatchik, short and stocky, already old beyond his years.

Yet there were other, more fundamental differences. Sasha, who had been a brawler in a tough Worker's Alley youth gang, famous for his powerful right hook, was a hard piece of work. Push him and he'd shoot back an unflinching stare; it warned—don't mess with me. And when things got dangerous, when, as he put it, "my heart would be in my heels," his instinct was to charge on, to show neither indecision nor fear.

When Yatskov stumbled into a sticky situation, he'd slow down, turn contemplative, trying to sort out all the possible consequences before making his next move. He was a man who felt comfortable with stealth, with subterfuge. And he had natural gifts that his friend couldn't even begin to challenge. Yatskov could learn any language in just months, or so it seemed. Give him an instrument, and he'd play it. Put him in front of a chess board, and he'd checkmate any opponent.

The two friends, however, were not troubled by their differences. They were certain that together, working as a team, each bringing his talents to the mission, they would make a single perfect spy.

But Moscow Center had other ideas. Yatskov was sent to New York, with the impressive cover identity of vice consul. While Sasha, to his dismay, was ordered to report to radio school.

RADIO SCHOOL WAS ENDLESS DRUDGERY. Sasha was put in front of a receiver and transmitter in Moscow Center's communications room, and the demands were exacting—a single mistake in a single digit and the entire encoded message was rendered unintelligible. And while he'd learned to speak some semblance of English during his year at spy school, it proved to be insufficient for what the KGB had in store for him. Every morning, under the watchful tutelage of an illegal—that is, a field agent without the protection of either diplomatic or trade cover—who had just returned from the West, Sasha was made to translate arcane intelligence reports from English to Russian, typing out the results in his stiff two-fingered way.

At first, Sasha was a disaster. With his KGB trainers leaning literally over his shoulder, he'd reach out to covert operators in neighboring countries. But he'd make such a mess of his transmissions—too slow, too many mistakes—that a "change operator" request would be abruptly sent by the annoyed receiving station. The entire experience, he conceded, left him "quite tense."

But KGB captains didn't have the option of going into another line of work; their destiny had been set when they were recruited. With a sojourn in Siberia looming as the consolation prize for failure, Sasha made up his mind to master all the nuances of radio work, and after two months of diligent practice he was close to succeeding. At least, he quietly celebrated, the insulting "change operator" codes had stopped appearing in the midst of his transmissions.

Then in early December 1940, the radio instructors decided it was time to put him through his operational paces. Sasha was given a specially designed radio transmitter and receiver, a device powerful enough to send signals across the world to New York. He was ordered to contact stations in Minsk, then Kiev. Finally, they instructed Sasha to transmit to a station at Ashkhabad, in the far reaches of Turkmenia, some 2,500 kilometers from his post in the middle of Moscow. When he passed all these trials with flying colors, next came the field test. Take the equipment and go to Batumi, in the depths of remote Georgia, and then contact us here at the Center. And he did it: the transmission came through loud and clear.

When he returned in January 1941, his sternest taskmaster, Fyodor Budkov, a stuffy KGB deskman, delivered the news without a hint of congratulation: Comrade Feklisov was being sent to New York. He must prepare to leave as soon as possible.

Yet before Sasha had a moment to rejoice, the rigid Budkov went on without missing a beat: If his wife could not be ready on such short notice, he must depart without her.

Sasha patiently explained that would not be a problem. He wasn't married.

Budkov turned somber; and then let loose with a long incredulous whistle. "How can you recruit any agents if you can't recruit a wife?" he challenged with the unshakable certainty of a man thoroughly persuaded by his own shaky logic. "Tomorrow we shall discuss this with Comrade Fitin."

The next day Sasha walked into a war council. Seated across from Fitin, the KGB commander, was Andrei Vlasov, the director of foreign affairs. At the head of the table was the man who would cast the only vote that counted, the all-powerful Molotov—and Stalin's henchman, the People's Commissar, wore the grave, resigned face of a hanging judge.

"You know that we never send bachelors overseas, especially to America," Molotov announced as the tribunal ground down. "The Americans will slip a blonde or a brunette into your bed very quickly and you'll be quite a mess."

As he stood at rigid attention, Sasha realized his dream assignment was floating away from him with every passing moment. There was no need for the tricky Americans to go to any further trouble. He was already "quite a mess."

But then Vlasov, the man whose service would provide Sasha with his cover job at the consulate, spoke up. Why did Vlasov dare to challenge Molotov? A combative nature? A sudden whim? All Sasha knew was that the foreign affairs director had boldly dared to interrupt Molotov. "Comrade Feklisov's superiors have every confidence in him politically and morally," Vlasov countered. "What's more," and now Sasha would swear he detected a salacious leer, "there are quite a few pretty girls in the Soviet colony in New York. He will have the luxury of a choice to get married over there."

Molotov mulled in silence, and whether he was considering Sasha's fate or the bevy of attractive Soviet women in New York was anyone's guess. When he finally spoke, though, his tone was conciliatory. "Go ahead, Comrade Feklisov. Do your best and don't betray the confidence we have placed in you."

Sasha was, by his own measure, "stolid by nature." "I am someone who is so fearless and so sure of myself that no one will ever see me jumping for joy." But he walked out of Moscow Center that afternoon feeling both exhilarated and for once scared. "New York is as far away as the moon," he couldn't help thinking.

10

S ASHA WAS RIGHT. IN NEW York, as things turned out, he had for all practical purposes been exiled to the moon—and the dark side, to boot. The New York *rezidentura* kept him at bay; he didn't even know where it was located, or who were its agents. Instead, he worked as a "clean" diplomat, doing his best to solve visa requests or bailing the occasional drunken Soviet merchant seaman out of jail. Even his reunion with Yatskov was no comfort.

Rather, it stirred all his competitive spirits. Yatskov's desk faced his in the consulate on Sixty-First Street, and his friend, too, had his share of diplomatic chores. He'd spend a good part of each day forwarding the legal documents and personal affidavits filed by the Russian community in New York to the proper authorities in Moscow. But Sasha couldn't help noticing that his friend would often disappear. He'd watch as Yatskov, a focused and determined look on his face, the time for small talk over, would rise from his desk without a word and vanish mysteriously. Sasha knew better than to ask what he was up to; a cardinal rule of intelligence work is that it is compartmentalized: you only know what you need to know. Nevertheless, Sasha had no doubt Yatskov, his contemporary as well as his rival, was doing something important. While Sasha was shuffling papers.

Bursting with his own sense of victimization, and feeling, Sasha would frankly say, "wronged," he confronted Yatskov.

"Don't worry," his friend insisted, working hard to soothe Sasha's dangerous anger. "It's standard procedure here. I went through the same thing myself. Right now they're observing you. Don't think about it anymore!"

But he did. It was nearly all he ever thought about.

"COME ON, WE'RE GOING UPSTAIRS."

It was a bright spring morning in May 1941, and Sasha had been sorting indolently through the papers on his desk when he looked up and saw Yatskov, a beaming, genial host, towering above him. Sasha didn't grasp what was happening, so his friend repeated his invitation.

Sasha at last stood and followed Yatskov. He led the way up to the third floor and then to a locked door. It was opened by someone on the other side and for the first time Sasha walked into the New York *rezidentura*.

A man he'd never seen before in the consulate welcomed him. He was old enough to be his father, and had a pitted face. He talked and carried himself like a soldier, a man accustomed to giving commands. His name, he announced as if he were reading a decree, was Pavel Klarin, and he was the number two *rezident* of the First Directorate in New York. In his hand, he explained, were Comrade Feklisov's orders; they had just arrived that day from Moscow Center in the diplomatic pouch.

He recited: Your mission is to maintain a clandestine radio link between the *rezidentura* and the Center. You must prove yourself capable before you can be trusted to manage agents. Now follow me!

Klarin led the way up to the attic. It was not much bigger than the outhouse his family had in Tula and the dropped ceiling only made the space seem tighter. Sasha was able to stand up straight, but just barely. An alcove fronted a small round window that had been boarded up. There, Klarin pointed, was where the radio transmitter should be placed.

Klarin found his commander's voice again. "Daily reports on the work done!" he barked. "You are dismissed!"

———

AND SO SASHA BECAME THE *rezidentura*'s radioman. His day would begin at five a.m. He'd tune into the Center's frequency and transmit in code, "I read you loud and clear." "Do you have any messages to send?" Moscow would reply. Afterward, Sasha would start sending the day's pile of encrypted messages, all written in numbers. When he finished, the Center would start sending its own traffic to New York. In the afternoon, he'd listen in to the Moscow radio news broadcasts and write up a summary that he'd deliver to Klarin each evening.

Sasha told himself he was doing spy work. He was at last part of the *rezidentura*. But at the same time he could not help reminding himself that his transmissions were just a bit of redundancy, the Center's wanting to make sure that the unscrupulous Americans were not tampering with the consulate's cables sent through commercial offices such as Western Union or RCA. Each day he spent in his attic hideaway in front of a radio transmitter he felt as if his reserves of ingenuity and commitment were being squandered. He wanted to be in the field, running flesh-and-blood agents in the streets of New York.

SASHA FINALLY GOT HIS CHANCE because his best friend was color-blind.

It was the silly season in the running battle between the Bureau's SE squad and the Soviets. As soon as anyone suspected of being a KGB hood walked out of the consulate on East Sixty-First Street, the Bureau, or so it seemed to the *rezidentura*, would be breathing down their necks. Sasha made a game of following the watchers on his trail, and in his estimation the FBI pavement artists were a pretty motley crew.

On a saunter across town to a steamship company to purchase tickets for some Russians heading home, he had no trouble spotting the opposition. The soldier riding behind him on the subway escalator. The man in shirtsleeves and no tie leaning on the counter in the ticket office. The man in the black raincoat and fedora in the cafeteria where he'd stopped for lunch. And that same soldier again as he walked back to the consulate. The enemy kept changing the guard, but despite the impressive show of manpower, the Bureau's handwriting, he judged with a professional's vanity, was entirely amateurish.

It was so heavy-handed that Sasha couldn't resist the urge to have some fun at the opposition's expense. There he was on a busy midtown street, and across the way a fellow in a topcoat and hat was staring at him. There was not even the pretense of artfulness. So Sasha, all mischief, crossed over and confronted the FBI man. "He looked," a bemused Sasha would always remember, "like a pickpocket caught in the act." The agent recovered, though, and walked off, ducking into the first doorway he could find. Sasha followed. The desperate agent now twisted the handle—but the door was locked. That's when Sasha started to laugh out loud. He was still laughing as the FBI man ran in embarrassment full-speed down the block.

But while Sasha, still on the operational sidelines, was enjoying these spy-versus-spy encounters, Yatskov was actually running agents. He couldn't afford to be observed. And that was why he turned to his best friend for help.

It was a meet at a coffee shop on the Upper West Side, and Yatskov worried about the drive uptown. He was color-blind, unable to tell the difference between the red and green traffic signals. He would need to focus all his attention on the flow of cars in front of him. There'd be no opportunity to glance in his rearview mirror to see if he was being tailed. So he asked his friend to drive with him, and keep a sharp eye out for the enemy. And when they reached the coffee shop, he had Sasha stand on the corner and babysit, as security operations were known in the trade. If he spotted the FBI, his instructions were to go to the counter and order a coffee, and Yatskov and his contact would know to run for the hills.

The meet went off without complications. After that, Sasha was given more opportunities to babysit for his friend. Then, one evening, without a hint of what was in store, Yatskov brought him to a restaurant on the East Side, near Thirtieth Street. Kvasnikov was already seated at a table in the back of the room. Speaking in a whisper so soft that Sasha had to lean across the table to hear him, Kvasnikov told him about Operation Enormoz.

At that moment he became a member of the KGB's most important covert team. He and his best friend would be running the networks stealing America's atomic secrets.

CONVINCED OF THE URGENCY OF his mission, Sasha went to work. He discovered that there was an army of possible recruits—scientists, intellectuals, and Party members—who believed it would be a disaster if America had sole possession of an atomic weapon. Some put their hopes for peace in a more equitable balance of power. Others were committed to the Soviet cause. And Sasha, playing caring friend, stern adviser, and shrewd accomplice, as if he had known no other life, was there in the shadows to help them.

But all at once, in the aftermath of the succession of defections in the fall of 1945, Moscow Center ordered that the ongoing operations in the United States come to an abrupt halt. Enormoz, although ripe with tantalizing promise, was shut down. And Sasha, for all operational purposes, was shut down, too.

IT WAS DURING THIS DORMANT period that a classified paper titled "A Review of the Uranium Problem" made its way to Laboratory Number 2 in Moscow. It had fallen into the New York *rezidentura*'s net—whether the credit should go to Sasha, or Yatskov, or to some other operative remains a mystery hidden in still-classified files—just before Enormoz had ground to a halt. It wasn't a scientific treatise, but rather a memo written for British and American policy makers, and so perhaps that explained why it had taken so long before it was shared with the physicists laboring on Pyzhevskii Lane.

But the young director of the Soviet atomic project, Igor Kurchatov, found the paper on his desk. Picking it up, he began reading but hadn't gotten very far before he abruptly stopped. Full of his sudden discovery, he dashed off an excited personal letter addressed to General Fitin at Moscow Center.

The brief note called attention to "the extremely curious remark on page 9" of the purloined report. And making sure the busy general would focus on the correct reference, Kurchatov patiently explained that this was a description of a secret facility in America called "Laboratory V" where scientists were calculating the physical properties of uranium-235 and plutonium "in connection with manufacturing a bomb."

And with that, the scientist's letter came to its brusque end. There were no specific demands, no recommendations about how Moscow Center should proceed. But arguably this was a shrewdness since clearly none were necessary. After Viktor had warily turned it over in his mind, a cable went out to New York: Kvasnikov and his team were to find out all they could about the mysterious Laboratory V.

Operation Enormoz was reactivated. And at the same instant, Sasha was back up and running, too.

11

As COINCIDENCE WOULD HAVE IT, not long before Operation Enormoz was secretly reactivated, at Arlington Hall the orders were issued, with similar stealth but a lot less importunity, to get the wranglers back working on the Blue Problem. This decision, just like the sudden one that had shut it down, seemed more a bureaucratic whim than a well-considered strategy. Nevertheless, the Army Security Agency got moving again on its attempts to break the Russian code.

Gene Grabeel, to her mystification, was abruptly pulled from her duties on the German desk and reassigned to the Blue Problem. And now she was joined by eight new female recruits. Like the industrious Grabeel, most were former schoolteachers, but the youngest had a leg up on the rest: she had taken a correspondence course in cryptanalysis during her senior year at the Mississippi College for Women.

The newly assembled unit went back to work sorting the intercepted Russian cable traffic—"discrimination," the more veteran cryptanalysts called it—into trade, diplomatic, and military groupings. They worked in a room with two long tables and a shoulder-high wall of filing cabinets that separated them from the impressively large teams dealing with the German and Japanese codes. Under orders, they talked to one another only in a hushed whisper, but even this sort of communication was rare. They spent each day staring blankly at thin pieces of paper filled with typed blocks of numbers—an incomprehensible language. The impossibility of their task left them enveloped in a nearly terminal listlessness. Yet with a numbing regularity, new piles of intercepted cables kept arriving on their desks, as many as 4,000 in a single week.

After eight dismal months, a frustrating period during which little more than a careful sorting of the Russian traffic had been accomplished, the team finally dared to ask for help. "The aim is to break the system and a staff of experts would be of value to the unit," it was tactfully suggested in a memo to the Arlington Hall brass.

It was a tempered plea, but it was also fortuitously blessed in its timing: the wranglers had already broken the back of the German and Japanese codes; and, more incentive to move on, the end of the war was in sight. So perhaps that was why it bore such quick fruit. But for reasons that the Army never bothered to explain, a half-dozen or so experienced cryptanalysts, most with impressive academic credentials, were soon assigned to the Russian unit.

And slowly, like the turning of a dial on a radio receiver, first tentatively, then more determined as it homed in on a signal, the new team began to make progress.

LIEUTENANT RICHARD HALLOCK HAD AN orderly mind. One of the new additions to the unit, he had studied archaeology at the University of Chicago and, more because he enjoyed poking into puzzles than for any practical scholarly purpose, he'd taken it upon himself to translate texts from various ancient Babylonian dialects. The key to making headway, he'd discovered after all his late nights, was to focus on repetitions: a word or phrase appearing in one dialect would have approximately the same meaning in another. It was a tool he employed time after time to wrench open whole sentences. And as he began to grapple with the Russian cables—blocks of numbers that were, at first perplexed glance, more abstruse than any language conceived by the ancients—he was guided by his own self-taught wisdom: hunt down the repetitions.

Only it was not enough. No sooner had he fixed on this strategy, than he realized he'd be setting off on a quest that was as unlikely to succeed as it would be unending; there were hundreds of thousands of pages, each filled with blocks of numbers. He needed to find a way to whittle down the odds. And that's when Hallock had his second insight.

The Russians—not unlike the stilted royals at the Babylonian court—often had standard, introductory doggerel at the start of each message. Time after time, they could be counted on to begin a cable with a formal phrase that, more or less, read, "Reference your message # . . ." And the sign-off was pretty formulaic, too.

Sensing an opening, Hallock rolled up his sleeves and went to work. Arlington Hall had one of the first IBM processing systems, and he set the staff to preparing punch cards for the beginnings and endings of 10,000 messages; the bulk of them were back-and-forths between Moscow and Washington sent years earlier, in 1942 and in the winter of 1943.

The chugging machine scanned the perforated rows and columns not unlike the way a player piano read musical scores. And the song the IBM wound up playing was music to Hallock's ears: there were seven cases where the Russians, going against all their rigid coding procedures, had enciphered two unrelated messages with the same additive block of numbers.

Could this have been a statistical accident, one of the vagaries of life, a happenstance akin to someone's picking the exact Irish Sweeps number five years in a row? The more mathematically gifted of the cryptanalysts did the sums: the odds of one-time pad numbers—random additives spewed forth by a cavalier machine in Moscow Center—being repeated seven times were about a billion to one.

And if that wasn't sufficient proof that the Russians' security procedures had indeed broken down, further scrutiny removed any lingering doubt. More duplicates, more examples of disparate Russian cables using the identical five-figure additives, were identified.

Which should have been impossible.

The entire point of one-time pads—and the source of their impenetrable security—was that they were used only one time. The cipher clerk sending the coded message added the random blocks of numbers taken from a page in his pad, and the recipient, using the same page, subtracted them. When each clerk was done, his page was to be incinerated, and that specific string of numbers would go up in smoke, gone forever.

Unless, against all their training, all their knowledge, all their institutionalized instincts, the Russians in the early years of the war had distributed duplicates of their one-time pads to their embassies and consulates.

Could that have happened? What had gone wrong back then?

THE GERMAN ARMY WAS AT the gates of Moscow. It was November 1941, and with the bone-chilling winter blowing in off the Russian steppe, the ground quickly froze. The tanks of the Wehrmacht spearheads, fifty-one divisions that had already blitzkrieged their destructive way across the Soviet Union, prepared to advance. The armored units would encircle the city, and then charge forward in unison to crush Moscow.

Stalin remained defiant, determined to rally his people. Against the admonishments of his generals, who feared Moscow would be left perilously exposed, he diverted troops to form a defensive line along the outlying cities of Klin and Tula. It was a gamble, and a desperate one. If the enemy broke through, Moscow's residents would need to take up arms. Yet with grim inevitability, Stalin's gamble moved closer and closer to becoming a losing bet. In the first icy week of December, the German tanks drove on, boldly splitting the Russian line of defense. "The enemy, ignoring the casualties, was . . . willing to get to Moscow by any means necessary," Marshal Georgy Zhukov, the chief of the Soviet General Staff, would recall. Stalin, his confidence now teetering, had no choice but to confront his generals. Could they keep the Wehrmacht out of the city? Could they successfully defend Moscow? With the German Seventh Panzer Division just twenty miles from the walls of the Kremlin, the generals' assurances were guarded, fraught with doubts.

It was at this perilous time, as the German tank commanders could see the twisting spires of the Kremlin in their field glasses, that the harried cipher clerks in Moscow Center who produced the one-time pads decided that the moment had its own unique priorities. With the Motherland imperiled, with so many pressing demands on resources, they decided it was necessary to risk a small accommodation to the usual code-manufacturing procedures.

In the past, the pages of random blocks of numbers rumbling out of the coding machines had employed a single sheet of carbon paper to make a single copy. They now used three sheets of carbon. As a result, the output of pads was tripled.

With that bit of time-saving, the one-time pads became another casualty of the war. Since there were duplicates, the blocks of additives no longer formed an unbreakable wall around the encoded message.

And a few years later the Arlington Hall code breakers would begin tearing the wall down, brick by loose brick.

As the wranglers proceeded with their arduous work, in one more stroke of good fortune another of the new recruits helped move things along by finding an ingenious shortcut. Cecil Phillips, a gangly nineteen-year-old, was an improbable candidate for such a fruitful discovery. He had wound up at Arlington Hall purely by chance.

A sophomore at the University of North Carolina, he had been cooling his heels at home for the summer when his mother suggested he'd better get a job. Obediently, he went off to the U.S. employment service in Asheville to see what the government had to offer a chemistry major. They had nothing, but suggested he speak to the Signal Corps lieutenant who was recruiting at the local post office. Phillips took a short IQ test, responded that of course he knew what the word "cryptography" meant (his parents had bought him a Little Orphan Annie Decoder Pin as a present for his eleventh birthday), and on the spot he was offered a job at Arlington Hall.

He did not return to college when the summer ended. Instead, for nearly the entire uneventful year, Phillips worked as a civilian clerk tackling the Japanese weather problem. Then, in May 1944, he was transferred to the Russian unit. Armed with paper and a well-sharpened pencil, he spent six diligent months scouring the pages lined with columns of numbers hunting for—well, something. And then he found it.

But his eureka moment would not have been possible without the interference of a Russian spy.

ELIZABETH BENTLEY'S LENGTHY CONFESSION, THE same 107-page document detailing Soviet espionage in America that had helped spark Bob Lamphere's mounting concerns, contained a single brief, almost throwaway, comment about a well-placed government official. Yet it was a revelation that left G-2 officers at Arlington Hall riveted.

"I recall one occasion," she had written, when one of the Soviet assets in the Washington ring, whose microfilms she'd been carrying to New York in her knitting bag, told her "he had informed Moscow that the United States was on the verge of breaking the Soviet codes."

The information was overly optimistic. The code breakers were a long way off. Yet as things worked out, the message the spy conveyed to his Soviet handler became, in time, a self-fulfilling prophecy.

On April 25, 1944, in response to the warning, Moscow Center sent an urgent directive out "to all Residents." As of May 1, the indicator system that showed the specific page from the one-time pad book the sender was using—the "key page," the wranglers called it—would be changed. The old two-digit key indicator at the start of every message would be replaced by a five-digit group taken directly from the page being used.

It was a tricky maneuver that Moscow Center thought would put the American code breakers off the scent. And it succeeded. For six months the Russian unit moaned that the sudden change in Soviet coding procedures had left them stumped.

But then Cecil Phillips noticed something. He realized the Russians had done them a favor.

"TOO MANY SIXES"—PHILLIPS EXCITEDLY ANNOUNCED to the rest of the outfit. At the start of some of the recent traffic sent from the Center, he studiously pointed out, there was a block of numbers that contained more sixes than seemed random. He had kept staring stubbornly at this oddity, and then it struck him: these numbers were not strings of enciphered code, but were naked, raw (*en clair*, as his more experienced colleagues put it) numbers. But why?

It was that question, he further explained to the code breakers who were now rushing along with him to the same giddy realization, that had brought him to his great discovery: Moscow Center was announcing the page number of the one-time pad they were using to encipher the message.

Since the team already knew that the one-time pads—the name now a fiction—were used for multiple messages, all they had to do was hunt for the traffic that had been enciphered with the same keys. The IBM sorter did most of the work. Still, it took several months to find the matches. Then they attacked.

It was a communal effort, with new readers being hurriedly brought on to the team. Shrewdly, they focused on cables that were Moscow's order lists for Lend-Lease supplies. The formats were identical, as were the commodities and quantities; this "item cycling," as it was known, gave the cipher strippers further advantage.

It was the edge they had needed. "The repetitious nature of the trade texts made it possible for the large cryptanalysis staff of fifty to seventy-five people, mostly young women, slowly to recover the code text," Phillips would explain.

But this was only the end of the beginning. Unraveling the Soviet code was similar to playing with a Russian nesting doll: you removed one, only to find another laying inside. The wranglers at Arlington Hall had, against all expectations, succeeded in stripping the cables of their encipherment. Yet that only revealed another deep mystery—the unreadable encoded message. The code breakers had traveled all this long, taxing way, and yet were still as far off as when they'd started the journey.

WHEN THE WAR ENDED, THE deep thinkers in military intelligence began to focus their attention, as well as their growing fears, on the Soviet Union. As a result, old hands from the other units at Arlington Hall were reassigned to the Blue Problem. In January 1946, Meredith Gardner was given a desk among dozens of others in the Russian unit that spread out across a large, open space in Building B. He was newly married to the woman, a fellow code breaker, who already thought him a legend, but now Meredith would prove it to the rest of them.

12

BOB LAMPHERE WAS ALSO NEWLY married, and, in the fall of 1947, was also off to a new posting. But he couldn't bring himself to feel the sort of unequivocal exhilaration that Meredith experienced in his love and work. For Bob, both these sudden changes in his life, he'd confide, had left him grappling if not with second thoughts, at least some moments of disquiet. Not for the first time, he feared he had gotten things all wrong.

After all, he had thought he loved his first wife, Geri, the college sweetheart whom he'd married five years earlier. But their marriage had quickly turned into a battle of wills; they were too alike to get along, he'd say. And for a gleeful spell he'd thoroughly enjoyed his nights as a bachelor on the prowl in wartime New York. But then— maybe it was growing up, or maybe it was just growing old, he'd wonder—Bob had reached the stage when he suddenly decided it would be nice to settle down again. And in this determined mood, all his thoughts turned to rekindling the flame of an old memory. Bob, in fact, persuaded himself that he had been seriously in love with someone else all along.

He had met Sarah Hosch when he was a young, footloose novice field agent in Birmingham. It was an energetic time, when his badge was still shiny and he could hightail across the state chasing down wartime desperadoes and also look forward to the long, playful evening ahead. Sarah had beauty, an infectious Southern charm, and when he was with her it was easy to be convinced that life held nothing better than hanging out till the wee hours in smoky roadhouses. Their glasses would be swiftly refilled, the band would mix honky-tonk with torch songs, and late into the evening they'd be dancing cheek-to-cheek. And come the new day he'd head out a bit red-eyed, but still basking in the fresh thrill of being a G-man. Throughout those dizzying months, one constantly recollected moment seemed to center all his thoughts with a pull as strong as gravity: Sarah singing "Linger in My Arms a Little Longer, Baby," her soft voice barely audible, yet still coaxing, and Bob at that perfect instant thinking he'd be happy to linger with her forever.

Yet as things worked out, their youthful relationship was destined to fall apart. Sarah married, and had a daughter. It was then that Bob, on the rebound, or so he now began to think, had married Geri, the adventurous woman he'd met at a college party in Idaho, only to wind up quickly divorced, living in New York, and once again passing his evenings in nightclubs and hotel bars, a drink in front of him, a smile on his handsome face, and doing his devilish best to chat up any woman who caught his wandering eye.

It was late one driftless night at the Astor Roof, a scotch resting on the bar and a singer with the face of an angel easing into *"linger in my arms a little longer, baby, don't think twice . . . ,"* that a once familiar memory reclaimed its place in his mind. All it took was a single long-distance call to find out that Sarah was divorced. And in the clear light of morning their reunion still seemed like a good—no, a fated—idea.

And now it was five whirlwind months later, September 1947, and, while Sarah's daughter remained with her father, they were newlyweds living, at least until they found something better, in a small, stifling room on East Capitol Street in muggy Washington, D.C. In the mornings their pillows would be damp with sweat and neither of them felt much like lingering. Adding to his woes, he'd doubted whether his new bride had the remotest idea of what life with him would now be like. How was fun-loving Sarah, he fretted, ever going to fit into his new straitlaced nine-to-five life as a supervisor in the Espionage Section at FBI headquarters? But for that matter, he was also wondering if he'd fit in, too.

THERE WERE THREE DISTINCT WORLDS in the FBI, Bureau veterans liked to remind young agents. There were the field offices, which offered an eclectic caseload and the much-prized autonomy to agents to pursue them pretty much as they saw fit. Then there was New York, where the possibility always loomed of being part of an investigation that would deliver career-making headlines. And then there was headquarters, which was totally unlike anyplace else in the Bureau. You sat at your desk all day, praying that whenever the director hurled one of his frequent thunderbolts down from Olympus, it wasn't aimed at you. "Dreamland"—that was what many who had done their time in the fortress-like Art Deco building on Pennsylvania Avenue called headquarters. It was a place where you went and dreamed about what your career might have been.

Bob, of course, had heard all this. He would never claim that when he'd filed his FD-638—the form requesting a promotion to a supervisor's role—he hadn't weighed any of the derogatory talk about what life at headquarters offered. But Bob had remained undeterred. He was convinced that all the verbal signals he'd been receiving about the changes in Bureau doctrine regarding the Soviet threat were sincere. He believed that not only did the top floor want to put an end to, as he called it, "the watch and wait philosophy," but that with his field experience and knowledge, he'd be the right man in the right spot to help wage the aggressive counterattack.

He had been recruited by Bill Harvey, the Bureau's counterintelligence "eminence rouge," as those on the SE squad called him because of his suspiciously rosy-cheeked glow. It was just after Bob had added to his growing reputation by representing the Bureau at the deportation trial of Gerhart Eisler, a balding, diminutive, ostensibly unemployed middle-aged man living in a third-floor walk-up in Long Island City, Queens, but who secretly was an active Com-

intern agent, crisscrossing the country to push the Kremlin's political
agenda. The Eisler case demonstrated to the skeptical lawyers at the
Justice Department that at least one FBI agent could provide them
the sort of watertight evidence they'd need to get a conviction in the
always problematic security cases. It also showed his Bureau bosses
that Agent Lamphere, when he was shoved into a corner, would ball
up his fists and fight his way out.

It was toward the end of what had proved to be a raucous trial,
when Eisler's frustrated lawyer jumped to her feet, pointed to Bob,
and roared, "This is a frame-up by you!" Without skipping a beat,
Bob shot back, "You're a goddamned liar!" The press was all over the
hot exchange, and so a very tentative memo went up to the director
reporting on Bob's outburst. People in the Bureau held their breath,
waiting for Hoover's response, and the consensus was that the intem-
perate Lamphere was toast. But when the director wrote back that
"the agent is to be commended," Bob's star at the Bureau rocketed
into its full ascendancy.

After the jury brought in a guilty verdict, Harvey made his pitch.
Bob listened, and he immediately felt as if Harvey had read his own
brash and impatient mind. The Bureau was "hamstrung, facing an
enemy that did not fight by rules of decency or fairness"—that had
been Bob's longtime mantra to his buddies on the SE squad. Now
at last one of the bosses was chanting it, too! Even better, Harvey
promised he'd back up his tough talk with all the naughty goodies he
had at his disposal—hidden microphones, telephone taps, electronic
surveillance, even black-bag jobs, as the warrantless "surreptitious
entry" ops were known. Harvey needed, as he flatteringly put it to
Bob, "new blood," knowledgeable supervisors who'd sit by his side
in Washington and help him direct the troops as they went off into
battle. Bob signed on without reservation.

But no sooner had he arrived at his new desk at headquarters,
than he found that Bill Harvey was no longer with the Bureau.
Mr. Harvey, Bob was succinctly informed, had decided his talents
could best be put to use at the newly formed CIA. After poking

around a little, Bob discovered what had actually happened. Harvey had gone off to a party, enjoyed himself too much, and on his unsteady way home, pulled his car into Rock Creek Park with the plan of sobering up before continuing on. Only he promptly fell asleep. He never made it home. In the early hours of the morning, his distraught wife, Libby, raised the alarm. When Hoover learned that his missing counterintelligence chief had not been sandbagged by the Russians but had just been sleeping it off in his car, he fired the errant Harvey. And so the Bureau's loss became the CIA's gain.

Bob's new boss, Lish Whitson, he soon recognized, was "almost the polar opposite" of the hard-charging Harvey. Whitson was a reserved, academic presence. He possessed an encyclopedic knowledge of the Russians working in the United States; throw a name at him and he'd give you the diplomat's or trade official's ostensible job, years of service, and marital status without consulting the file. But Bob couldn't help fearing that Whitson's studious approach to counterintelligence would result in only more of the same largely ineffective, largely passive responses to the KGB. Bob was left shaking his head, wondering about the rightness of his choice to walk away from the streets to sit behind a desk.

THEN THERE WAS HOOVER—AND, AS improbable as it was disconcerting, the director's apparent concerns about Bob's new wife.

In any circumstances, a summons from Hoover loomed as a nerve-wrangling encounter. Bob had no idea what had precipitated the director's wanting to see him, but he prepared for the appointment as carefully as if he were going into battle, which, he knew, might very well be the case. His suit pressed, shoes shined, tie precisely knotted, Bob was led down the long corridor by Sam Noisette, the director's unsmiling staff assistant. As instructed, he waited until Noisette announced his name, and then, feeling as reluctant as if he'd been ordered to step into a vat of boiling water, he crossed the threshold into the director's office. At once the door closed behind him.

Hoover approached, shook his hand perfunctorily, and directed Bob to a black leather chair.

The seating arrangement was pure theater. Hoover's desk was mounted on a platform, and Bob had no choice but to look up at him, a supplicant gazing at the king on his throne. He waited in intimidated silence for Hoover to begin.

What came forth was a diatribe about Bob's wife. Or was it about Bureau wives in general? Bob was too blindsided to tell. He simply nodded and grunted judiciously, as the director went on and dogmatically on. While all the time Bob's racing mind was screaming: *Can this be really happening?*

The gist of the nearly thirty-minute rapid-fire lecture was this: Wives talk. And when they do, their ill-considered chatter often jeopardizes ongoing investigations, and no less damaging, can also dent the Bureau's scrupulously crafted image. Wives, the famously unmarried director lectured, should never, ever be told by their husbands what they were working on. It was true for all agents, but even more for those in counterintelligence, he added emphatically.

The next thing a perplexed Bob knew, Noisette had once again materialized, and he was being escorted to the door.

On the way back to his desk, two floors below, a stampede of questions galloped through Bob's mind. Had Sarah said something to someone? Did this mean the wives routinely spy on one another? Could it be that Hoover was suggesting, however obliquely, that Sarah might not be a suitable Bureau spouse? Did he actually know something? Or perhaps, Bob tried to convince himself, it might not have been about him at all. It very well could have been a cautionary lecture Hoover routinely dished out to everyone at headquarters.

Bob had no answers, and lots of suspicions. But that night, and not for the first time, he had a sickening notion. He lay in bed next to Sarah unable to sleep, his thoughts circling from his new job to his new marriage and then back again. And once again he wondered what he had gotten himself into.

BUT, BOB DISCOVERED, THERE WERE at least two pleasing advantages to life at headquarters. First, he now had regular access to the Bureau's voluminous files. Shoot off a query slip with a subject's name and aliases, and before you knew it, a mountain of material would be piled on top of your desk. And, second, though not least to a grateful Bob, he was assigned a young clerk to help dig through the landfill of information.

Their paper chases—always a team effort—often proved gratifyingly productive. Take, for example, the time Bob was pulling together information on Mikhail Chaliapin, a particularly slow-witted KGB thug whom Elizabeth Bentley had first ID'd. Bob had been going down that long trail when, unexpectedly, he found himself doglegging off in pursuit of another Soviet contact Bentley had encountered when she was with Chaliapin.

For the past three years, Bob, who was convinced Bentley's 107-page confession was full of clues that would lead to buried treasure, had been trying to get a handle on "Jack." All they had was this cover name and Bentley's intriguing description of a man with "dark-blond kinky hair, unusually thick eyebrows" and who "walked with a slight limp in his left leg which was noticeable when he moved rapidly." Jack's identity, though, remained a mystery.

But Bob's clerk noticed something that had been previously overlooked in the thick Chaliapin files. Bureau watchers had been tailing the KGB man when he met up with an unidentified subject—"unsub," in Bureau-speak—on a New York street corner. On a hunch, or perhaps simply out of boredom, they abandoned Chaliapin and followed the unsub to a brownstone in Greenwich Village. And that's where the trail ended. There was no further follow-up on the man Chaliapin had met on the street. But the report included a brief description: he had a limp.

When his assistant pointed this out, Bob was quickly on the phone to the New York office. That day an agent, hiding behind a routine cover story to justify his inquiries, spoke to people in the building on West Eleventh Street. And the man with the limp was given a name: Joseph Katz. When Katz's photograph was shown to Bentley, she confirmed that he was "Jack." A long-running mystery was finally solved. And Bob, although still straining against the shackles binding him to his desk, couldn't help but enjoy a small sense of triumph for the role he'd played in bringing another covert member of the KGB operation out of the shadows.

BOB ALSO HAD THE FRUITS of another weapon at his disposal—and it was a secret one. In fact, it was so secret it wasn't officially supposed to exist. A strident Bureau memo made that clear: "We do not obtain authorization for 'black bag jobs' from outside the Bureau. Such a technique involves trespassing and is clearly illegal." Only Hoover or Clyde Tolson, his deputy, could sign off on a surreptitious entry—an op undertaken without a legally required warrant—into Soviet facilities. The authorization memo would be prominently marked "Do Not File," and it carried the instructions that the paper must be destroyed once the operation had been completed.

Nevertheless, as Harvey had promised, the black-bag teams were kept busy. In the dead of night, sound teams spiked the Soviet consulate in New York with microphones. And after posing as New York City elevator inspectors to get the lay of the land, over a series of weekends another crew targeted the office of the Soviet Government Purchasing Commission. With the lock-school agents leading the way, they succeeded in breaking into the code room. Then the photo teams took over, and they had a field day, snapping shots of everything that the Soviet cipher clerks had filed away. By dawn they were gone, without leaving a trace.

Bob was cheered that the Bureau was beginning to fight back. But at the same time, he didn't know what to make of the information that was coming in. The wires seemed to produce nothing of any operational value; the Soviets were apparently too canny to talk openly. And he'd look at the photographs of encoded cables and shrug. Then he'd get on with other work.

IT WAS AN UNCOMFORTABLE TIME for Bob. He knew he should be proud of what he'd accomplished—at twenty-nine he was both newly remarried to a pretty wife and already a supervisor at Bureau head-quarters. Outwardly, as he went about his days, Bob was his usual stolid, hardworking, pipe-smoking self. But inside he was having dif-ficulty coming to terms with a sense of his own uselessness.

Bob was convinced that, as he unhesitatingly put it, "the So-viets were the enemy." He had envisioned himself as "a man on a mission"; that was why he'd come to Washington. But now he had come to suspect that he had been sidelined. Supervisors must live by the golden rule of their profession: Don't get your hands dirty. Bob, however, wanted to get into the thick of things. He wanted to break away from his desk and check the flow of evil. He wanted to make a contribution, and he blamed the Bureau for not knowing how to use him.

13

Unknown to Bob as he tried once again to make sense of his life, just a few miles away, Meredith Gardner was staring at a bullet hole. Or *was* it a bullet hole? It certainly looked like one. Still Meredith Gardner, always one to value accuracy, couldn't be sure. When asked, he would be of two minds. But even Meredith had to concede the events that had brought the KGB codebook to his desk at Arlington Hall certainly made the likelihood a genuine possibility.

It was quite a story. And, Meredith was sternly warned, a top-secret one. Yet the way his superiors told it, it might have been a fairy tale. Once upon a time, they near enough began, on a wind-swept promontory in Finland, a long-forgotten hero bravely reached into a roaring fire as bullets whizzed all around him. . . .

June 22, 1941. A chaotic day when German troops marched into Russia, and Finland once again changed sides in the country's musical-chairs-like struggle for survival. Two years earlier, in what became known as the Winter War, the outnumbered Finns had stood up to an invading force of twenty-six Red Army divisions, fought them tooth and nail for 105 days, and in the end earned a compromise that was no small victory. The Russians wound up occupying a small, icy, albeit strategic, isthmus due north of Leningrad, but the rest of the country remained as it was before the war. And Finland and Russia made peace.

But the Finns' embrace of the Russian Bear would be short-lived. They had simply pretended to let bygones be bygones; yet all the while their silent thoughts ran to revenge. In early 1941, the foreign minister sneaked off to Berlin and the country took the first tentative step toward reclaiming the territory it had lost. The pragmatic Finns forged a secret alliance with the Nazis. It was agreed: when Germany invaded Russia, Finland would join the assault.

On that June day, as the first waves of German troops and tanks rolled into Russia, the Finns charged into action, too. In a maneuver inspired as much by pride as sound tactics, one of the initial Finnish military objectives was to retake an isolated building overlooking the deep harbor in Petsamo. It had been serving as the Soviet consulate. At just before nine in the morning, the Finns stormed the building.

Scrambling Russian security forces formed a makeshift battle line across the consulate's entrance hall. In the cipher room, the lone duty clerk had no time to initiate Moscow Center's careful emergency procedures for the destruction of the coding materials. Instead, racing about in full panic, with the assistance of a couple of armed guards, he got a fire going and started throwing whatever he could into the flames. But just minutes later, the heavily armed Finnish troops broke through the consulate door, and the Soviet guards raised their hands in surrender. A special squad, led by Finnish intelligence officers who'd been previously briefed about the classified treasures to be had, hurried to the cipher room.

A valiant last stand ensued. The Russians desperately hoped they could win the time needed for the blazing fire to complete the incineration. But even as the bullets flew about, the Finns were determined to claim their prize. Four singed Russian coding books, one after another, were gingerly plucked from the flames. It was an unprecedented trove of Moscow Center material. The real jewel, however, was a partially burned codebook from the First Chief Directorate of the KGB—the intelligence group that directed spying abroad.

The victorious Finns dutifully shared photostats of the Petsamo haul with their new ally, the Germans. And then—nothing. The Wehrmacht did not attempt to exploit the secrets the codebooks held. For all operational purposes, it was as if the Petsamo material had simply vanished.

As THINGS WORKED OUT, WHEN the codebooks finally reappeared four years later, it wasn't the work of a magician pulling them from a hat, or even a fire. But it might as well have been magic. They were found buried in a pile of abandoned papers in the damp basement of a medieval German castle.

The Target Identification Committee—TICOM, to those in on the existence of this top-secret Anglo-American unit—had been set up as the war drew to a close. Its mission: to recover German cryptographic material. And what they couldn't take, they were to destroy before the advancing Russian army got their hands on it. From its inception, the brass at Arlington Hall considered the entire operation fanciful; the Nazis were too shrewd to let any of their coding material be seized. And their skepticism was confirmed, when in April 1945, an eager TICOM team rushed to the site of a Wehrmacht sigint unit in newly liberated Leopoldsburg, Belgium, only to find the facility had been meticulously destroyed—except for a welcoming note in English the Germans had tauntingly left.

Nevertheless, as the war was in what would be its final weeks, when the commander of the One Hundredth Infantry sent a flash signal about some intriguing civilian prisoners they had captured fleeing from a tenth-century castle in Saxony, TICOM Team 3 rushed into action. Under the command of Colonel Paul Neff of the Army Security Agency, a convoy of trucks left Paris that day. They drove at mad speed through Verdun and continued on without stopping in Germany, arriving with the new morning at the ancient castle towering above the Unsutt River.

A narrow bridge led to the *Schloss*, and as Colonel Neff headed across with his men, he had few expectations. Despite the haste, his trip to Saxony had been largely dutiful, at best a bit of wishful thinking. Deep down he suspected the prisoners, civilians after all, would be of little value. If anything of cryptological importance had been stored in the remote castle—of all unlikely places!—the retreating Wehrmacht troops would have made sure it was destroyed. But for once everything worked in TICOM's favor.

The dozen prisoners were indeed civilians, but they were Reich Foreign Ministry officials who had fled in January from a secret base near Breslau. Hoping to avoid both the advancing American and Russian forces, they took refuge behind the closed gates of the castle. For four carefree months, they lived in splendid isolation; incredibly, the castle had been untouched by the war. But when the American infantry took control of the tiny village outside the castle walls, the Germans decided the time had come to move on once again. Only they ran straight into an American patrol.

Now they faced Colonel Neff and his team. The TICOM interrogators were all sigint specialists and so when the anxious prisoners revealed they had worked with the *Balkanabteilung*, an alarm might just as well have started clanging. This was the German cryptographic unit tasked with "solving the Russian problem." They were the Nazi wranglers who tried to make some sense of intercepted Russian signals.

Still, the colonel did his best not to betray his growing excitement. As if there were nothing in this revelation that was of any genuine interest, Colonel Neff asked his next matter-of-fact question. When you left the Breslau base, had you, by any chance, happened to bring any papers along?

Not much later the astonished TICOM team was in the castle's clammy basement, staring at the entire records of the *Balkanabteilung* cryptographic unit. There were rows of boxes arranged in tall towers, one carton neatly balanced on top of another.

Over the next busy days, the boxes were transported to the nearby Kolleda airfield. From there they were flown by special plane to England. By the time the Russians marched across the bridge leading to the castle on June 23, the cache of valuable papers had made its way to Arlington Hall. It was a mother lode that included the codebooks the gritty Finns had rescued from the flames during the taking of the Soviet consulate at Petsamo.

AND NOW A COPY OF KOD 14—the Russian KGB First Directorate's codebook—was on Meredith's desk. Day after day, he sat bowed over it, poring through it with an intensity so deep that it seemed to isolate him from all the others at the rows of tables in the large room. From time to time, he could be observed staring blankly into space. At other moments, he was seen absently tracing a finger around the small, irregular black oval on the singed cover. When any of his fellow code breakers dared to ask about the mark, his answers varied. One time he said it was caused by a bullet. Another, by the fire. Perhaps his judgments kept changing; but just as likely, he enjoyed having a bit of fun with his inquisitors before he got back to work.

He understood the magnitude of the specific challenge he was facing. The cipher strippers had done their job. Thanks to brains, ingenuity, and an incredible stroke of luck—the Russians having committed the sin of all cryptological sins by reusing their one-time pads—the encipherment had been wiped away. Now it was his turn. He had to decode the blocks of numbers that remained. He must translate seemingly random digits into words.

Meredith knew too well the codebook could not serve as a crib; the underlying code in the cable traffic he was grappling with was something newer, a different language. All the Petsamo codebook could offer was insight; a familiarity with the structure of a Soviet codebook, with its vocabulary. It was as if someone had given an aspiring writer a copy of *Moby-Dick* and said, "This is what a novel looks like. Now go write one." Yet when Meredith finally returned to the task of breaking the Soviet code, it was with a newfound confidence.

14

O F ALL THE WRANGLER'S DARK arts, bookbreaking was the oldest—and the most challenging. At the same time, it offered the greatest prize. The lofty goal was to reconstruct the enemy's codebook. If you succeeded, a world of secrets would be revealed: you'd have a dictionary that'd allow you to read an adversary's mail.

Like other puzzles, bookbreaking had its own time-proven strategies. They were not so much foolproof rules as bits of leverage, procedures that experience had shown could, in the right hands, help jimmy open a code. The cardinal one: There's always a weakness. The canny bookbreaker shakes the pieces until he finds this weakness, and then he exploits it for all it's worth. Or, as the Arlington Hall wranglers, partial to wartime analogies, put it: You establish a beachhead, and day after day you continue to extend it.

And so as Meredith, a man apart, a bookbreaker locked into the clarifying calm of his own solitude, took on the Russian code, he set out to look for its weakness. To his credit, he did not rush. His hunt began with preparation, the tedious preliminary work that's the elbow grease behind any decoding success. The tortoise always beats the hare, code breakers were fond of saying.

His desk was a battlefield, and across it stood five columns of papers in neat, parallel rows. To his left were the original cables: impenetrable five-digit blocks of numbers. Next in line were what the professionals called the "message prints"; that is, the cables reduced to their basic code groups, the concealing encipherments stripped away.

Occupying center stage was the "Index." This was invaluable: a list of the specific five-digit code blocks that appeared more than once in the cable traffic. Over several weeks the IBM machine had done the heavy lifting, and now there was an inventory that logged each of the messages in which the identical groups of numbers occurred, highlighted the position in that message, and—another rich potential clue—showed the code groups that preceded and followed it. Then, in an attempt to narrow the problem even further, came his fourth column of papers—the "Inverse Frequency List." This ranked the blocks of codes by how frequently they appeared in messages, the most-often-repeated five-digit groups put at the top of the list. And, finally, on the extreme right flank of Meredith's desktop battlefield, was the "Lane Log." This allowed him to see at a glance the circuit—military, trade, or diplomatic—over which any message had been sent, and the date of the transmission as well.

These were his tools; and, at the same discouraging time, also his scant clues. He started out trying to recognize sentences, only he had no idea which blocks of numbers were the verbs, adjectives, and nouns. And, giving the problem a further malicious twist, the original words would have been written in Cyrillic. Still, the Russian language had rules. It was rational. He had no doubt it would yield to a systematic interpretation. That's what Meredith kept telling himself as he went to work.

The days were long and slow. There were periods when nothing much seemed to be happening, when he'd stare vacantly toward the ceiling and those around him would quip, "There's Meredith praying to the heavens for guidance." Perhaps that was true; there were certainly days, he'd later confess, when he'd have been glad for a little divine inspiration. But even when all seemed lost, he never quit playing with the pieces of the puzzle, juggling them in his head and on his work pad, trying to find the pattern.

When an identical block of numbers had been repeated in a single message, he compared the locations in the text, and he came up with some preliminary, and perhaps promising, findings. Since the block was always preceded by two different groups, it might very well be a verb. So then the block that follows should be, according to the rules of Russian syntax, the subject, a noun. Which Meredith found interesting, a handle to grab on to. But in the end, the handle slipped from his hands. *What* verb? *What* noun? He was certain of his logic, but he still had no answers. He couldn't take things any further.

Now he backtracked. Over several focused weeks, he returned to the lists of repetitions. He compared; he annotated; he cross-referenced. And in the process he noticed something curious, something that had escaped his scrutiny. Previously, he had been attempting to work out the role a single five-digit block might play in a sentence, whether it would logically translate into, say, an article, verb, or noun. But when he looked again he saw that entire blocks of numbers—long bodies of text—were introduced by the identical five digits. And at the end of this long chunk of text, another five-digit group, also always the same numbers, would appear.

Could it be that these were the encoded digits that announced "to" and "from"? But no sooner had he considered this possibility than Meredith realized it didn't make sense. The cipher clerk would put that sort of information at the beginning and end of a transmission— not in the middle. So what could they be? Two code groups always used in conjunction with each other, one at the start, the other at the end of a block of text. He lived with the question for a couple of days, and for a while he thought he'd cracked it: They must be quo- tation marks, one block of code signaled "open quote," another "close quote." Only the frequency with which the blocks appeared seemed to undermine this theory. With some disappointment, he put this hypothesis aside. Don't force the pieces, he reprimanded himself. Still, Meredith felt he was on the right track: the two code groups worked in conjunction with each other. But how?

And then suddenly he was there.

All at once, it was obvious. Why hadn't he seen it before? The Rus- sians were sending their messages to and from America. It was only

reasonable to assume the traffic would contain words in English—
names, places, transcripts of conversations, official documents—that
could not be rendered in Cyrillic. QED: the initial five-digit block
told the cipher clerk: Start spelling with Latin letters. The concluding
one announced: All done; return to Cyrillic. They were the "spell"
and "end spell" indicators.

Which meant, Meredith deduced in a triumphant jolt, *there was
a code within the code!* The Soviet cipher clerks, he realized, had a
separate dictionary that assigned numeric code groups to letters, even
phrases, that were to be transmitted in English.

At last he had found the weakness. And his entry point: he would
concentrate on re-creating this English dictionary. It would be a
considerable challenge, but one that, over time, would be susceptible
to analysis. All at once he felt that the entire Russian problem had
abruptly become more manageable. With renewed confidence, a plan
of action took shape. He would make his beachhead, and then, with
one determined push after another, extend it.

IN A CROSSWORD PUZZLE, YOU fill in the blanks. One letter leads
to informed suspicions about the next. The discovery of a repeated
vowel can be the key that opens an entire word. And the placement
of a word can lead to the recognition of a familiar phrase. So it is in
codes. The bookbreaker deduces unknown values from the known.
Guided by logic and common sense, he, too, fills in the blanks.

Over the next six plodding months, one daunting letter at a time,
Meredith began to reconstruct the coding dictionary that the Soviets used for sending words and phrases in English. "My hunt for the
Great White Whale," was how he'd remember the time; and the
description, several observers would agree, was an accurate measure
of the self-absorbed, obsessed mood in which his restless days were
spent.

It was in the winter of 1946 that Meredith decided the time had
come to put his creation to the test. He selected a message that, if his

theory was correct, had been transmitted entirely in English; it began with the "spell" code block and concluded with the "end spell" indicator.

Slowly, with studious attention to each new letter, he translated one block of numbers into an English word and then moved on to the next. The process of watching the message slowly come to life on his work pad, of numbers becoming words, of words becoming sentences, filled him with an incredible excitement. He had started in a state of total ignorance, and even as he continued he had no idea what would ultimately be revealed. It was as if he had set off on a long voyage across a murky sea, all the time wondering what strange land he'd find at the far side of the world. And in his desk-bound way, Meredith was a true explorer. No one had ever gone where he was heading.

In the end, what he discovered, after all his strenuous efforts, was not only mundane but also demonstrably wrong. The revealed message read: "If election were held today R [President Roosevelt] would probably obtain slender majority of popular vote but lose election due heavy concentration his vote in South."

Yet Meredith was elated. With a professional's pride, he quickly made a list of what he'd learned.

Fact: The message was political, an explanation of how Roosevelt would lose the election in the Electoral College despite receiving more votes in the ballot boxes.

Fact: This meant that the traffic on the cable circuit he was attacking—designated JADE by Arlington Hall—was not concerned with trade but with diplomatic issues. And this offered the encouraging possibility that future decoded cables might provide significantly more interesting reading.

Fact: Since it was transmitted in English, that suggested the unknown source who was being quoted was an American. Which could mean the Russians had signed on a journalist or even a politician as an asset.

And finally, his one great, glittering fact: He had done it! He had broken the Soviets' spell code for English words. He had demonstrated that what had previously been impossible was indeed possible.

It did not matter to him that the decoded message was trivial. Meredith had little interest in what the men in impressive military uniforms who ran Arlington Hall portentously called "strategic importance." The value of the information he'd unearth, where it fit in the push-and-pull game being played out between the Americans and the Russians, was irrelevant. He simply solved puzzles. And now, spurred on by this first heady success, he would continue to recover more code groups. He would hunt for other repetitions, and then chart their interplay. He would go forward, and he would go back. He would not stop until he could read entire messages, not just the words from the Soviets' English spell dictionary. He'd stay at it until every blank was inked in. That was all that mattered.

YET AS THE MONTHS PASSED and Meredith continued to fill in the blanks more, he began to suspect that all his initial instincts had been too parochial. His success remained limited; a word here, a phrase there. Decoding entire messages was still beyond him. Nevertheless, what Meredith read started to fill him with apprehension. Word after decoded word woke up a new suspicion. Yet stubbornly he refused to acknowledge it. But in the spring of 1947, after he succeeded in reading a message sent from New York to Moscow, he could no longer deny the larger significance of the puzzle he'd been piecing together. He could no longer take refuge in the belief that he'd been toiling away at a purely academic pursuit.

He read, in part: "For correspondence with Arthur a book in the Spanish language, 'Una Excursion a Los Ranqueles,' was used as a code.

"For correspondence with Aleksandr the books 'My Sister Eileen' and 'Defense Will Not Win War' were used as codes."

It was now clear to Meredith that he had broken into Soviet espionage traffic, most probably KGB. He was reading a cable announcing the book code that Soviet spies would use to transmit messages. He had no inkling who the well-read "Arthur" and "Aleksandr" were. But he knew these were the code names of Russian agents.

Over the weeks that followed, as Meredith continued to grow more confident in deciphering the cable traffic, the trail of incriminating footprints led him deeper and deeper into the secret world. Yet once again, there were mysteries buried within other mysteries. For even after he'd managed to turn numbers into words, he was left staring dumbfounded at a new, seemingly incomprehensible language. There were cover names for agents, for politicians, for sources, for locations. It was an entirely new vocabulary of intrigue.

When Meredith had first started grappling with the Blue Problem, he'd told himself, *This is going to be fun.* The prospect of cracking a big, complicated code, a problem that had defied all previous attempts, had filled him with a childlike joy. But now his assignment had taken him into unsuspected territory. He had stumbled onto something chilling, even dangerous. He wasn't all the way there. There were still plenty of loose threads that remained to be tied. Yet he knew it was not too early to sound the alarm.

On August 30, 1947, Meredith wrote the first in what would be a series of top-secret memos. With a deliberate vagueness, it was headed, "Special Analysis Report Number 1." And the subtitle was only a bit more forthcoming: "Cover Names in Diplomatic Traffic."

The memo opened with a careful diffidence, full of caveats that were intended to batten down tight restraints on any reader's expectations.

"Any report at this time on the contents of traffic encrypted by the system," Meredith cautioned in his opening sentence, "must necessarily be fragmentary and subject to correction in detail." And if that weren't warning enough that this was very much a work in progress, he offered yet another dose of candor: "Only about 15 per cent of the equivalences [of the Soviet codebook] are identified, some only tentatively."

But once the qualifications were out of the way, his hesitancy vanished, and the report rolled on with a compelling speed. Readers were rewarded with not merely theory or speculation about the enemy's tradecraft, but the real thing—an insider's tour of the KGB.

Meredith had pulled a long list of cover names from the cable traffic. Some were used for locations. Others indicated either the senders or the recipients of the messages. And, most ominous, there were dozens of work names of Soviet penetration agents, living and breathing enemies buried deep in the nooks and crannies of American life.

Still, the report offered lots of clues but no specifics. At that preliminary time, it was impossible to infer what sort of espionage activity these networks were conducting; the targets of specific KGB operations remained frustratingly beyond Meredith's grasp. Equally infuriating, the traitors were well protected by their cover identities; it was impossible to put a name or face to any of them. All that could be established was that they were out there, working in the shadows.

Yet in retrospect, one clue, although thin and stuttering, stands out. Years later, when events would give his report a riveting clarity, Meredith would recall what he had written with a shudder:

"LIB?? (Lieb?) or possibly LIBERAL: was ANTENKO [ANTENNA] until 29 Sept. 1944. Occurs 6 times. 22 October–20 December 1944. Message of 27 November speaks of his wife ETHEL, 29 years old married (?) 5 years, '. . . . husband's work and the roles of METR(O) and NIL.'"

But back then, this was as far as Meredith's analysis could go. And after having stirred things up, after having as good as shouted its implicit warning that networks of Soviet spies were running pellmell about the country, the report ended by taking a big, admonitory breath. "In its present state," Meredith reminded his readers, "the traffic tends to arouse curiosity more than it does to satisfy it. This unsatisfactory state of affairs makes it imperative this report be supplemented at intervals."

Then having said his piece, Meredith, quite happily, went back to work.

AS MEREDITH CONTINUED HIS DAILY struggle to make further inroads into the code, the Signal Corps spymasters at Arlington Hall pondered what to do with his report. They were suspicious by both nature and profession, and Meredith's findings had only reinforced their doubts. They no longer knew whom they could trust. But one thing, they felt, was a certainty: the larger the distribution list, the larger the chances the Soviets would learn what they were up to.

They discussed sending a copy to the president, but this was quickly rejected. The White House, it had to be assumed, was riddled with Soviet spies. And the newly formed CIA? Its wartime predecessor, the OSS, had leaked too many valuable secrets. Why should things be any different merely because the initials had changed? After a good deal of heated debate, it was grudgingly decided to share a single copy, along with a few supporting pages containing the cryptic phrases and sentence fragments that Meredith had so far been able to extract, with the Army colonel running G-2. But before they handed this package over, they made it clear that their concession was bound by a strict understanding: the documents would not leave his office at Military Intelligence. Colonel Harold Hayes agreed.

The deputy chief of Military Intelligence, however, did not. Colonel Carter Clarke thought the FBI might be able to help lift the masks concealing the faces in Meredith's report. On his orders, the memo and the challenging pages were hand-delivered by special military messenger to the Bureau's Washington headquarters.

Pat Coyne, the head of the FBI Soviet Espionage section, read the documents. There was a brief discussion with two of his deputies, but it was swiftly decided the clues were too slight and too fragmentary to be of any operational value. Satisfied, Coyne locked the papers in his office safe.

15

THE SAFE WAS BIG, OLD, and battered, a Mosler with a spindial combination lock and a handle as long as a child's arm that you'd push down to open the creaking door. And every time Bob Lamphere went into Pat Coyne's office, he felt it pulling him like a magnet.

He'd heard the stories same as everyone else on the SE desk. How more than five months ago the Army Security Agency had sent over a top-secret report including a few pages of the cryptographer's work notes; apparently they had made some inroads into a KGB code. But it had turned out to be just scraps of messages, sentence fragments, really, and some cover names. Nothing worth pursuing. And so the dull pages had been shoved into the Espionage Section chief's safe, and that was that.

Still, Bob was curious. These days he had been shunted off to the side, assigned to monitoring the low-grade Soviet satellite states. And at home, things with Sarah had gotten off track, too. Often he found himself complaining about her drinking, and then she'd shoot back with digs at his hair-trigger temper—and they both knew the other had a point. Yet neither felt like changing, neither felt like learning from past mistakes. They had moved out of the stuffy downtown apartment to a new development in Silver Spring, Maryland, which was probably a good thing. Now they had more space to hide from each other. So perhaps, as Bob would later concede, he was just *looking for something*. He certainly had no specific sense of what was in the safe, nothing tangible that he could even hang a suspicion on. At best, Bob would hedge, he had an "operational intuition." But whatever the reason, even before he'd read a single page that Meredith had written, he was intrigued. Every professional instinct he'd nurtured in the field, as well as all his unsatisfied ambitions, were shouting to him they held promise.

Then one afternoon Bob finally got up the nerve to confront Coyne. He might have been a prisoner approaching his jailer; the section chief, after all, was the boss who had locked him away in the backwater that was the satellites desk. But Bob was no timid supplicant. His pitch was surprisingly blunt; it just wasn't in his nature to kowtow.

"I'd like to take charge of the messages the ASA sent over. See what I can do with them," he said straight out.

"Which I suppose means you're asking to be relieved of your present duty?" Bob would remember Coyne shooting back.

That led to some further sparring. But when Bob walked out of Coyne's office, it was with the agreement that he no longer had to put in any time monitoring the low-priority Soviet satellite countries. He had Meredith's pages clutched tightly in his hand. And he had Coyne's parting warning ringing in his head: *You have your chance, now you'd better deliver.* Bob hurried to his desk to read the prize that had fueled his imagination.

It didn't take him long. What he read, Bob judged as his heart sank, was not just thin—it was useless. He could not see how he—how anyone!—could be able to make sense of these meager, incomprehensible scraps. Not for the first time in his roller-coaster life, Bob wondered if he'd made a colossal—and this time perhaps career-ending—blunder. He'd gambled his professional future on the contents of the safe, and he'd lost.

He lived with these wretched thoughts for the rest of the afternoon. On the commute back to Maryland that evening, still locked in this dismal mood, he decided to seek refuge in some dark bar.

One scotch helped to level things off. And by the time he'd drained the second, his whole world had started to come back into focus. Now raised from the depths, he found the perspective he needed.

All things considered, he told himself as his spirits rallied, he'd accomplished a very large victory that day. He was "back to fighting the main threat—Soviet intelligence." That was the important thing, he felt. For how long had he been saying that it was "every counterintelligence man's dream to be able to read the enemy's communications?" Well, now he'd been given that very opportunity. True, the cards he'd been dealt were not very encouraging; the odds were stacked high against success. But, Bob reprimanded himself, he'd always been a battler. When had he ever backed away from a challenge? You don't grow up doing pick-and-shovel work in the bowels of a silver mine and expect things to be handed to you. Besides, what was the alternative? To rot doing the hackwork on the satellites desk? He decided: this was the bright, shining opportunity he'd been waiting for. He'd take those scant pages and do something with them.

OVER THE NEXT FEW DAYS, as he sat in his distant corner in the sprawling SE section, his commitment grew into a plan of action. Bob realized: if he was going to assist the code breakers in widening their narrow breakthrough into something more substantive, he'd need to meet with them. This, however, became a more complicated process than he had imagined.

The FBI's bureaucratic fiefdoms were protected by vengeful lords, and Bob knew it would be a mistake not to pay them the homage they expected; otherwise, they'd make his life hell. So he sent off a request to meet with Wes Reynolds, the sleepy-eyed agent who was the Bureau's designated liaison to the ASA. According to headquarters protocol, Reynolds would need to make the initial contact with Frank Rowlett, the chief intelligence officer at the signals agency. Yet it must have been the busy time of year at Bureau headquarters, because a week passed before Reynolds could find the time to see him.

When Bob was finally granted a face-to-face, their conversation was stiff, but mercifully quick. A man who had more important things to get on with, Reynolds agreed to reach out to Rowlett, and then briskly escorted Bob to the door.

The meeting took place nearly three long weeks later, and it was, at Rowlett's insistence, "on neutral ground." Bob, mystified but wise enough not to look for a fight, especially one he knew he wouldn't win, went as directed to the Pentagon. He entered a small, windowless room as clean as a surgical theater, just a metal desk, two straight-back chairs, and nothing else.

Rowlett was a gruff, confident man who had no time for fools, yet even those who had felt the brunt of his disdain would concede that he'd earned the right to his arrogance. In 1930, Rowlett, barely twenty, had been hired as one of the three civilian cryptanalysts at the fledgling Signals Intelligence Service, and over the subsequent decade, despite having no formal training, he'd been a key player on the team that had broken the Japanese code. Now he sat behind a desk in an office that Bob assumed had been borrowed for the occasion and, without any of the usual niceties, launched straight off into a lecture on security.

Rowlett must have been aware that the man across from him was an experienced Soviet hand who held the rank of supervisor, yet he made no concessions. All Bob could do was listen, and silently bristle.

They were meeting off-site, Rowlett explained, because before Agent Lamphere could be allowed entry into "the facility"—a euphemism meant to suggest that even its name was classified—he had to agree to the ASA's rules. First, and this, Rowlett made clear, was the holiest of holies: the attempt to break the Soviet code system was top secret. It could not be spoken about, nor could its existence even be hinted at. The other rules, all recited in Rowlett's rapid machine-gun way, were stringent corollaries of the initial one: the FBI could not quote directly from a deciphered cable. The source of the paraphrased information could only be described as "a highly sensitive source of known reliability." And the actual messages could only be shared with individuals who had a special top-secret clearance, regardless of the rank they held at the FBI.

Do you agree to all these conditions? Rowlett demanded.

Bob agreed. Nevertheless, as if he had not heard the response, Rowlett repeated his speech, rule after dogmatic rule. When he finished, he once again asked if Bob accepted the conditions. Growing weary of this game, Bob offered a curt yes. But this time Rowlett seemed satisfied, and so he moved on to new ground.

"The man you'll need to work with is Meredith Gardner," Rowlett announced, according to Bob's vivid memory of the meeting. "He's unusual and brilliant. He speaks six or seven languages, and is one of the few Western scholars who reads Sanskrit." And in the prickly silence that followed, Bob couldn't help but complete Rowlett's thought: While you, Agent Lamphere, are neither unusual nor brilliant.

When Rowlett continued, he picked at the same sore spot. His words were another deliberate taunt. "You'll find Meredith Gardner to be a shy, introverted loner. You'll have a hard time getting to know him."

Bob listened, but he was not about to let Rowlett's warnings throw him. Instead, he chose to focus on a more hopeful reality: the operation, his chance to do something of consequence, was moving forward. Besides, when had he ever met someone whom, when he put his cheery heart into it, he couldn't charm? A code breaker stuck at his desk all day would probably be glad for a little company, some convivial conversation.

The next morning, Bob headed off to Arlington Hall. The day was bright, and as he drove his Bureau car into Virginia, his foot heavy on the pedal, the window cranked open so he could enjoy the breeze, he felt certain he was driving down the road that would take him back into the thick of things.

16

OB WAS NOT SURPRISED BY the security, the barbed wire, the armed guards, the checking and rechecking of his credentials each time he entered another of the brick-and-wood-frame buildings on the Arlington Hall campus. After Rowlett's harangue, he had anticipated finding things under tight control. But he had not been prepared for the legions of young women scurrying about. They seemed to be everywhere. Walking about the grounds, striding officiously through the halls, poised over the long tables that served as communal desks—a secret female army hidden in the Virginia woods, he happily observed. As he made his way along the path that led from the main building, he took sly measure of one passing woman after another. A few, he noticed with a small ripple of vanity, openly stared back. On a different day he might have felt a stronger pull, contrived an excuse to daw-dle, perhaps spark a conversation by asking for directions, but not this morning. His gaze remained alert, and he continued walking briskly to Building B.

Meredith, in recognition of his accomplishments, and no doubt with a nod to security, now had his own office. Bob gave a knock on the door, waited for a response, and when there was none, he simply entered.

The room was tiny and as dark as a cave. A man sat hunched over a wooden table that served as the desk, papers strewn all about, and he was so motionless that Bob's first thought was that he had caught him napping. His second thought, as he stepped closer, was that Rowlett's description had been altogether accurate: Gardner was tall and gangly. And when he finally raised his head to look up at Bob, his eyes were brimming with hostility.

Meredith still hadn't spoken, and for an uneasy moment Bob wondered if he had been informed an FBI agent would be coming by. But then he remembered that he had been present the day before when Rowlett had called Gardner. It had been agreed; ten a.m. sharp. So Bob decided to plow on.

He introduced himself, then improvised a small speech about what an honor it was to work with Meredith, and how eager he was to do all he could to help. Bob believed he had a gift for hail-fellow intimacy, and he laid it on with thick, florid cheer. He was determined to win Meredith over.

If Meredith had heard any of it, he gave no indication.

Bob didn't retreat. But he didn't press, either. Instead, more instinct than strategy, he offered his hand, and Meredith politely reached out and shook it.

A small victory, Bob decided, and he swiftly tried to build on it. Without waiting to be asked, he brought the wooden chair that had been shoved against the wall up to the table and sat down opposite Meredith. Their eyes were now on the same level, and Bob felt they would be able to talk as one professional to another.

He asked if Meredith had made any further progress on the codes.

A moment passed in heavy silence. When Meredith finally spoke, the words came slowly, and with great reluctance. "I don't think it's appropriate to discuss that."

At least a dozen possible responses shot through Bob's mind, but none of them were polite. He waited until his rash mood had passed. Then he tried another tack.

"How can I be of assistance to you?" he asked, hoping to sound both eager and considerate.

Meredith once again appeared to give the question considerable thought. But whether that was really the case, or perhaps something else was going on in his mind, Bob could only guess. He found the man across from him inscrutable.

"I don't know," Meredith announced an eternity later, or so it seemed to Bob. The words were flat. Not plaintive. But neither were they dismissive. So Bob tried again. "I could mount a research effort to help you get information."

Meredith nodded. But whether that meant yes or no was far from clear.

Bob, though, soldiered on. "I could write up a memo about one of the message fragments. The FBI might have a glimmer of understanding on the subject matter being discussed by the KGB."

Again Meredith was noncommittal.

Bob considered trying another approach, but Meredith had apparently lost interest. His eyes had returned to the papers on his desk, signaling that the dismal conversation was over.

But Bob was determined not to betray his annoyed mood. He acted as if things had gone swimmingly. He told Meredith that it had been a pleasure to meet him and that he looked forward to their working together. "Think about my offer to help," he suggested, all the time feeling like some nagging salesman trying to close a deal.

At the door, he announced that he'd return soon. "I look forward to continuing our chat," he lied.

Meredith's head remained hovering over his papers. For all Bob knew, his thoughts were a million miles away. Bob walked back on the twisting, pebbled path leading to his car. Unlike his earlier cross-campus trek, now he was too upset to pay attention to the people passing by. Worse, his anger had slid into despair.

YET BOB REFUSED TO GIVE up. He returned to Arlington Hall a week later. "You give any thought to how I might be able to help?" he asked.

Meredith looked past Bob toward the opposite wall, his eyes fixed on an invisible target. At last his gaze focused on Bob, and he offered a small shrug.

When Bob left minutes later, he chose to remember that Meredith hadn't said no. He hadn't totally rejected the possibility of their working together.

ANOTHER WEEK, AND AGAIN THE same question. "You give any thought to how I might be able to help?" Bob asked. As he spoke he tried not to sound too beseeching, as if he'd not abandoned all of his pride.

Again the interminable silence. And then Meredith responded.

He did not explain why he finally chose to answer. That would come later. Only in retrospect would Meredith reveal that at the time he had run out of alternatives. He had taken the deciphering as far as he could on his own. Stymied, with nothing to lose, Meredith had decided he might as well try anything. Even the FBI.

Was there any possibility, Meredith wondered, his words so hesitant they might as well have been dragged out of him, of obtaining the plaintexts of Soviet cables? Perhaps traffic that had been transmitted from New York to Moscow? Say, oh, in 1944?

Bob understood the significance of the request. If Meredith had the *before* as well as the *after*, he could really go to town. The comparison of the same texts, one in Cyrillic and the other wrapped up tight in its blanket of encipherment, would be any code breaker's dream come true. Give it to someone like Meredith, and he'd tear the Soviet code apart.

"Let me see what I can do," Bob responded, trying to appear confident. But even as he offered this small assurance, he knew it was hollow. In truth, he had no hope at all. The texts Meredith wanted were over three years old. How was the Bureau going to get their hands on them?

Still, like Meredith, he was willing to give anything a try. When Bob returned to headquarters, he sent a flash request to the New

York office: "Need soonest plaintext Soviet cables circa 1944." And
while you're at it, he felt he might just as well have added, "How
about the key to the vault at Fort Knox?"

A thick package from New York arrived a few days later. It was
sitting on top of Bob's desk when he came in. There was no accompanying note, nothing to hint at the contents other than the "Classified
Material" stamp on the standard gray Bureau envelope. Could it be?
He ripped open the seal as eagerly as any child attacking the wrapping
on a Christmas Morning present.

Inside were photographs of hundreds of cable messages from
the Soviet Government Purchasing Commission on West Twenty-
Eighth Street in Manhattan. All before they had been enciphered.
And all had been transmitted to Moscow in 1944. How, he wondered, had the New York field office happened to have this pile of
goodies sitting in its files?

An SE colleague with whom he had worked surveillance details
years ago on the streets of New York gave him an oblique answer.
There's no explanation, his buddy said carefully, because officially
these photographs don't exist. Get what I mean?

At once Bob did. They were the warrantless, forbidden fruits of a
black-bag job. Worthless—no, less than worthless—in any American
courtroom. But the only judge Bob had to go before sat in a tiny
room in a barracks-like building in Virginia.

Later that day he presented the package to Meredith. Bob did not
know if the photographs would prove helpful; breaking a Soviet code,
as Rowlett had pointed out in his superior way, required the sort of
brain that belonged to someone else. All Bob said was that he hoped
this was what Meredith had wanted.

Thank you, Meredith answered in his dead-fish voice.

Bob dropped the package on the desk, and turned to leave.

TWO WEEKS PASSED, AND BOB had counted every day. But he had
deliberately waited before returning. He wanted to give Meredith

time to go through all the plaintext messages; he could only begin
to imagine the complexities of the trial-and-error process that would
be Meredith's hunt for matches with the encoded cables. Also, Bob
was in no hurry. He suspected his first chance could end up being his
last one. If he had failed to provide the valuable information Meredith needed, he knew the code breaker would never come to him for
help again. Their partnership would have ended before it had truly
started. It was with considerable trepidation that Bob entered Meredith's room.

At once Meredith looked up from his pages. "We hit the jackpot," he said. His voice was still soft and hesitant. His posture as
he sat at his desk remained so stiff and so self-contained that in
someone else it would've been judged as downright antagonistic.
But Bob didn't care. A single word, a word received as gratefully as
any answered prayer, kept echoing in his mind: *We, we, we.* We hit
the jackpot!

They sat and talked, and for all operational purposes it was their
first conversation. Meredith was careful to avoid making any guarantees. The small accomplishments he did share were couched in his
natural modesty. But despite these restraints, Meredith managed to
reveal that he had made some real progress. His efforts to reconstruct
the Russian codebook were beginning to pay off. And he acknowledged that the plaintexts Bob had provided were invaluable.

"Thank you," Meredith said. This time he was the one who offered his hand.

When they shook, Bob felt the moment had its own deep solem-
nity, and a kinship had been forged.

A WEEK LATER WHEN BOB returned to Arlington Hall, he was
greeted by what he immediately recognized as a different Meredith.
It was not the reticent, inaccessible code breaker of their initial encounters. Nor was it the man who at their last meeting had, in his
guarded way, allowed himself a small victory lap. Meredith's mood

today was something totally different, and for reasons he could not identify, it left Bob unnerved.

Look at this, Meredith finally got around to saying. He handed Bob a thin piece of paper. It was a deciphered cable sent from the New York KGB station to Moscow Center. The date was December 1944. Bob glanced at the cable; and as he did, he grew filled with alarm. He read:

"Enumerates the following scientists who are working on the problem—Hans Bethe, Niels Bohr, Enrico Fermi. . . ."

The list ran on for a total of seventeen names. Each was a physicist and each had worked on America's most closely guarded wartime secret—the construction of the atom bomb. Their identities, as well as their top-secret laboratories, had been so classified that they were only referenced even in U.S.-government documents by their cover names. Yet the Soviets had penetrated the Manhattan Project. They knew who had directed the critical research and fabrication laboratories in the New Mexico desert at Los Alamos. They had the names of the scientists who had made the essential breakthroughs at the university centers of Berkeley, Chicago, and Columbia. They had the names of key scientific personnel at the massive Oak Ridge, Tennessee, compound with its mile-long electromagnetic separation plants that provided the uranium-235 needed to make a bomb.

It was at that moment that all Bob's professional suspicions, the sporadic drumbeats of clues he'd been collecting over the years, hardened into a new resolve. Any lingering doubts that it was a false peace, any attempts at denial, any bouts of indecision were cast permanently aside. "It became immediately obvious to me that the Russians had indeed stolen critical research from us," he recalled. At the same time this clarity brought with it another profound conclusion: Bob was equally certain the Russians were still at it. And now when he looked at Meredith, he was able to put a name on what the code breaker had been feeling, because he felt it, too. It was fear.

Six days later, on October 19, 1948, a meeting took place that made their partnership official. With Frank Rowlett and Colonel Hayes there to give the ASA's blessings, and a sullen Wes Reynolds representing the FBI, it was formally agreed that Agent Lamphere would work hand-in-hand with Mr. Gardner to exploit the deciphered Russian cable traffic.

Then Bob and Meredith walked off together, returning to the dark little room in Building B, the light of battle shining in their eyes.

MEANWHILE, ON THE STREETS OF New York, two old friends, each as committed to their cause as Bob and Meredith were to theirs, already had much to show for their collaboration. Alexander Feklisov (Sasha to his comrades) and Anatoly Yatskov, the two KGB handlers who had been running the Operation Enormoz networks, had dispatched "about 3,000 pages," according to the Center's proud count, of stolen documents to Moscow.

The flow of reports, a detailed how-to collection of diagrams, mathematical formulae, and atomic theory, had been so constant that their boss at the New York *rezidentura*, Leonid Kvasnikov, became skeptical of the entire enterprise. A man whose suspicious mind ran to plots within plots, he feared that the haul might be too good to be true. He wondered if the foxy Americans had concocted a load of fake science with the aim of putting the Soviet physicists off the scent.

His concern was understandable. "If this is disinformation, I'll send you off to the basement," Lavrenti Beria, the chairman of the new Special Committee on the Atomic Bomb, had threatened. And Kvasnikov, the old KGB hand, knew only too well that it was a journey from which you didn't return.

But the product passed all the tests with flying colors. The team of scientists at Laboratory Number 2, the official report announced, "had conducted the research and experiments necessary to confirm that the information provided by intelligence was true and not disinformation." And Igor Kurchatov, the young physicist directing the Russian bomb makers, went even further, nearly swooning with glee: "Wonderful materials, they fill in just what we are lacking."

Formal notification was sent to the Special Committee: Laboratory Number 2 would proceed to construct a Soviet atomic bomb "on the basis of materials received from the KGB."

Part II

"In the Enemy's House"

Part II

17

THEY WERE NOW A TEAM. Huddled in Meredith's monk-like cell, an isolation that reinforced the realization that they were on battle footing, the two men began to search for a way to move forward. As in any new relationship, there was a tentativeness to their conversations, an elaborate politeness born out of caution, an unwillingness to offend. This awkwardness was further reinforced by the large differences in both demeanor and natural talents that shaped their approaches to the looming challenge, as well as to each other.

But as they got to know each other, as each took appreciative measure of the other's unwavering commitment, what separated them began to recede. The contrasts became unimportant. Instead, they acquired an informed, increasingly respectful admiration for what the other had to offer. It was almost as if they each sized up the man across the room, one the prideful brawler and elbow-on-the-bar carouser, the other the devotee of unfathomable puzzles who hid behind an armor of social inhibition, and wondered, What if I could walk in his shoes? What if I could bring such gifts to my duties? Who knows what I'd accomplish?

In this curious way, a union of shared purpose was forged. There was no grumbling, no censorious judgment made by one partner of the other. Rather, these were extraordinary days. Working together, they filled the dismal space with an electric intensity.

And in time they did nothing less than re-create the KGB codebook. Bob would venture out into the real world of official Washing-

ton and track down the texts of documents—cables from Churchill
to Truman, wartime notices—that had been transcribed with meticulous care in the KGB cables and, like a hunting dog returning from
the field, drop these goodies on Meredith's crowded desk. Then he'd
sit back and marvel at the alchemy.

"I'd give him something," Bob would recall, "which was, say, the
real text of something that was in his message, and that would give
him a new word in his codebook. Right away, he's over there with
his pen writing it in there. He was as pleased as a little kid. One more
word!"

In that workmanlike way, one valuable word at a time, there was a
constant thrust toward tangible progress. Slowly, the KGB codebook
took fuller shape on Meredith's desk. And as this dictionary grew, as
it provided more and more of the vocabulary they needed, they began to succeed in reading nearly complete texts of Moscow Center's
cables that had been sent years earlier.

The military intelligence generals, soldiers who had little if any
hands-on experience with code breaking, were astounded by this
accomplishment. That a lone, and for that matter, rather eccentric,
bookbreaker and a plodding FBI agent had pulled off such a feat was
nothing short of a wonder. Yet both Bob and Meredith knew better
than to indulge in self-congratulatory outbursts. This was not the
time. They had read the cable that hinted at the Russian penetration
of the top-secret American project that built the atom bomb. They
knew what was at stake. They understood the severity of the covert
threat aimed against America.

Grimly, Bob and Meredith weighed the significance of their accomplishment in strictly operational terms. They both realized they
were stationed on the front lines in a secret war. And now they could
launch their counterattack.

"I stood in the vestibule of the enemy's house, having entered by
stealth," Bob would later say, although such was their shared intensity
of purpose that he could very well have been speaking for Meredith,
too. "I held in my hand a set of keys. Each would fit one of the doors

of the place and lead us, I hoped, to matters of importance to our country."

They had—quite literally—filing cabinets full of clues. But at the same baffling time, they had no way of knowing which of Moscow Center's newly revealed twisting trails might lead to a mission involving the theft of atomic secrets, which led to other, still unimagined precincts of intrigue, and which ones, no less a possibility, led to an inconsequential dead end. The chase itself would be another mystery.

Bob, the experienced fieldman, understood the complexity of what he was up against. "I had no idea where the corridors in the KGB's edifice would take us, or what we would find when we reached the end of the search," he conceded.

Meredith, although a newcomer to the rough-and-tumble world of secret agents, shared this realization. Their tactical predicament, he explained as he reached for another metaphor, was like the old parable of the blind men and the elephant. Like the naïve blind men who'd reach out to feel a tail or a tusk and think that that was all there was to the animal, they could grapple with a single Soviet cable and believe they were homing in on the enemy's main thrust. And yet this insight could be absurdly narrow. It might not reveal how their discovery fit into the entire operational puzzle that Moscow Center had assembled. More dangerous, it could just as well give them an entirely skewed view of what the enemy was up to: they'd be as mistaken as the blind men.

And another profound anxiety: the clock had already been ticking away for years. Since the cables they were working with were several years old, they did not know if the enemy's spies were still active, operating at this very moment in the shadows, or if they had completed their missions. It was a very tricky business.

There was really no choice, however, but to proceed. And no sooner had they addressed the task when Meredith, in a flurry of sustained activity, deciphered a series of apparently interconnected cables. His discovery was a further call to action.

IT HAD BEEN MEREDITH'S TURN to deliver the goods. He had been working away for days, bleary-eyed, oblivious to Bob, maintaining the silence of the self-absorbed, and now he finally was done. There were no shouts of eureka, no attempts to coax a celebratory pat on the back from his partner. He simply handed the pages of his "Special Study" (as he'd officiously titled it) to Bob with a businesslike courtesy, knowing all the while that the words on the page were as potentially explosive as a ticking bomb.

Bob read:

"For some time the cover name 'Enormoz' (which is not a word found in the Russian dictionaries, but is obviously based on the English *enormous*) has been known to occur in one or two New York–Moscow messages of 1944 in the system but previously the context has not been readable enough to limit the possible reference of the name. Recently enough context has been recovered to suggest a possible link between Enormoz and war-time nuclear fission research."

So there it was! The translation of four still rather cryptic cables filled out this study and each one reinforced Meredith's deduction that Enormoz was Moscow Center's cover name for its plot to steal atomic secrets. Now that Bob's worst fears had been confirmed, he was less surprised than appalled. How could the nation have allowed itself to be so easily victimized? And was it too late? Could his efforts hope to be something more than an after-the-fact closing of the barn door? Or were the Enormoz spies still at work, having moved on from pilfering the science of the atom bomb to the secrets of the next "super weapon," the hydrogen bomb that Bob had heard mentioned in deliberately vague references in several Bureau counterintelligence briefings? Were these Soviet agents planning to make off with other closely guarded technological treasures?

Hand in hand with those questions, another concern burned in Bob's already overheated mind: Was it simply vanity to think that the two of them—a relatively junior supervisor on the SE desk and a head-in-the-clouds code breaker—could lead the assault against a well-entrenched Moscow Center operation? Would they have the strength of body and mind to get the job done?

These misgivings, while natural enough, threatened to boil over into a near panic after Bob tried to rally the Bureau to join him in this quest. Part of the problem, he realized, was of his own making: he was bound by his promise to the ASA not to reveal that the KGB ciphers had been cracked. Yet even with that restriction, he could not grasp why his "superiors did not appreciate the worth of the work very much." The bosses, he'd recall with despair, "believed little would come of the work and the research." And while he had written the requisite memo to the director and other top officials giving a more revelatory glimpse into the extent of Meredith's accomplishments, it, too, had elicited not a ripple. No word of encouragement made its way down from the fifth floor.

Bob was mystified. The Bureau's complacency was not just bewildering, but also, his every professional instinct shouted, dangerous. *Context has been recovered to suggest a possible link between Enormoz and wartime nuclear fission research.* Yet before he had time to brood, Meredith summoned him. The code breaker knew better than to say too much over the phone; and anyway, by now that sort of directness was unnecessary between the two friends. Bob only had to hear the animated tone of Meredith's voice and he immediately understood, he'd later explain, that "a sense of urgency and importance" had suddenly taken hold of their hunt.

18

"WE MIGHT HAVE AN ACTIVE spy on our hands!" Bob decided.

Not much more than an hour had passed since he had received Meredith's call, but it had been an hour that had raced away as if it were an instant. One moment he was driving pell-mell through the D.C. traffic; the next he was hurrying across the Arlington Hall campus in a walk that was near enough to a run as to attract curious stares; and then, as soon as he'd entered the gloomy room, Meredith, for once rising from his desk in greeting, had handed over the deciphered cable. And now Bob had just finished his reading. Still clutching the thin page in his hand, he let a single operational thought sink in: there was at last the possibility of a living, breathing target in his sights.

Yet despite his excitement, Bob chose to store that intelligence in the back of his mind for now. He needed, he realized, to get a firmer grasp on the entire puzzle. With the dispassionate scrutiny of a veteran counterintelligence analyst, he held the page up to his glasses and started to reread the message that had been sent more than three years earlier, on July 26, 1944, with a slow and deliberate concentration.

"To Viktor," it began. "In July Antenna was sent by the firm for ten days to work in Carthage."

Bob now paused. It was important to get all the working parts clear before going any further. "Viktor," Meredith had previously deduced, was the cover name of Pavel Fitin, the spymaster who pulled all the strings in the Foreign Intelligence Division at Moscow Center. Or, as the cable put it, "the firm." And "Carthage," as in "Carthage must be destroyed!" was the KGB's cover name for Washington. But "Antenna"—who was he, or she, for that matter? All Bob knew, again thanks to Meredith, was that the Center, as part of its routine security procedures, had recently changed that cover name. "Antenna" had been rechristened as "Liberal." Other than that, Bob had no clue; and so he decided to put the problem aside for the time being and continue reading.

"There he"—Antenna/Liberal—"visited his school friend Max Elitcher, who works in the Bureau of Standards as head of the fire control section for warships. He has access to extremely valuable materials on guns."

Indeed he must, Bob thought. No KGB hood would dare to embellish in a cable to his no-nonsense boss. And Bob pondered something else: Elitcher's name had been sent *en clair*; his identity was not hidden behind a code name. Which meant he was not working for the Soviets—at least not at the time the cable had been sent.

Bob resumed his reading. There was a summary of Elitcher's education; he had a degree from the Electro-Technical Department at New York's City College. Now Bob's mind flitted back to the beginning of the cable: Since Antenna/Liberal was a "school friend," this might prove to be helpful in identifying him. Filing that away, he continued: Elitcher "entered the Fellow Countrymen's organization after finishing his studies." And all at once Bob's heart sank. The "Fellow Countrymen's organization," according to Meredith's exhaustive report on cover names, was KGB-speak for the Communist Party. At the very least, the stage was set for a potential national security disaster: a card-carrying Party member had access to military secrets.

Plowing on, he read some details about Elitcher's wife, "a fellow countryman" who worked, he discovered with one more stab of dismay, "at the War Department." Yet what followed struck Bob as

even more ominous: "Max Elitcher is an excellent amateur photog-
rapher and has all the necessary equipment for taking photographs."
In other words, Bob realized, Elitcher had the makings of a fully
operational spy.

All, though, was not yet lost. The cable's concluding sentence offered a small hope: "Please check Elitcher and communicate your
thoughts on his clearance." So this message, Bob noted with some
solace, had simply initiated the vetting process. It informed the Center that the New York *rezidentura* had a potential recruit, and wanted
to get permission before attempting to reel him in. But there was no
confirmation that Elitcher, fellow countryman or not, had agreed to
betray his country.

And with that, the cable came to an end.

Bob now focused his full attention on Meredith. Was the FBI
man looking for help? The assistance of his friend's invaluable mind
in formulating a tactical strategy to grapple with this new information? Or was he using Meredith as a sounding board, trying to bring
clarity to his own meandering and alarmed thoughts by speaking
them aloud? Bob never shared his motivations. The record that ex-
ists is simply cool testimony to this moment when Bob, as if a commander briefing his troops on the upcoming mission, enumerated
what must be done.

"First, we needed to know," Bob would recall of this charged
occasion, "whether Elitcher had ever agreed to work for the KGB."

"Second, if he had been recruited, whether he was still active."

"And third, whether we could identify the person who had tried,
successfully or unsuccessfully, to recruit Elitcher."

It was this final challenge, pinning a name and face on the Moscow Center talent spotter working under the cover name Antenna/
Liberal, that held the promise of real gold. "This last was the most important objective," he'd explain with the unfailing wisdom of hindsight, "because the recruiter might lead us to others in a network."
But even at the time, working only on instinct, he was driven by the
possibility that this network would somehow be tied to the unsettling

words that kept seizing up inside him: *a possible link between Enormoz and wartime nuclear fission research.*

The operational goals laid out, Bob was ready to take charge. At this challenging juncture, he realized only too well that all his big questions remained to be answered. And another reason for pessimism: every fieldman knows that making an airtight espionage case is often as much a matter of luck as of diligence. The SE desk was scattered with the carcasses of abandoned investigations. Here the legal hurdles would be even higher: the deciphered cables couldn't be introduced as evidence in a courtroom; they were such a closely kept secret that even President Truman had no inkling that the Russians' mail was being read. Still, when Bob left Meredith that afternoon he felt like a hunter who finally had caught the scent of his prey. There was a Soviet network out there, a ring of spies coordinated by a talent spotter, quite possibly an American, code-named Antenna/Liberal, who had graduated from New York's City College. Bob drove back to headquarters with the deciphered cable in his suit jacket pocket, close to his heart.

But THE SPARSE CABLE COULD only hint at the furtive war that was being waged in the shadows. The New York *rezidentura* had been, as Bob and Meredith had increasingly come to suspect, a busy nest of spies. Operating simultaneously on several fronts, the KGB had successfully penetrated the atom bomb project, while also running an ongoing network of well-placed agents who were making off with bundles of technological and scientific secrets. Liberal—just as Bob's gut had suggested—was the linchpin of this secondary ring.

Liberal's recruitment had been a cautious dance of veils straight out of the Moscow Center handbook. First, a friend from his student labor movement days—who also was an occasional talent spotter for Soviet intelligence—had, as if it were the most natural of occurrences, introduced him to a KGB fieldman working out of the consulate in Manhattan, under diplomatic cover. Next, this professional, not pushing, just having a casual talk, yet all the while discreetly taking the potential recruit's pulse, discovered that the prospect was not only a passionate supporter of the Soviet experiment, but also worked for the Army Signal Corps. When that tantalizing information was shared with the New York station, Kvasnikov, the KGB deskman running the XY line (as the operation aimed at both atomic and technological secrets was known at the Center), was swiftly brought in. It was Kvasnikov, as perceptive as he was cautious, who gave the orders to slip off the final veil.

The approach to the spy who would be code-named Liberal was made during the Labor Day Rally in Central Park in 1942. Fifty thousand people jammed the park on a sunny afternoon, and in the midst of this crowd, standing shoulder-to-shoulder in solidarity with workers everywhere, was a comradely trio: the potential recruit, his friend from their shared labor-movement days, and his new buddy, the talkative Soviet diplomat. And with a serendipity that couldn't have fooled anyone, who should bump into them but the diplomat's good friend, "Henry," who happened to be another Russian national. No sooner had Henry and the targeted recruit started talking, than the other two men—one the original talent spotter, the other the Soviet diplomat—hewing to the prearranged script, exited.

Henry and his new friend went out for lunch that afternoon. The unbreakable rule is that you never go to bed on the first date; it's best to leave some mystery, some anticipation wafting in the air. And the Center also preached that time spent being prudent was never time wasted; you don't want to wind up in the false embrace of a double agent. So in the fall of 1942, on their third get-together—fast work by the puritanical standards of the KGB—the relationship was artfully consummated. In a well-rehearsed argument, Henry complained that America, despite its professed commitment to the Soviet wartime effort, was not sharing its technology with its besieged ally.

"I find it unfair that you should be fighting the common enemy alone. If I can do anything to help you, you can count on me," replied Julius Rosenberg, swallowing the dangled hook without hesitation.

At their next meet, the novice secret agent delivered his first shipment of purloined documents. And throughout the months ahead, he kept at it with unflagging efficiency. By the time his code name had been switched to Liberal, Rosenberg was regularly passing over, according to the boastful Soviet accounts, between six hundred and a thousand pages of often top-secret technical documents at each encounter. Also, himself an intrepid recruiter, he'd built up a valuable network. They were a youthful, largely under-thirty group of friends and relations—each knew the other members in the ring; that is, they were "inter-conscious," as the jargon of his new trade put it—who were, in their zealous hearts, dedicated to the socialistic goals of Mother Russia. And now, as the KGB cable Meredith had deciphered three years later had reported, Rosenberg hoped to pull his old school friend and fellow Communist, Max Elitcher, into his network of strategically placed idealistic spies.

But as Rosenberg in May 1944 prepared for his recruitment mission in Washington, D.C., Moscow Center, the sternest of employers, had decided he required a new handler. For Liberal, the move was, in its indirect way, a promotion. In recognition of his ring's success— the yield, according to the Center's consistently pleased evaluations, varied from simply "good" to more often "extremely valuable"—and with an eye toward an even more promising future, the spymasters decreed that the phlegmatic Henry must be replaced. A more resourceful professional, an agent who would know how to exploit the ring's many burgeoning connections into the defense industry, a case officer who'd inspire the confidence that was necessary for daring undertakings, was needed to run the group.

Alexander Feklisov—Sasha—got the job.

19

SASHA PRIDED HIMSELF ON THE calm he showed in the field. He had grown up living by his fists in the hard streets of Worker's Alley, and he didn't fear the dangers that came with his new profession. Let the enemy test him! "If they broke an arm or a rib while they beat me," he'd say, "I'd laugh at their blows." He was confident he could be reduced mentally and physically to the limits of any man's endurance and yet he would not crack. His death would be his honor. His loyalty to the Center was absolute.

Yet Sasha lived with a secret fear that was worse than any physical pain. His greatest anxiety, the imagined death that left his heart racing and had him staring at the ceiling unable to sleep at three a.m., was being outwitted by the opposition and, in the humiliating process, letting the Center down. He still worked under diplomatic cover at the Soviet consulate on East Sixty-First Street in Manhattan, and there was no sign that the FBI had any suspicions that he was anything other than what he pretended to be. And he was determined to keep things that way.

Pondering his new assignment, Sasha was, by his own embarrassed admission, nervous. With so much at stake, there was no room for error, for any rash or impetuous move. His tradecraft must be meticulous. But from the start, his concerns centered on one large problem: How would he establish contact with this agent?

The simplest way would be to call Liberal at home. But all his training warned against such an approach. Liberal had access to secret documents; it had to be assumed that the Americans, as a matter of routine security, had a tap on his phone. With a single telephone call he could wreck a productive network, and, in the inevitable aftermath of such a disaster, earn himself a long stay in the Lubyanka basement. No, Sasha decided after some deep thought, "the best solution was to meet him at home."

He knew better, however, than to rush off and knock on Liberal's door. First, he went to reconnoiter the location. A discreet, no-contact reconnaissance. With a professional's scrupulous eye, he weighed the potential dangers: a busy Lower Manhattan street in the long shadow of the Brooklyn Bridge. A dark brick apartment house, Building G, part of a complex of ten-story buildings that made up Knickerbocker Village. Liberal's three-room apartment was on the eighth floor; Sasha tried to locate its windows. And there was the building's lobby: to enter, a code needed to be punched; or, one used the intercom and asked to be buzzed in.

It was a setting that in its unextraordinary way was like much of this low-rent residential neighborhood in New York's Lower East Side, a community whose streets were alive with families striving to make ends meet, constant big-city hustle and bustle, and streams of immigrants firmly tied to their Old Country ways, muttering a cacophony of languages. Yet for Sasha, an agent behind enemy lines, it held countless perils, provoked a constant wariness. No fieldman heads out on an operation without his active mind warning that at any moment something unexpected can happen, that around the next corner a trap could be sprung.

Sasha, nevertheless, formulated his plan, and Kvasnikov signed off on it. It was, in its direct way, nearly as matter-of-fact as a telephone call. He'd go to Liberal's apartment unannounced at two on a Sunday afternoon; it was a time when Sasha imagined he'd find him home. Then he'd quickly introduce himself: "I come from Henry." It would work. Yet, just as likely, a dozen things could go wrong. He tried to find solace in the disturbing truth that his two brothers, infantrymen in the Red Army, faced greater risks each day on the battlefield. "What," he asked himself in an attempt to add fuel to his flickering courage, "was I doing that was so dangerous in the peaceful traffic of the New York streets?"

On the day of the meet, with his mood shifting each mercurial moment, from stiff confidence to the certainty of impending doom, he left his apartment on West Eighty-Ninth Street an hour and a half ahead of his predetermined schedule. He strolled down Central Park West, the image, he hoped, of a man enjoying a pleasant New York Sunday. Then, he suddenly bolted across the street, weaving through the traffic as enraged drivers honked their horns and slammed on their brakes. This was, he'd boast, "his favorite move." "It allowed you to see, without showing it, what the situation around you looks like." After taking stock and finding no apparent cause for alarm, he continued on foot to Columbus Circle, where he boarded a downtown subway train.

He rode it down to Little Italy, all the time trying to catch a purposeful glance from one of the opposition's watchers. No one had been flushed, but Sasha felt he couldn't be sure that he hadn't missed something. He took a diversionary bus back uptown to Grand Central.

Grabbing a hot dog from a vendor inside the terminal, he gobbled it down without interest while his eyes scanned the crowd for the telltale signs of people loitering artlessly about. He saw nothing suspicious. With his rumbling doubts now somewhat at rest, he boarded a downtown bus, got off at Rivington Street, and, following the sidewalk at a sedate pace, arrived at the entrance of Liberal's building at two p.m. to the minute.

He pushed the intercom button.

"Yes?" questioned a man's voice.

"Hello," said Sasha with all the authority he could muster. "I'm looking for Julius Rosenberg."

"That's me."

"I'm a friend of Henry's," he announced. "May I come up for a minute?"

The door buzzed open and Sasha headed to the elevator. The ride to the eighth floor was its own heart-pounding adventure; if Liberal had been doubled, if, despite all Sasha's caution, he'd been followed, an army of FBI agents might be waiting to greet him.

The door opened and there was Julius Rosenberg, a skinny man with black hair and a wispy mustache, staring at him mournfully through a bookkeeper's steel-rimmed glasses. He was alone. His firm handshake was further reassurance.

Without prelude, Sasha dived in. "I'm the one who will come to see you from now on," he said.

Rosenberg calmly absorbed the news, and when he spoke his words did not betray his feelings. Instead, apparently resigned to the change, he offered his new handler a terse apology. "Excuse me, but I can't let you come in. We're entertaining a couple of friends."

Together they walked down the eight flights of stairs to the lobby, talking all the time, their voices holding a normal pitch; if someone entered the stairwell, whispers would've attracted suspicions. It was agreed that they would meet next Tuesday at Childs' (a decidedly proletarian restaurant on West Thirty-Fourth Street, where the blue-plate special was, famously, a stolid rectangle of gray meat doused in a brackish gravy; the menu insisted it was Salisbury steak). The rendezvous was set for 7:30 p.m., since Rosenberg worked during the day.

Sasha had a final word. He instructed his new agent not to bring any stolen papers with him. A first meet, the rigid protocols of good *konspiratsya* insisted, should be an occasion where both handler and his new charge take full measure of each other. After all, when your life is at stake, you'd better be able to trust the man with whom you're working.

Tuesday evening, across the narrow table at Childs', after Sasha made the requisite toast to his companion and to the success of their future collaboration, he proceeded to the next item on his checklist. The Moscow Center psychologists wanted him to "open his heart," believing that candor cemented allegiance. Finding the confiding tone that had won over a small legion of previous "joes" (as handlers uniformly referred to their agents), Sasha spoke about his down-at-the-heels childhood in Moscow, his worries about his brothers at the front, his sisters digging trenches at Bryansk directly in the thundering path of the advancing German forces. Rosenberg reciprocated with confidences about his adored wife—he closed his eyes and blew a kiss into his hand, when he spoke about her—and his young son (a second boy would be born in 1948).

In that way, a product of shrewd manipulation, a shared antipathy toward Nazism, and a common faith in the Soviet socialistic ideals, a bond grew. The two men would meet about fifty times over the next three years, passing documents on rush-hour buses, at a boxing match in Madison Square Garden, at restaurants and on street corners in Manhattan, the Bronx, and Brooklyn.

Sasha provided Rosenberg with a Leica carrying a special lens devised by Moscow Center and shipped over in the diplomatic pouch; the focal length of the lens could be expanded, and that made microfilming documents a perfunctory exercise. The eager agent photographed everything that came his way, and his yield continued to fill the Center's coffers. His dedication was such, his desire to do more was so strong, that Sasha had to hold him back. Rosenberg routinely took risks that his handler begged him not to take.

In the course of their work together, they became, as Sasha grew to appreciate, "a real team." Sasha was the professional, but time after time, he conceded operational details to the agent: "He knew his own country, his fellow citizens, their frame of mind and their reactions, and workplaces, far better than I did." And, another rarity in a harsh world where agent runners value success far higher than any inhibiting concerns about their joes' safety, Sasha could not help liking Liberal. He took to calling him by the affectionate nickname of "Libi"—an intimacy that would've shocked his stern bosses.

And what did Rosenberg get out of all this? Once, above the concealing din of a crowded cafeteria, he shared more of a clue to what was driving him than his usual homilies about the war-beleaguered Soviet state and his sanguine visions of the Marxist-Leninist paradise that would come to pass in the future. "I know you may not be aware of it," he confessed to Sasha, "but our meetings are among the happiest moments of all my life. . . . I have a wonderful wife and a son whom I adore. But you are the only person who knows all my secrets, and it's very important to be able to confide to someone."

A N D S O I T H A P P E N E D T H A T Liberal confided to his handler one more secret: the details of his own attempted recruitment of Max Elitcher. It was a brief report, as summaries of failed missions tend to be. But to Libi's credit, Sasha thought, he told it with the stoicism of someone who remained unprepared to give up.

Rosenberg had telephoned Elitcher, whom he had seen only once in the five years since their graduation from college, and asked if he could come over to say hello; Signal Corps business had brought him to Washington, he'd lied.

There was some talk over coffee in Elitcher's apartment, all sounding even to Rosenberg's own ears embarrassingly forced. So, abandoning whatever small pretense remained of this being merely a casual visit, he bluntly asked his school friend's wife if she would be kind enough to give him a few minutes alone with her husband. Once she left, he made his pitch.

Rosenberg had two cards to play, and he laid them both out with a succinct yet earnest passion. He began, as Elitcher would remember the conversation, by highlighting "the great role Russia was playing in the war and the great sacrifice she was making." Then he quickly followed with the revelation that "some persons were contributing to the Russian war effort by giving secret material and developments to the Russians, which they would not ordinarily receive." The pointed way he said it left little doubt that by "some persons" he meant himself and some of their mutual City College friends.

He asked if Max would contribute in this way, too.

Rosenberg, by now a veteran recruiter, knew this was the most dangerous moment. A person could say "yes." He could say "no." Or, a secret hero in his heart, he might pick up the phone and call the FBI two minutes after you left. It was always difficult to predict how someone would respond to the question of whether he'd betray his country.

Yet Elitcher said neither yes nor no. He was firmly noncommittal. But he certainly didn't seem as if he'd be running to the FBI.

Rosenberg later told Sasha that it would just take some time. He'd try Elitcher again.

I trust your judgment, Sasha said with a genuine confidence.

When Rosenberg made a second approach to Elitcher, now over a dinner in Manhattan at Manny Wolf's, the result was more of the same indecision. Only this go-around, Rosenberg had his own second thoughts.

"Elitcher has changed," he reported to Sasha.

Sasha was concerned enough about this "change" to share his anxieties with his superior. And Kvasnikov, another professional, agreed. He, too, was at once on alert.

"Forget about Elitcher," Sasha told his agent at their next meet. "It's not that important."

His instructions, while an order, were offered with an apparent indifference. He chose a casual, even convivial tone. He did not wish to share that he was thinking of a future that he didn't want his agent to dare imagine. He did not explain that in Elitcher's sudden transformation he had a premonition, still faint, still instinctive, of the enemy one day closing in. But as things would work out for Liberal and his ring, perhaps he should have.

20

BUT BOB, SETTING OUT ON his hunt nearly three years later, had no knowledge of these events. He was ignorant of the drama that had taken place between Elitcher and Liberal, or the puppet-master role Sasha had played in the wings. Yet, using just the thin clues in the deciphered cable sent back in 1944—a lifetime of secrets ago, he feared—he went on the offensive. His first step was to try to mobilize the Bureau—again.

Bob was well aware of the irony in this attempt. It wasn't that long ago that he'd been the salesman trying to convince a disinterested Meredith that the FBI could offer the code breaker a wealth of deductive resources. Now he'd be going to the Bureau, trying one more time to stir them out of their doldrums, and his best argument was the promise in the leads Meredith had uncovered. A further complicating wrinkle: he could not reveal either the source of the information, or how it had been obtained. The most he could do, he'd decided after some tortured pondering, was attribute the clue to a "confidential informant of known reliability." At least that euphemism, while modest, would be an accurate description of Meredith and his conjurer's skills.

Nevertheless, as Bob prepared to go, fedora in hand, and try one more time to rally his bosses to the chase, he felt surprisingly prepared to take on the dismissive arguments he fully expected to hear. A large contributing factor to his buoyant mood, he'd later confide to intimates, was that the ambiguity in his married life had been, for now at least, resolved. A son, George, had been born and in their joy both he and Sarah had found reason for a renewed commitment to family happiness. Yet too often Bob would find himself looking at the innocent baby boy, and his thoughts, like a recurring nightmare, would slink away to Enormoz and the dangerous world in which George would grow up.

In that driven yet remarkably steady mood, Bob burst into Al Belmont's office. Belmont was the assistant director of domestic intelligence and, Bob would say, "FBI through and through." On some days, that description was meant as high praise, a recognition that Belmont shared Bob's steely commitment to bringing all the villains to justice. On others, especially when Bob was seething after his exertions trudging through the bureaucratic morass, it could just as easily mean that Belmont was reluctant to authorize any innovative action. That day Bob could only make his case as forcefully as the expurgated facts would allow, and then wait to see which version of the assistant director was sitting behind his impressive desk.

Belmont answered without hesitation: "Bob, we're going to increase the number of guys on your unit."

"Who are you kidding?" Bob shot back, incredulous. He'd girded himself for a knockdown brawl, and, deprived of this opportunity, he compensated by not taking yes for an answer.

"What do you mean, 'who we're kidding'?"

"It doesn't work that way. You know damn well it doesn't work that way, Al."

Now it was Belmont's voice that rose suddenly in anger. "Goddamn it, Bob. I just told you. You name them, we'll get them!"

Bob named them, and within days, still not quite believing his unexpectedly easy victory, he got them. The handpicked force, although tied to their desks in the SE unit at headquarters, hit the ground running. On Bob's instructions, they reached out to both the Washington and New York field offices and ordered an investigation into Max Elitcher. The priority telex was headed, again on Bob's say-so, "Espionage R." R stood for Russian, and he could only hope that the designation would spur on the men in the trenches.

No sooner had Elitcher's name gone into the system than lights might just as well have started flashing. The request, Bob was stiffly informed, was redundant: the Bureau was already looking into Elitcher. Only rather than being reassuring, this news filled Bob with a new dread.

The facts that were shared were these: back in 1941, gimlet-eyed Naval Intelligence investigators had spotted Elitcher and a fellow Navy employee, Morton Sobell, packing demonstrators into Sobell's car to ferry them to an anti-draft rally sponsored by the American Peace Mobilization Committee. Since there were several Communist Party members sprinkled throughout the committee's leadership hierarchy, the Navy sleuths wondered if the two men, both of whom had access to military secrets, were also Party members. The FBI was brought in to conduct a "loyalty check."

The Bureau's background investigation had meandered along over the years. It had never determined if in fact the two men were Communist Party members (which could've resulted in a perjury case, since both had sworn they were not when they'd started working for the Navy). All they had come up with was that Elitcher and Sobell had both attended City College from 1934 to 1938, and that they had roomed together for a while in Washington. Then the investigation had petered out. Besides, while Elitcher had continued to work for the Navy during the war, Sobell had moved on, first to the General Electric laboratories in Schenectady, New York, and more recently joining the Reeves Instrument Company in New York City.

But these small pickings were enough for Bob nearly to scream, *Stop!* No sooner had the word come back to him at headquarters that the Bureau's inquiry into Elitcher was, technically at least, still on an active footing, than he sent down the order that rather than gearing things up again, the investigation should come to an immediate halt.

He didn't explain his decision to the agents in the field offices; for all they knew, this was just one more example of the supervisors at headquarters running hot one day and cold the next. To his own team, however, he revealed a bit more of his thinking.

A reinvigorated loyalty check, talking to neighbors, to bosses, could scare the prey, he explained. Elitcher would learn, as targets invariably do, that questions were being asked, and he'd bolt. If Elitcher was a Russian spy, the investigation had to be handled with extraordinary care. The operational goal was to catch him in the act—stealing documents, passing these secrets to his handler—and that would require a far more tactful strategy.

Bob issued a new series of orders. With the discreet cooperation of the post office, a "mail cover" went into effect; photocopies of the outside of all envelopes and postcards mailed to Elitcher's apartment arrived on Bob's desk before they were delivered. A record of Elitcher's long-distance calls was obtained, and agents began combing through them, hoping to find something that might catch their interest. And after weighing the matter, Bob finally decided to order visual surveillance on Elitcher. Bob knew the Bureau's watchers were of variable quality; there was always the chance Elitcher might catch on. But he judged the risks to be worth it: the prospects of nabbing an active Soviet agent in the act were too enticing.

Yet even as he shared all this with his men, there was something that he kept buried deep. It was an investigative secret to which only he and Meredith were privy. Because all the time that he was running his "bandstand operation," to use the watchers' term for round-the-clock scrutiny, his own thoughts were fixed on Sobell. He made the connection between the "school friend" who lived in Carthage in the deciphered cable and the scant but confirming details unearthed in the Bureau's background investigation, and he wondered if he had found a talent spotter. And a leader of a Soviet spy network. Was Morton Sobell Antenna/Liberal?

A "BRUSH PASS," AS SASHA's tradecraft instructor at the KGB training school in Balashikha had lectured, offered many operational advantages for the clandestine transfer of small objects. Even if the opposition's surveillance team was breathing down your neck, the skillful agent could still pull off an exchange without being detected. The maneuver's success, however, required that the fieldman obey certain rules: the delivery should occur only in a crowd; the two agents must never look each other in the eye; and (this one etched in stone at the top of the list) don't stop walking. Like a baton in a relay race, the pass from one hand to another must be done in a flash, with no one breaking stride.

Over the years, Sasha had perfected this covert art, and it had become his preferred procedure for collecting palm-sized canisters of microfilm from his joes. And so every month or so since he had taken over the Liberal network, walking with seemingly aimless intention through the bustling lunchtime or rush-hour streets of midtown Manhattan, he'd receive a roll of film from the agent code-named "Senya."

Code names are usually bestowed with the tricky intent of adding one more misleading clue to an agent's identity. Hence, a tall man would be called "Dwarf," the rotund spy might be "Thin Man." "Senya" meant "God heard me" in Russian, and Sasha reflected that for once the KGB's covert shorthand was accurate: Senya was a most productive asset, an answer to all the Center's prayers.

He had been recruited by Rosenberg in 1944, and his yield, year after year, had continued with an impressive fecundity. He had consistently delivered documents praised as "very valuable" by the Center, thousands of pages of secrets about sonar, infrared rays, and missile guidance systems. The classified reports he'd passed on from the U.S. government's Coordinating Committee for Radio Technology revealed precisely what the nation's scientists knew, and, of even greater interest to the Russians, what they were aiming to accomplish in the future.

Morton Sobell—code-named Senya—was not the ringleader Bob

had been hunting. He was just one more of Liberal's well-placed recruits, another spy in the bread-and-butter operation Sasha was coolly
running with remarkable efficiency.

YET AS BOB STRUGGLED TO get a context for the new clues that
were coming his way, he was summoned once again by Meredith.
Another cable had been deciphered and, Meredith soberly hedged, he
might just be jumping at shadows. But then again, it could take them
straight into the very operational heart of the ring of spies.

Arlington Hall. Once a girls' finishing school, Arlington Hall became the top-secret headquarters for the government's attack on Russian codes. *Wikimedia Commons*

The Arlington Hall bowling team. After a long day of trying to crack the Soviet codes, many of the young code breakers would relax on the lanes. *Wikimedia Commons*

The Lamphere children: Bob, Art, and Alice on a snowy winter's day in Mullano, Idaho, in 1922. Bob grew up as the overlooked middle child. There was nothing he liked better than heading up into the hills with his rifle and hunting dog to be "out of sight of people from dawn to dusk." *Lamphere Family Collection, courtesy of Theo Schaad*

The Lamphere children: Bob, Alice, and Art. Growing up in the hardscrabble mining town of Mullano, left Bob, he'd say, "always ready to put up a fight." *Lamphere Family Collection, courtesy of Theo Schaad*

A twelve-year-old Bob. He was both of his parents' son. He inherited his temper from his dad, Joe, and his fondnesss for books from his mother, Lilly. *Lamphere Family Collection, courtesy of Theo Schaad*

Bob and Sarah's wedding day photo. Bob met Sarah Hosch when he was a young, foot-loose, novice FBI field agent in Birmingham, Alabama, and she became his second wife. *Lamphere Family Collection, courtesy of Theo Schaad*

Meredith Gardner was a long, lanky, ascetic man, partial to a deliberately donnish attire. A man whose very thinness seemed to suggest that all the fun had been squeezed out of him. *Gardner Family Collection, courtesy of Michele and Arthur Gardner*

Meredith Gardner at Arlington Hall. Gardner worked amid a "sea of women" at Arlington Hall, but he was not just the rare man—he was the only legend. *Gardner Family Collection, courtesy of Michele and Arthur Gardner*

Blanche Hatfield, a Mount Holyoke Phi Beta Kappa grad and a code wrangler at Arlington Hall, introduced herself to fellow code breaker Meredith Gardner with a flirty, "I thought you were just a legend!" And in German, to boot. It was pretty much love at first sight. *Gardner Family Collection, courtesy of Michele and Arthur Gardner*

Gene Grabeel. A high school home economics teacher, Grabeel went to wartime Washington to "shuffle papers" and wound up at Arlington Hall working on "the Blue Problem." *Wikimedia Commons*

After a thirty-six-year career for the Army Security Agency (which later became the National Security Agency), Gene Grabeel was recognized as "an American hero" by the CIA. *Wikimedia Commons*

The KGB seal. While the Soviet Union was an ally of the United States in WWII, the spies of Moscow Center were already waging a covert war against America. "The Russians were operating all around us," Lamphere finally realized. *YAY Media AS/Alamy Stock Vector*

Harry Gold, the Soviet courier known as Raymond. When he broke, Moscow Center presciently feared, all the dominoes would start to fall. *nsf/Alamy Stock Photo*

Bob Lamphere (*right*) heading off to London with Hugh Clegg, the assistant FBI director he called "Trout Mouth," to interview atomic spy Klaus Fuchs. "The whole pressures of the world were on my shoulders," Lamphere moaned. *Bettmann/Contributor*

Ethel and Julius Rosenberg after their arraignment for conspiracy to commit espionage, August 1951. Julius, as the Soviet spy code-named "Liberal," ran a network of productive agents. Ethel, according to the cable Gardner had decrypted, "does not work." Yet both died in the Sing Sing prison electric chair. *Everett Collection Inc/Alamy Stock Photo*

Bob, nearly forty, after he had left the FBI. He had written a memo to FBI director J. Edgar Hoover arguing that Ethel Rosenberg should not be executed, and Hoover had shared it with the judge—to no avail. After that, Bob's heart was no longer in the hunt for spies. *Lamphere Family Collection, courtesy of Theo Schaad*

Meredith and his daughter, Ann, on the boat to England. After the execution of the Rosenbergs, he felt a deep guilt that his puzzle-solving had culminated in their deaths. He went to work at Cheltenham, the British code-breaking facility, because he wanted to get away from America for a while. *Gardner Family Collection, courtesy of Michele and Arthur Gardner*

Arthur Gardner and his sister, Ann, when the family was living in England. Years earlier a mischievous Arthur, mystified by his parents' conversations, had constructed an electric chair to give Ann the shock of her life. *Gardner Family Collection, courtesy of Michele and Arthur Gardner*

21

I T WAS NOT IN MEREDITH'S nature to appear pleased with himself. In public, he was far too modest. While in private, he was too self-assured to portray his shrewd feats as anything more than natural—for a man who was a legend. Still, when Bob arrived at his friend's desk and Meredith handed over his latest decryption, the FBI agent couldn't help but feel that for once he detected a small glimmer of professional pride in his colleague's smile.

And while that might have been so, what was also animating Meredith, as he'd explain when the passing years had provided him with additional insight, was that he, too, had become caught up in the thrill of the hunt. Before he'd teamed up with Bob, his sedentary (and thoroughly fulfilling) existence had been measured out in academic challenges. He had thought the trajectory of his life and career had been long settled. But like the happily married man whose world is turned inside out by an unexpected passion, Meredith's "dalliance" with Bob had given him a fresh perspective on things. In this second spring, he'd discovered that he enjoyed the relevance of his new, consequential life. Every day he grappled with puzzles that brought him deep into a real-world mystery. The words that, after all his painstaking labors, took shape on his work sheets were not merely nouns or verbs, but clues to a ring of spies. And all the while, spurring him on, thoughts of Enormoz, of the precarious balance of international power being upended, were never far from the center of his mind.

That afternoon, there was still a bit of pedantry in the report he

shared with Bob. "Otvod," Meredith had written, carefully trans-
literating the cable's Cyrillic, "means recruitment in KGB parlance.
Similarly, the verb 'otvesti' would mean 'to recruit.'" But all this
was simply prelude—and a stagy one at that—to his big reveal. He
reported that Moscow Center had been notified back in 1944—four
long years earlier!—that Liberal also had his eyes on another recruit.
His name, sent *en clair*, was Joel Barr.

Bob listened, and now it was his turn to experience a sudden
burst of encouragement. He had begun with Max Elitcher, who had
brought him to Morton Sobell, and here was another rich clue: Joel
Barr. Bob knew, of course, that this was just more of the beginning;
he remained at the starting gate and had no notion of how far off in
the distance the finish line was. At this point, Barr was only one of
Liberal's targets; Bob had no knowledge of whether he'd become part
of the ring. His investigation, woefully preliminary, further handi-
capped because the deciphered cables recorded events that had taken
place years earlier, had not yet allowed him to draw any of the firm
connective lines that he'd need to guide him in the summer of 1948
to the mysterious Liberal, the ringleader. And it was so far only his
conjectures that had tied the ring in to the enemy's theft of atomic
secrets. But now that he possessed another name, he felt the plot
had considerably thickened. For a counterintelligence man, it "was
a golden time." "I could look ahead and see us coming closer and
closer, not only to Russian agents whose trails the intervening years
had muddied, but also to spies who were actually still at work among
us."

Nevertheless, in the long nights that followed, while he lay in his
bed in Maryland surrounded by darkness and his unsettled thoughts,
Bob had trouble sleeping. In his bedroom, away from the activity at
headquarters, his conferences with the uncanny Meredith a receding
blur, he found his optimism harder to sustain. He feared the enemy
was beyond his reach, and always would be.

———

BUT IN THE RESTORATIVE LIGHT of day, there was an investigation to run, and, seemingly unencumbered by any of his nocturnal doubts, he threw himself into it. Even as the operational wheels still turned on Elitcher and Sobell, he focused his attention on Barr. Meredith had given him reason to suspect that Barr would lead to Liberal. Perhaps Barr even was Liberal, the busy anchor of the ring. And so Bob took a gamble.

Ignoring the concerns of his circumspect bosses on the fifth floor, and skirting very close to the edge of the agreement he'd made with the brass at Arlington Hall, when he turned his men loose on the new target, he pretty much let them know what was at stake. He believed the agents in the field would be more diligent if they had some sense of the prize.

The formal request for information he sent through the FBI pipeline was headed "Joel Barr and UNSUB," the designation Bureauspeak for "unknown subject." And while Bob knew better than to reveal the code name Liberal, or how he had learned of the ring's existence, he nevertheless lifted the cloak of official secrecy to share what this unsub was involved in. Barr, he wrote in his accompanying report, possibly "acted as an intermediary between person or persons who were working on wartime nuclear fission research and for KGB agents."

When the fifth floor got wind of Bob's indiscretion, they went into full damage-control mode. A bristling directive went out under Hoover's signature to the field offices ordering that no further references were to be made to the unsub "for security reasons." And as for Bob, he received an official reprimand.

But Bob quickly forgot about this administrative slap on the wrist as the field reports poured in. Pieced together, they formed an intriguing story. Barr had an electrical engineering degree from City College, same as Elitcher, Sobell, and, if the clues were pointing in the right direction, Liberal. He'd also been a member of Branch 16B of the Industrial Division of the Communist Party, and so he'd been a "fellow countryman" same as all the other potential recruits in the

ring. His employment history set off even more alarms. Barr had
worked at the U.S. Army Signal Corps laboratories in Fort Monmouth, New Jersey, only to lose his job when the Army learned about
his Communist ties. Still, he was quickly hired by Western Electric,
a major defense contractor, where he helped develop a classified radar
bombsight for B-29s. And after the war, he'd moved on to become
a project engineer at Sperry Gyroscope, working daily with "information secret and unlimited." Just as the New York *rezidentura* had
boasted in its cable about Elitcher, so, too, did Barr have "access to
extremely valuable materials." Adding it all up, Bob moved toward a
confident conclusion: Barr had all the makings of another member of
the well-placed ring.

His burrowers had dug up something else that caught Bob's interest. When Barr had worked at the Signal Corps lab, his close
friend had been Alfred Sarant. Sarant had graduated from the Coo-
per Union, not CCNY like all the other suspects. But Sarant had
also been a member of Barr's Communist Party cell, and when he,
too, had been dismissed from the Army lab, he'd also found a job
at Western Electric. His work was focused on APQ-17, a secret
airborne radar system being developed for the military. And during
their wartime bachelor days, Barr and Sarant had shared an apartment on Morton Street in Greenwich Village. All of which, Bob
readily conceded, proved nothing; it was a biography that could
have no intelligence value. Or, as his professional's hunch shouted,
Sarant's life had been too closely cut from the same cloth as Elitcher's and Barr's not to have attracted the attentions of the ring's KGB
talent spotter.

When Bob shared all this with Meredith, the code breaker felt
enough had been unearthed to allow him to return to old mysteries
and tackle things from another vantage point. He tracked back over
the messages he'd already broken and, armed with this new knowledge, something caught his eye. In one of the early messages sent from
the New York *rezidentura* to Moscow back in the spring of 1944,
there had been a reference to a pair of friends. Liberal, the cable in-

formed the Center, "has safely carried through the contracting of Hughes who was a good friend of Meter." At the time, Meredith had no doubt that by "contracting" the KGB meant "recruiting," but he'd been totally stymied by the cover names "Hughes" and "Meter." The only clue he'd had during his first go-round was their friendship. Now, extrapolating from the fresh intelligence Bob had gathered, he felt he had the kernels of a budding theory.

It went like this: in early 1944, Meter had preceded Hughes into the ring; at least that was how Meredith read the cable. And since Barr, like Elitcher and quite possibly Liberal, had been "school friends," then QED: Barr = Meter. Which meant that Sarant, the new acquaintance who'd earned his degree at another college and would've needed to have been introduced to old school pal Liberal, was Hughes.

This supposition became arguably more solid, and certainly more menacing, after Meredith managed to break down a fragment of another message between New York and Moscow, sent on December 5, 1944: "Expedite consent to joint filming of their materials by Meter and Hughes." It was a request that made further operational sense if, like Barr and Sarant, the two operatives were not only best friends but also shared an apartment. And the cable's concluding sentence made it disturbingly clear why Moscow needed to give the okay for the two agents to film their yield sooner rather than later: "We are afraid of putting Liberal out of action with overwork."

The case, once filled with only imponderables, was now taking firmer shape in Bob's mind. He believed that his gut instincts and Meredith's hypothesis were parts of the same whole. It was time, he decided, to see how it all might hold up if he brought Barr in for questioning. Only now he couldn't find him.

Sperry Gyroscope had finally gotten around to doing their own background check on the engineer; and when Barr's Communist affiliations became known he was stripped of his security clearance and, days later, fired. Barr, according to what the New York field office unearthed, had realized his days of getting work in the defense industry were over. Reluctant to endure years of unemployment in America, he had decided to reinvent himself. The story he told acquaintances was that he was going to Paris to study piano.

Bob needed to know more. On his orders, the New York office dispatched an earnestly fulsome agent to make contact with Barr's mother. Trotting out the thin cover story that he was a school friend of Joel's, the agent asked the unsuspecting woman where he might find his old buddy. Her amused response was that his guess was as good as hers. The last she had heard, her son was traveling through Finland, playing the piano to support himself.

When Bob read the report, he promptly felt that all his suspicions had been confirmed. Finland was just a short hop from the Russian border—and it was precisely the sort of circuitous itinerary an agent would follow as he made his covert way to his Moscow Center spymasters. It was a journey that would end with his disappearing without a trace.

Bob was stymied. He had neither the resources nor the authority to track down Barr now that he was abroad. All he could do was pass on a heavily censored explanation of his interest in Barr to the CIA. Perhaps they might be able to pick up his trail. As for Sarant, Bob had nothing on him. No, he glumly realized, less than nothing. The decrypts were thin gruel; the messages had been sent four years earlier. Worse, they couldn't be introduced as evidence in court. Further, whatever leverage he might once have had was gone; Sarant had left Defense Department work for the groves of academe, teaching physics at Cornell. As for his being Barr's friend and roommate, well, even the ever condemnatory Hoover, Bob admitted, couldn't begin to make a federal case out of that.

What, Bob glumly asked himself, had he accomplished? "So far," he'd say in answer to his own troubling question, "the inquiries had been tantalizing but inconclusive." "Both Elitcher and Barr might have been spies in 1944, or neither of them might ever have been a spy."

WHILE BOB COULD ONLY WONDER, Sasha knew the truth. And what he knew had kept him for years in a constant state of high alert. Barr and Sarant—Meter and Hughes, as Meredith had accurately surmised—had been a reckless pair of spies. They had continually broken the most basic rules of operational security. "Danger," Sasha, their beleaguered case agent, would moan, "was never very far away." His steady fears were further compounded by his helplessness: his two young charges refused to obey his orders.

The problem was sex. Now, Sasha was no prude. He was married and had a young daughter, but it had not been that many years ago when he'd been a footloose bachelor. More to the point, he knew firsthand about ill-advised romances. While he'd been stationed at the Center's spy school, he had entered into a risky arrangement with a certain Lydia, who taught English. She was six years older and about to marry a divorced university professor. Yet Lydia feared that if on her wedding night her new husband discovered she was still, at the ripe age of thirty-two, a virgin, he might reevaluate his infatuation; why should he want what no other man had wanted in all these years? And so Lydia focused her attentions on handsome Sasha, and the would-be spy, despite the explicit prohibition against fraternization between teachers and students, responded with an ardor that she apparently found a revelation; their liaisons continued even after Lydia had returned from her honeymoon. It was Lydia, with her more mature practicality, who finally ended it. "I do hope that you did not lose anything because of our affair," she told the secret agent in training as she waved goodbye.

Looking back at the experience, Sasha knew he'd dodged a bullet. If the spymasters at Moscow Center had known what had been going on, his career would have ended before his first mission. But that was nothing when measured against what Meter and Hughes were jeopardizing by their parade of one-night stands. Every time the two young lotharios entertained the latest in a series of seemingly unending conquests, they put the entire Liberal network at risk.

The honey trap was one of the oldest tricks in the counter-intelligence agent's book, and, Sasha had been taught, one of the enemy's favorites. In the bedroom, even the most prudent spy was bound to let his guard down; there were few secrets in a double bed. Sasha lived in a state of perpetual anxiety that one or perhaps both of his agents would reveal something as he lay next to a woman he'd met earlier that night in a Village bar, and that with the new day the FBI would be hot on their trail.

But while it was a genuine cause for concern when your agents were spending their nights with a chorus line of strangers, it was a complete five-alarm disaster when the love nest was also their operational headquarters. Barr had a makeshift darkroom in the two-room apartment, where he routinely photographed and then developed both his and Sarant's haul.

The best Sasha could do to ensure some small measure of security was to come by the apartment and work with Barr to find hiding places for the tools of his secret trade. Together, they pried up a few floorboards and cached the camera and its accessories in one spot, the rolls of microfilm in another. Still, it was just rudimentary tradecraft and Sasha could not help fearing that it was only a matter of time before the FBI came crashing through the door of the Morton Street flat.

There was, however, one saving grace, and it was a substantial reward that put all the risks in perspective. Once a month, Barr would slip Sasha a package containing about twenty exposed rolls of film, a total of between four and five hundred pages of often highly classified defense-related material. On other occasions, he'd provide the photographs of the actual documents.

Even better, the two spies were remarkably prescient. Without needing to be told, they seemed to know what their masters were hoping for. For example—

Early one morning over a coffee in the *rezidentura*, Sasha read a cable detailing the Center's latest urgent request: "Just outside London, an ultra-modern device, the SCR-584, automatically determines the speed and path of German V-2 rockets and sets the firing of antiaircraft batteries. Take every step to obtain more information on this facility."

The next day at seven a.m. Sasha was sitting with Barr in a midtown cafeteria when he passed his agent a slip of paper describing what the Center wanted.

Barr read it, and then offered a small, cryptic smile that left his handler perplexed. But in the next satisfying moment the mystery was solved.

"That's funny!" Meter said. "We must have a crystal ball. Five days ago we read your minds and got the technical manual of this facility. We finished photographing it last night at two a.m. There are six hundred pages of texts and drawings."

He passed Sasha several canisters of film under the table.

Two days later the films traveled in the diplomatic pouch to Moscow. And one week after the cable had been sent, the much-desired documents were on Pavel Fitin's desk in the Lubyanka.

As long as the flow of product remained constant—and of such high quality—Sasha felt he had no choice but to resign himself to the risks created by his two agents' imprudent behavior. But all the while, Sasha couldn't help pondering how much longer they'd be able to continue to get away with leading their secret lives. Or if the entire network would soon come crashing down.

22

EVEN TODAY, THERE REMAINS SOME mystery as to why
Meredith, at this point in the investigation, decided to
replow old ground. At least one of the intelligence historians
who reviewed the files insists it was simply Meredith's new knowledge about the relationship between Meter and Hughes that had sent
him scurrying back on this detour. This explanation is further bolstered by the undeniable fact that Meter is specifically mentioned in
the cable to which Meredith's attention returned.

Yet there is another school of thought that suggests the revelations in the first flurry of decryptions that had set up the two spies
as friends working in tandem had little to do with Meredith's next
move. Totally irrelevant, they huff. In fact, they assert, it's impossible to gauge with any kind of accuracy how a unique mind like
Meredith's worked. Genius, they point out with an argument-ending
smugness, has its own intuitive logic.

Still, whatever the reason, it is a matter of record that even as
the Bureau continued its pursuit of several targets, from his desk at
Arlington Hall Meredith issued a new "Special Study." It was titled
"Revised Translation of Message on Antenna—Liberal's wife Ethel."

"Further work on this message has so improved the text," began
Meredith, for once taking the slightest self-congratulatory bow, "that
a revised translation is in order." His new version of the cable sent on
November 27, 1944, from the New York station to Moscow Center
now read:

Intelligence on Liberal's wife. Surname that of her husband. Christian name Ethel 29 years old. Married 5 years. Finished middle school. A fellow countryman in 1938. Sufficiently well-developed politically. She knows about her husband's work and the role of Meter and Nil. In view of her delicate health does not work.

Meredith's second go-round did not shed any further light on Meter (the man Bob was convinced was Joel Barr). And Nil still remained a complete and total puzzle; the agent's identity was as impenetrable as it had been in the earlier translation. Nevertheless, Meredith believed he had found something he'd previously missed. It was a clue that took him deeper into the inner machinery of Liberal's ring. And to an understanding of the role of Liberal's wife. The key was a single verb.

Meredith, a linguist in his previous life who still felt on firmest ground when dealing with syntactical notions, had initially zeroed in on the use of the verb "work" in the message. The word in Russian, *rabotayet*, had, Meredith had recently grown certain, "a special meaning" in the cable. It referred, he wrote in his report, to "conspiratorial work in the interests of the U.S.S.R." And, therefore, the sentence "In view of her delicate health does not work" took on a special meaning, too.

"In the same way," Meredith reasoned, "the work that Ethel cannot do in view of her delicate health may not be the earning of her bread and butter, but conspiratorial work."

With that deduction, the network of spies took on a greater physical shape. There was the ringleader and talent spotter, Liberal. There were agents, productive operatives like Meter and Hughes. And then there was the head man's wife, Christian name Ethel, who was apparently fully cognizant of what was going on but at the same time stood on the sideline. *Does not work.* A passive spectator to the treason being played out around her.

———

FOR BOB, THE INVETERATE CASE man, there was little appreciation of his friend's semantic feat. He had no time for digressions into
the use of Russian nouns and verbs. The knowledge Bob took from
the revised translation was purely tactical: He had a new unsub. A
woman. And she was at the very heart of the ring.

Once again cavalierly ignoring the restrictions both Arlington
Hall and his superiors in the Bureau had placed on the investigation,
he let the field offices know why he was so keen on tracking her
down. Like Barr, she was thought "to have acted as an intermediary
between person or persons who were working on wartime nuclear
fission research and for KGB agents."

Bob reasoned that if he nabbed "Christian name Ethel," and if in
the process she led him to Liberal, then let the bosses come gunning
for him. He'd have something to shut them up all right. In his obsti-
nate way he sent a supplementary letter to the Bureau offices detailing what he knew, thanks entirely to Meredith, about the ringleader's
wife:

"ETHEL, used her husband's last name; had been married for five
years (at this time); 29 years of age; member of the Communist Party
USA, possibly joining in 1938; knew about her husband's work with
the Soviets."

But although this description offered, as Bob fervently wanted to
believe, "a considerable amount of positive information," it wasn't
enough. Not a single promising tip reached his desk. The identity of
the female unsub remained an enigma. He needed to find another
way to get to her.

Desperate, Bob began grasping at straws. He theorized, despite
the fact that the deciphered cable had clearly stated "Christian name
Ethel" was Liberal's wife, that she might be involved with Barr. His
rationale, as much as he had one, hinged on a belief that this network
of fellow countrymen might also have liberated sexual ideals. A bour-
geois concept like matrimony might not be too restrictive in Marxist
circles. Thus began the investigation, as Bob would primly describe it,
"of Barr's women friends."

It was quickly established that Barr didn't have a wife, but at the head of his list of many girlfriends, there was one longtime relationship. And when the Bureau started poking into Vivian Glassman's background, they found themselves following a trail similar to the ones they'd previously traveled while attempting to identify members of the ring. Her life had been lived in near lockstep with Barr's and Elitcher's, and, even more tantalizingly, perhaps with Liberal's. She was the daughter of immigrants, attended City College, worked at the Army Signal Corps laboratories at Fort Monmouth, had access to classified defense information, and had ties to Communist groups. But as much as Bob wanted to make the match, he came to the conclusion that there was nothing that could tie her to the female unsub.

Then, just as Bob was ready to surrender, a new bit of information came in: one of Barr's friends claimed that, in fact, he *was* married. Could his wife—a secret wife, since few people appeared to know about her—be "Christian name Ethel"? And what if, Bob now found himself wondering, and not for the first time, Barr was really Liberal? Had all the girlfriends just been one more bit of Moscow Center subterfuge to throw the enemy off the scent in the event they ever discovered the ringleader was married? To conceal that Joel Barr was the agent pulling the network's strings?

Elaine Goldfarb was the name of the woman alleged to have been Barr's wife, and the FBI pulled her biography apart. Yet in the end, Bob had to concede that Goldfarb and Barr had never been married, and there was nothing furtive about their relationship. True, they had lived together for a short time. But Goldfarb had not set eyes on Barr for seven years. The premise that she was the elusive unsub he'd been hunting could not, even Bob had to agree, be logically sustained.

"We came to a dead end on the investigation into 'Christian name Ethel,'" Bob decided, full of a certainty he'd live to regret.

BUT THERE WAS STILL MAX Elitcher. He was suddenly on the move, and the FBI, as Bob had instructed, was sticking closely to him.

It was July 30, 1948, a muggy midsummer morning, and Elitcher, his wife, Helene, and their young daughter were in their two-door Chevy, driving from Washington up to New York. Elitcher had given notice to his superiors in the Naval Ordnance Department that he'd be leaving soon; a school friend, Morton Sobell, had helped him land a better-paying job at Reeves Instrument Company in New York. The purpose of this trip was to check out the progress on the new house in Queens the Elitchers would be moving into as of September. Its backyard bordered Sobell's home, and the convivial plan was for the Elitchers to be weekend houseguests at the Sobells'.

They were heading through Baltimore when Helene Elitcher noticed the car trailing behind them. It was a dark sedan and both the driver and the man next to him in the front seat wore ties, jackets, and fedoras. It was as identifying as any uniform, and she excitedly told her husband that the FBI was following them.

Elitcher tried to lose the tail. He sped up; he slowed down; he switched lanes. The dark sedan relentlessly kept pace.

Near Philadelphia, another team of FBI watchers took over. And for a while, the Elitchers appeared at ease; they hadn't spotted the new tail. But as he drove into New York City, coming down the expressway along the Hudson River, Elitcher looked into his rearview mirror and saw a dark sedan on his bumper. There were two beefy men sporting fedoras in the front seat.

Elitcher quickly improvised a new plan. He wouldn't lead the FBI to his friend's home. Instead, he'd wait out the storm at his mother's apartment on upper Lexington Avenue. If they wanted to arrest him, they could do it there. At least his family would be safe.

It was a long, uneasy stay for the Elitchers. The husband and wife went repeatedly to the living room window, looking furtively up and down the street. The slightest noise and they wondered if it was the sound of the FBI stomping up the steps, preparing to pound on the apartment door.

Hours passed, but nothing happened.

As the sky darkened, the Elitchers grew convinced the FBI had abandoned their surveillance. They'd be able to continue undetected to the Sobells in Queens.

They were wrong. When the Elitchers arrived at their friends' home, Agents William McCarthy and John Ward were still on their backs. But it didn't matter. The two FBI men did not stay for long.

The next morning Bob read their surveillance report:

"It should be stated that on the trip from Manhattan to the Sobells' home, it was confirmed without a doubt that the Elitchers were 'tail conscious,' and, therefore, the surveillance was discontinued."

And so Bob never knew what happened next.

MORTON SOBELL WAS FURIOUS. HOW could his guest have led the FBI to his doorstep? What if they come charging in and arrest you? With or without a warrant, they'll have the excuse they need to search my home, he worried.

The two families sat down to an uneasy dinner. Conversation was difficult. They were on high alert, listening for a sudden noise, an unnatural sound that rose above the passing traffic. Max and Mort, two old friends, could not help feeling that this might be their last supper as free men.

The table was cleared, and still nothing, no intrusions, no arrests. But Sobell's nerves were frayed. He took Elitcher aside and spoke to him in a low voice. He had some material in the house that was, Elitcher would remember his saying, "too good to throw away." But it was too dangerous to keep it, not with the chance that the FBI could barge in at any moment. He needed to get it to Rosenberg *now*! And he wanted his friend to come with him. He was too tired to drive into Manhattan alone.

In the car, Sobell convinced the reliably subservient Elitcher to drive. But first Sobell took a small canister, the size that would hold a roll of 35mm film, out of his jacket pocket and placed it in the glove compartment.

Elitcher drove carefully, and all the while his eyes were constantly darting to the rearview mirror, checking for unwanted company. He followed his friend's directions, heading down the East River Drive. Sobell told him when to exit, and then guided him to a deserted stretch in Lower Manhattan. It had an odd name for a city street, a woman's name—Catherine Slip. "Park," Sobell ordered. From the car the two men could see the dark ribbon of the East River in the distance. The night seemed unnaturally quiet. Elitcher sat behind the wheel as Sobell made his way on foot toward Knickerbocker Village.

Sobell walked the two blocks neither fast nor slow. The film canister was now deep in his pocket.

Meanwhile, Elitcher waited. He quickly lost track of the time. Minutes? An hour? A lifetime? In his churning mind it was as if a chaotic chorus were screaming mad, incoherent thoughts. He felt completely unnerved.

Then the car door opened and Sobell climbed in.

"What did Julie think about it?" his friend swiftly asked, not even trying to disguise the panic in his words.

Sobell, though, was all calm. "Julie says there's nothing to worry about," he answered.

And there wasn't. The Bureau's watchers had already returned their car to the garage. The evening came and went without either Bob or Sasha knowing just how close the Bureau had come to breaking the ring.

In their blindness, the hunters and the hunted continued on.

23

THEN, WITHOUT ANY WARNING, THE high-flying investigation went into a tailspin. For Bob and Meredith, there was the before, and then the after. And in the aftermath, America's hegemony came to an unexpected end, and the world changed forever. Bob would always remember the day he'd heard the shocking news, and the deep sense of personal failure that swiftly followed.

His eventful week had started off badly, and in that still innocent time he might very well have thought things couldn't have gotten any worse. Bob had been tethered to his desk at headquarters, poring over the latest batch of decrypts, when in a sudden flash of insight, a piece in the puzzle fell into place. The code name of the KGB agent mentioned in one of the new cables had been gnawing at him for days. Why did he keep returning to it? he wondered. But Bob couldn't find the answer. The connection eluded him.

Then there it was—he had seen it before, more or less. The name in the cable was similar to the cover name of a Soviet operative the Bureau had unearthed in a previous investigation. He ran to check the files and, digging feverishly, he tracked it down. The two names were so close it couldn't be an accident. They had to be the same man.

It was a finding, Bob was firmly convinced, that would open up new investigative paths, reveal previously undetected Soviet espionage activities.

But beyond the operational significance, it was also a personal triumph. Bob had come up with this new, important clue on his own. For once he hadn't relied on Meredith to make the breakthrough. They were a team, but nonetheless it bothered the competitive Bob that Meredith had been leading the way. Bob felt he'd be able to show the code breaker that he wasn't the only one who had the acuity to penetrate Moscow Center's secrets.

Flush with pride, Bob hurried to Arlington Hall. And all the way there he was beaming—"Waiting for compliments," he'd candidly recall.

Meredith listened with an impassive concentration. When he finally spoke, he was, Bob would concede with gratitude, "gentle." But at the same unflinching time he made it clear that Bob had gotten it all wrong. The problem, explained Meredith, seeming truly embarrassed to be in the role of teacher correcting the naïve pupil, was that Bob didn't know Russian. Although the two names did look alike, they were worlds apart when pronounced *correctly*. There was no connection at all.

Chagrined, Bob slunk out of his friend's office. Over the days that followed, the rebuke, despite the elaborate politeness with which it had been delivered, continued to sting. But Bob was never one to brood for too long; he possessed too much self-confidence. In time he managed to find the philosophy to shrug it off. Looking back at the conversation, he now could be "amused at my own stupidity."

And then, without warning, this rosy perspective, along with everything else he'd been working on, or so it seemed at the terrible time, no longer amounted to much. The "stunning news," as Bob would say with a measure of momentousness as much as shock, changed everything.

FROM THEIR BASE IN ALASKA, the B-29s of the 175th Weather Reconnaissance Squadron routinely patrolled a patch of the Pacific that stretched all the way to Japan, before circling back over the Arctic, just windward of the Soviet Union. As the B-29s flew below the jet stream, their specially designed fuselage ducts scooped up the air through paper filters. The planes were, in Air Force parlance, sniffers. The unit's secret mission: to detect long-range atomic explosions.

On September 3, 1949, one of the squadron's B-29s flying east of the Kamchatka Peninsula gathered evidence that set off the plane's red warning lights. Back at the base, measurements of the filter paper residue confirmed what had previously been unthinkable: radioactivity that was the result of atomic fission.

Five days earlier, on an isolated grassy steppe in northeast Kazakhstan, the Soviet Union had detonated an atom bomb. For four years the United States had been the only nation with this unprecedented weapon in its arsenal. America had dropped atomic bombs on the Japanese cities of Hiroshima (more than 140,000 dead) and Nagasaki (more than 70,000 dead) confident that no country on earth could respond with equally dreadful force. Now that monopoly was broken. There were two atomic superpowers.

President Truman, though, didn't believe it. It seemed impossible to him that "those Asiatics," as he dismissed the upstart Russian scientists, could build a device as sophisticated as an atom bomb. Adamant, he refused to make a public announcement until the members of the detection committee signed a statement, one of the participants recalled, "to the effect [that] they really believed the Russians had done it." And even after the committee dutifully affirmed the evidence was irrefutable, the president grumbled that "German scientists in Russia did it." That was the only explanation that made any sense. After all, just weeks earlier he'd received a report from the CIA repeating its previous estimate that the "most probable date" for a Soviet atomic bomb was "mid-1953."

But Bob, who had learned of the disaster at a hastily called intelligence briefing that swiftly turned as mournful as a wake, had another suspicion. And while people left the session in stunned silence, their eyes averted from one another, Bob saw things clearly. His collabora-

tion with Meredith over the past year, all the leads he'd been following, had convinced him that he was not inventing conspiracies where
none existed. *A possible link between Enormoz and wartime nuclear fission.* He believed, just as Meredith believed, that Russian scientists
had "been aided in their effort to build it by information stolen from
the United States." But believing was not the same as knowing. Or,
for that matter, proving.

It was a difficult time. His conjectures weighing heavy on his
shoulders, Bob was summoned the next day to another meeting
at headquarters. It would be three weeks before a somber Truman
would share the news with the American people, but an interagency
committee had already been formed to try to get a handle on "the
implications of the Russian bomb," as the shell-shocked intelligence
specialists put it. Lish Whitson, the studious new chief of the Espionage Section, was the Bureau's representative, and before he faced
the other committee members, he wanted to hear from his own unit's
supervisors.

Three of Bob's colleagues had already taken their places at the
round table, and as soon as Bob entered the room he could tell by the
stony stares that greeted him that something was not right. Whitson,
breathing anger and frustration, started things off with a barrage of
hostile questions. They were all aimed at Bob. Every one of them,
each in its separate yet accusatory way, wanted an answer to pretty
much the same thing: Had the Russians built their bomb using information they had stolen from us? And if they had, why weren't the
culprits behind bars?

Bob sat there, absorbing the attack, waiting for Whitson to finish. But from the opening salvo, he'd understood what was going
on. He was the man, it was well known in the Bureau, who was
leading the charge to track down Soviet spies. It didn't matter that,
if scientific information had indeed been taken, the thefts had occurred during the war—long before Bob had gotten on the case.
This was not a time for logic. Whitson wanted a scapegoat. And
since the Bureau didn't have an actual Russian to fit with a noose,

they'd settle by placing the rope around the neck of the next best thing—the supervisor of the Soviet Espionage desk.

At last it was Bob's turn to speak. He did his best to fight back. But it wasn't much of a battle: he couldn't reveal too much about what was going on at Arlington Hall, what Meredith had discovered about Enormoz; even the president was still in the dark about the operation. Flailing away, he offered a painfully brief catalogue of espionage activities that "resulted in some information—probably of minor value—being transmitted to the Russians." But in the end, with a condemned man's resigned candor, he had to admit that "it wasn't possible for us to assess accurately how much direct help these penetrations had been to Soviet scientists who had fashioned the Russian A-bomb." His direct answer to Whitson's direct question was a hapless I-don't-know.

When the torturous meeting finally came to an end, Bob left with his head hung low. He felt he'd let the Bureau—no, the nation—down by failing to round up the Soviet agents Meredith's magic had revealed. Worse, his sense of shame was compounded because his defeat appeared irreparable. He'd never find the definitive proof he needed to track down the atomic spies. And he'd never be able to stop them before they made off with more of his country's secrets.

YET TRUMAN, WHILE MUDDYING THE matter with his xenophobic slur, had nevertheless been onto something when he'd argued that making an atomic device was a complicated business. Uranium would be at the fissionable core of the prototype weapon, but one critical manufacturing problem was that uranium in its natural state is made up of two isotopes, U-235 and U-238. Isotopes are like fraternal, rather than identical, twins. They're elements with the identical chemical makeup, but at the same time they're unique. And as with twins, it's these variations, however small, that make all the difference. U-235 was the more highly radioactive twin, and the one that packed the wallop necessary to power a chain reaction that'd culminate in a nuclear explosion. Only—it was rare. In a chunk of natural uranium, less than one percent of the entire element would be the sleek U–235. The remainder was the heavier, inert U–238.

The scientists working on the bomb were faced with a daunting technical challenge: How do you separate these two conjoined uranium twins? How can the vital U–235 be extracted from the uranium element?

American and British scientists had experimented with a variety of complex methods—electromagnetic separation, chemical extraction, and gaseous diffusion. Gaseous diffusion, in the original theories scientists presented, was a sort of Rube Goldberg project involving a high-pressure system with pumps and tubes arranged in an interconnected cascade of more than four thousand stages. Uranium gas would course through this network, making its way through a series of membranes with submicroscopic openings, and the lighter U–235 would complete the journey before its heavier twin. It was such a promising theory that even before all the glitches had been worked out, the Manhattan Project had agreed to build a $100 million gaseous diffusion plant in Oak Ridge, Tennessee.

And now Meredith sat at his isolated desk reading a KGB cable announcing the delivery of a theoretical paper on the top-secret gaseous diffusion process. For while Bob had been lumbering about like a bereaved man, Meredith had been working. After laboring long hours well into the night, he had succeeded in deciphering a series of cables starting back in February 1944, between the New York *rezidentura* and Moscow Center that all involved the activities of an agent code-named "Rest."

A message dated June 15, 1944, fused all his inchoate findings into a single cry of alarm:

"... received from Rest the third part of Report 'SN–12 Efferent Fluctuations in a Steam [and here Meredith had stumbled for a moment; he couldn't unlock several code groups] Diffusion Method'— work his specialty."

With that, Meredith knew, and all his suspicions became certainties.

Just as Bob knew when he read the deciphered cable reporting what the agent code-named Rest had delivered. "It became immediately obvious to me," he'd say, the words crackling with resolve and anger, "that the Russians had indeed stolen crucial research from us and had undoubtedly used it to build a bomb."

As if in an instant, Bob was lifted from his doldrums. His theories had been proven; they were no longer speculations, but cold, hard facts. And there was an additional reason spurring him on. Just a day earlier at an intelligence briefing he'd attended a secret had been shared, albeit in purposefully imprecise, layman's terms, that gave his activities a new critical urgency. In the aftermath of Russia's detonation of an atomic device, President Truman had issued the order to build a new superbomb, a hydrogen bomb. "Go to it, and fast," the president had instructed the Atomic Energy Commission. Bob now feared that the Soviet spies who had stolen the Enormoz secrets would make off with the plans for this new superweapon, too—unless he and Meredith stopped them.

In his revitalized mood, he swiftly made an operational decision. Elitcher, Sobell, "Christian name Ethel"—all the inquiries into the potential members of Liberal's ring were to be put aside. That investigation suddenly seemed to Bob to be a diversion, and at best one that offered the prospect of only small rewards; there was nothing in their backgrounds that linked any of these suspects to atomic research. His priority was to track down the spies who had stolen the atomic secrets, Russian agents who could very well still be in place, pilfering the secrets of this new superweapon. His first step in this renewed hunt was to find the answer to the question that now burned inside him with the fiery glow of a vendetta: Who is Rest?

24

THE WORLD OF A KGB agent runner was one of frequent
change. Stay too long in one place, working one set of joes, and
the greater the likelihood the opposition will get a bead on you.
And so Moscow Center had pulled Sasha from his posting in New York,
praised him for a job well done, and, before too long, had sent him off
on a new assignment. On September 27, 1947, Sasha's destination was the
Nag's Head pub just across from the Wood Green tube station in North
London, where he was to meet Rest for the first time.

Every agent runner has his own "handwriting"—that is, his own
style of tradecraft—and Sasha was fond of bars for making visual
contacts with his agents. He could wait without attracting attention;
what could be a more natural cover than bellying up to the bar, glass
in hand? While, at the same time, he could keep an eye on the door
to see if the opposition's watchers had tagged along. The Nag's Head
offered all this and more. It was on a busy street, directly across from
a bus stop—the perfect observation post for a discreet reconnoiter before entering. Inside, three low-ceilinged rooms ran into one another,
and each was smoky, dark, and crowded, boozy voices roaring up in
a constant din on this Saturday night that made eavesdropping impossible. Another blessing, a bell above the door conveniently jingled
when someone entered.

Yet despite all the operational cards he was holding, on the day
of the meet, Sasha was uncharacteristically wary. Just three months
earlier, newly arrived in Moscow after his five and a half years in
America, he had been summoned to the Center and found him-

self facing an impassive Lieutenant-General Sergei Romanovich Savchenko, the head of intelligence, and Leonid Kvasnikov, his old boss in New York who had become the head of the KGB's Tenth Directorate for Scientific and Technical Intelligence. They advised him of his new mission. Comrade Feklisov was to take control of the agent who was "one of the key elements in the construction of the Soviet A-bomb." The agent code-named Rest had previously worked at Los Alamos and had made regular deliveries of secret materials that had proven essential to Russian scientists. In July 1946, he returned to England as head of theoretical research at Harwell, the center for the British atomic weapons program. For the past fifteen months Rest had been out of touch, but he'd recently sent word that he had new material. Sasha was to be assigned to the London embassy, once more masquerading under diplomatic cover, to handle the reactivation of Rest. He was specifically ordered to "satisfy all his requests." And at the same time, Sasha was to convey to Rest specific questions from the Soviet team that was trying to keep pace with the Americans' surprisingly public development of the new superweapon, the hydrogen bomb.

The session with the two spymasters concluded with a mission statement that was delivered with an icy hardness: "An arrest would be in and of itself a serious setback; any kind of problem could be potentially disastrous for Soviet scientific research." Sasha understood: He'd received a warning. And with so much hanging in the balance, he did not need to be informed of the penalty if he was the cause of Rest's apprehension.

Sasha proceeded to the eight p.m. meet with a professional's care, leaving, as was his practice, hours in advance. He had always preferred to act alone. His customary maxim: The more agents at a secret rendezvous, the greater the risk. But this time, with the stern warning he'd received in the Lubyanka still ringing in his ears, Sasha decided a more cautious tradecraft was necessary. After cabling the center for permission, he'd recruited Volodya, the good-natured young embassy chauffeur, to act as both his legman and babysitter.

And so, with Volodya watching his back, he traveled to the southern edge of London, before reversing course and heading north by a combination of buses and underground trains. When Sasha had set out, a thin sun had been shining through the autumn clouds, but by the time he emerged from the Wood Green station, the sky was dark and the operational gods had further blessed the evening with a concealing fog.

Still, Sasha waited. Prudent tradecraft required that he look before he leaped. If the opposition had been trailing him, or, an even more dire thought, if they had been following Rest, their surveillance teams would be in position along the street in front of the Nag's Head. He walked slowly to the bus stop, and stood there, pretending to read the newspaper, while all the time praying a bus wouldn't come before he had time to check for all the watchers' telltale signs. He looked for smoke trailing from the exhausts of parked cars; vans with an array of antennas on their roofs; or clumps of drinkers scattered on the street who never touched their pints or exchanged a cheery word with their mates. He kept a sharp eye but saw nothing that gave him any cause for alarm.

With an impressive punctuality, at precisely eight p.m. a tall man with a thin wisp of blond hair above a broad dome of a forehead that seemed high and wide enough to hold an encyclopedia of scientific secrets entered the pub. He walked with a martial erectness, shoulders back like a soldier on parade. He was the very image of the photograph Sasha had scrutinized at Moscow Center of the agent code-named Rest. Sasha waited an additional five minutes or so just to be sure no one was trailing behind, and then he crossed the street to join the lively Saturday-night crowd inside the Nag's Head.

Rest sat on a high stool, a beer in front of him, as he skimmed the pages of the *Tribune*. The newspaper had been the recognition signal ordered by Moscow Center, but Sasha's stomach dropped precipitously as he realized the choice had been an operational mistake.

The *Tribune* was too left wing for a scientist with the highest security clearance to be seen reading in these suspicious Cold War days.

Sasha carried a book with a red cover clutched in his hand—another previously ordained sign—and Rest acknowledged his arrival with a small nod of his head. Sasha quickly looked away, and found a place at the other end of the bar. And once again he waited. He knew this was a crucial moment. If the enemy had been following, now would be when they'd enter the bar. Either all his fears would remain locked in his imagination, or in an instant his worst nightmare would become very real.

Suddenly, the bell above the door jingled and in Sasha's shaky mind it clanged like a fire alarm. The door flung open and two men walked in. In a series of observations that passed so rapidly as to be a single instant in his mind, Sasha saw that they were old enough to be retirees; their faces shone with the rosy glow that comes from a night's drinking; and, with voices jolly and booming, they greeted the bartender like old friends when they ordered their pints. Although never partial to beer, Sasha took a long, relieved swallow from his glass, and for once the tepid, bitter taste was a pleasure.

Rest was the first to leave his seat. There was a corner of the dark room where the wall was decorated with framed photographs of British pugilists, their fists raised menacingly as if ready to do battle, and, as per the plan, he walked over and focused his attention on them. The Center had decreed that in addition to the recognition signals, a word code should be exchanged. Before leaving Moscow, Sasha had memorized the dialogue.

"The stout is not as it should be," was his line.

"Nothing can compare to Guinness," would be Rest's response.

But once he arrived in London, the local *rezident* informed him that Rest had vetoed the exchange. He had taken it upon himself to come up with a new script, to which Sasha had agreed without protest. Once in the field, the agent, not the handler, is always in control; he sets the rules.

When Sasha approached, Rest murmured, "I think the best British heavyweight of all times is Bruce Woodcock." He said the words as if he were merely thinking out loud, talking to no one in particular. His eyes remained glued to the photographs.

Sasha replied: "Oh, no. Tommy Farr is certainly the best!"

Rest didn't continue the argument. He returned to the bar, but suddenly he was in a hurry. He finished his beer in a single gulp, paid his tab, wished the barman a good evening, and was on his way. Sasha moved toward the window, a man finding a place to stand. But his gaze looked out toward the foggy street: there was no one on Rest's tail as he walked slowly down the block.

Sasha caught up with him several minutes later.

"Hello. My name is Eugene," he said, adding one more cover name to a lifetime of aliases. "I'm happy to see you."

"Hello, Eugene. I'm happy as well," said Rest with a smile that seemed genuine. "I thought you had forgotten me."

The two men shook hands and continued down the nighttime block, talking all the way as cars hummed along the High Road.

IT IS THE DUTY OF case officers to get to know their agents. And it is a practice that is driven by more than mere curiosity or good manners. It is necessary for survival. A professional has the training and the experience to sort through the clutter of his agent's life and make judgments about security, about what might set off the chain of events that will culminate in the enemy's counterintelligence team crashing through the door.

On that first evening stroll through the foggy streets of Haringey, Sasha peppered Rest with questions. He wanted to know about the scientist's life at Harwell. The British atomic research center, as Rest described it, was a compound surrounded by barbed-wire fences and checkpoints, a world of "endless security requirements." But his handler was cheered to hear that Rest had moved into a nearby boardinghouse and, thanks to the generous salary he earned, had his own car.

Sasha also discussed the risks Rest would be taking, and in doing so he had to walk the fine line that is the handler's constant balancing act: he wanted the product, but he didn't want his agent to get caught. "How will you be able to take out documents, calculations, graphs, and sketches?" he asked. What if they are discovered "while checking your ID card just as you are leaving Harwell?"

Rest was full of daring. "Simple," he said as if he really believed it was. "I'll tell them: 'But no one ever said I have no right to take my own notes with me. I work nonstop for twenty-four hours, and an idea can come to me at home just as easily as in the lab.'"

Sasha, his interest purely operational, also wanted to know with whom his agent was sleeping. One of his greatest fears, lodged deep in his anxious mind by the spymasters at the Center, was that Rest would get caught in a honey trap dangled by the opposition.

Rest's answer was vague, both hesitant and embarrassed. Sasha thought the implication was that he went to prostitutes from time to time. The handler decided not to press. Instead he tried a different tack.

"Why don't you get married? Aren't you tired of being a bachelor?" Sasha wanted the suggestion to sound genial, the advice of one concerned friend to another. But his professional's mind was thinking that a wife would be a useful bit of cover. Marriage conveys trustworthiness. With a wife by his side, Rest would get invited to social occasions at Harwell. There'd be more opportunities to meet the sort of people who would further his career.

"I think about it from time to time," Rest said. "But, you know, I'm walking through a minefield. One false move and it will all blow up. I can accept the worst-case scenario, but I can't involve a wife and children."

Sasha listened, and suffered through a moment's guilt. He felt ashamed by his small attempt to manipulate his agent's life for his own reasons. But in the next instant, he was once again the KGB professional.

He had a list of memorized questions that had been passed on to him by the Center. Like all the graduates of the KGB spy school, his memory had been drilled until he could repeat the license plates of at least nine cars that passed in rapid succession. But this was a completely different task. He had been tutored in atomic theory before he'd left Moscow, but it had been basic concepts. The questions posed by the Russian scientists were quite specific, and full of terms that might just as well have been in an incomprehensible language. Sasha could not trust himself to remember more than five of their carefully crafted inquiries.

Rest listened without interrupting. His answers, too, were patient. He spoke in a slow, calm voice, while at the same time gauging his handler's reaction. When he saw that Sasha seemed lost, he'd start over again, repeating the information with a deliberate precision.

Sasha's concentration was immense. He filed each response, he'd say, "in different drawers within my memory." Yet the exchanges were taut, filled with the constant fear that if he made a single mistake, forgot a phrase, or erred with a number, the Center would extract an unforgiving punishment. His only hope was that after he returned to the *rezidentura*, he'd "empty each drawer one by one, and put on paper what had been said."

When the five specific questions had been answered, Sasha gave Rest a list of additional, more complex technical areas that the scientists working in Laboratory Number 2 wanted him to explore. The list was written on cigarette paper; it could easily be swallowed. He instructed Rest to bring the information at their next meet.

Rest read the list. "No problem. You'll get all this next time."

Then he handed the slip of paper back to Sasha. He didn't need it; it was all locked in his mind. Rest's dossier had stressed his nearly photographic memory, but still Sasha was uneasy. Yet he decided that he could not at this first meet challenge his joe; it was more important that a bond of trust develop between them.

As the meet was about to end, Sasha asked for the documents Rest was carrying. The agent had wanted to hand them over as soon as they'd left the pub, but Sasha had refused. It was another of the inviolate rules of Moscow Center tradecraft that exchanges occur only at the very last moment. If the opposition suddenly emerged from the shadows, the agent would stand a better chance of talking his way out of the incriminating predicament than if the secrets were found on a foreigner.

Rest handed over a notebook with about forty pages in small but carefully legible handwriting. It revealed the latest information on the workings and manufacture of the plutonium bomb.

"Thank you," said Sasha as he was about to leave.

"My pleasure," answered Rest. "I shall always be indebted to you."

Then they went off in separate directions, handler and agent disappearing into the night's fog.

OVER THE NEXT TWO YEARS, Sasha would meet with Rest every three or four months. They would meet at pubs, or at the cinema, or on the street, using brush passes to exchange secret documents. For a while the Center grew concerned that the enemy was on to Rest. It was decided that a DLB—the professional's shorthand for a dead letter box—would offer greater security. A KGB asset, an Englishman by birth, lived in a cottage surrounded by a well-trimmed hedge on a quiet suburban street. Rest was instructed to toss a package containing his next delivery over the hedge and onto the lawn. But at the last minute, the Center overruled its own plan. Despite the risks, the spymasters ordered Sasha to continue his meets with Rest. The yield was too valuable to jeopardize.

And as Bob and Meredith began their hunt for Rest, an ocean away Sasha prepared for his next face-to-face rendezvous with the very spy who had just come into their sights.

25

F ROM BOB'S OFFICE IN THE Justice Department headquarters, it was a short walk up Constitution Avenue through the bureaucratic heart of official Washington to the broad limestone building on Nineteenth Street. On the outside the structure was as solid as a mausoleum, and inside it was no more comforting. There was a maze of dimly lit corridors whose walls were painted in a lugubrious shade of green, and the officious clickety-clack of typewriters reverberated from behind closed doors. During the war a cluster of high-ceilinged rooms had been home to the newly formed Joint Chiefs of Staff and their army of aides, but with the peace they had moved on to grander suites in the Pentagon. The offices had been recently taken over by another breed of intrepid warriors—the Atomic Energy Commission (AEC). And now Bob, not knowing where else to begin, had come here hoping to get the help he needed to find the Russian spy known as Rest.

The cable Meredith had deciphered offered, Bob was convinced, one potentially promising clue. It stated that Rest had passed on to his handler the third part of "Report Sn," and while Meredith had struggled to get the complete title, he had managed to make out that it concerned "fluctuations in . . . the diffusion method." Bob decided that if he could identify the actual report, then he might be able to get something that could direct him to the spy who'd passed the document on to the KGB. Specifics still eluded him; he was running on pure instinct.

After making a few calls, he'd been told to try the AEC; they had custody of all the Manhattan Project files. Yet even as he walked across town on that late October day in 1949, Bob was gripped by the disturbing awareness that he might not get too much cooperation. For one thing, he couldn't reveal why he was looking for the report, how the fragmentary title had come to his attention, or even the fact that the KGB cable sent from New York had been dated June 15, 1944, and therefore that was why it seemed likely that the report had also been written about that date. Adding to his uncustomary level of professional trepidation, he knew he'd be entering a realm that was beyond his grasp. The prospect of using some scientific mumbo-jumbo about "fluctuations in the diffusion method" as his avenue of attack had him seriously doubting he was up to the task. The best he could do was remind himself that he'd won Meredith over; these AEC pointy-heads couldn't be more difficult, or, for that matter, more brilliant, than his new friend at Arlington Hall. He'd come a long way from the days when his biggest intellectual challenge was hammering away with a pickax in the dark pit of an Idaho silver mine, he once again reflected with some amusement.

It took Bob a bit of doing, a judicious mixture of his natural charm and what he called his "G-man stare," to get the AEC officials to agree to look through their files. But once they went into action, it didn't take them long to find the document. All the pieces neatly fit: it was dated June 6, 1944, and titled "Fluctuations and the Efficiency of a Diffusion Plant."

Bob thumbed through the pages, more a reflexive gesture than any determined hunt, with only a faint hope of finding something incriminating. All he discovered were dense paragraphs, often mixed with mathematical formulae, and he swiftly came to the conclusion that the entire report was as incomprehensible to him as the encoded cables that Meredith somehow managed to decipher. Perhaps the AEC official (his identity a lost footnote to this story) saw the bewilderment on Bob's face, and that was why he offered a brief and indulgently simplistic explanation of how the diffusion process was essential to manufacture the sort of uranium necessary to create an atom bomb. Bob listened, and while he didn't follow all the science, he did grasp the bottom line of what the official was telling him: this was precisely the sort of valuable information that this government wouldn't want the Russians to have.

Bob next focused his attention on Part III of the report, but it was no less daunting. The section was headed "The Effects of Fluctuations in the Flow of N_2." He remembered enough of his high school chemistry to know that N_2 was nitrogen, but the rest of the section was way beyond anything he'd learned in school. He gave up quickly.

His cursory tour of the report over, Bob returned to the cover page. And there it was: an author was listed! A "K. Fuchs." Bob knew that simply because this "K. Fuchs" had written the report, that didn't necessarily mean he'd handed the report to the Russians. Someone else could just as easily have stolen the document. Still, grasping at whatever sliver of encouragement he could, Bob remembered that the cable had described Rest by stating that "work"—and here Bob assumed the KGB meant the diffusion process—was "his specialty." Who, he asked himself, would be more of a specialist than the author of the report? Bob at once decided his next step would be to identify this "K. Fuchs." It would be too much to hope that Fuchs was Rest, but he should at least be able to give Bob an idea of who had access to the document.

Despite all his initial apprehension, Bob felt he'd accomplished something. He had no definitive answers, but he had determined the direction he'd be taking. And experience had taught him that was all a fieldman could ever do: keep putting one foot in front of the other until he reached his destination. Standing still killed more investigations than anything else.

In this optimistic mood, Bob waited for a photocopy of the report to be made. Once he had it, he'd head back to his office and direct his troops to chase down all they could about "K. Fuchs." He was eager to get going, but he had time to kill and so he absently picked up the file folder that had held the report. It was crammed with other documents, and on the file cover was the designation "MSN." Why did those three letters trigger something in his mind? Bob wondered. Then he remembered: inked across the front page of the report that he'd just read was a handwritten "MSN-12." Okay, he now deduced, it'd been the twelfth report in the MSN series. But what was MSN?

The letters MSN, the clerk explained when he returned with the photocopied pages, denoted documents prepared by the group of British scientists who had come to New York during the early days of the war to work on atomic energy research.

IT WAS LATE NOVEMBER 1943, just as the SS *Andes* was preparing to sail from Liverpool, when a protective detail of military police led fifteen men in civilian clothes onboard. Before the bewildered captain could complain, he was handed an envelope marked "Secret." Inside was a brief note written beneath an impressive Whitehall letterhead and bearing the even more impressive signature of a cabinet member. It was imperative, the note stiffly informed, that these passengers arrive safely in America. Nothing less than the entire Allied war effort was at stake.

Over the tense days that followed, as the captain steered a circuitous path west toward Virginia across an Atlantic patrolled by German U-boats, he could only wonder as to the identity of his last-minute arrivals. Were they soldiers? No, they didn't have the look. Nor did he think they were pilots. And they certainly weren't sailors. Perhaps, he finally decided, they were civil servants who were working with the Yanks on Lend-Lease shipments. That would explain why they were so crucial to winning the war. Yes, he congratulated himself, that had to be it.

He was wrong. They were much more important than he had imagined, or could ever have imagined.

They were scientists who had been handpicked by J. Robert Oppenheimer, the director of the Manhattan Project. They were chosen to work with a team at Columbia University to solve the remaining questions in the essential gaseous–diffusion manufacturing process. If they could not provide answers to the engineers from the Kellex Corporation, whose multimillion–dollar facility was already under construction in Tennessee, the Manhattan Project would be unable to produce the specific uranium needed. And America would not be able to build an atomic bomb.

Six years later, as Bob studied the boat's passenger manifest, he suspected that one of the fifteen British scientists was also a Russian spy.

After the initial soft–pedaling round of burrowing, Bob's team had discovered plenty of reasons not only for suspicions, but for wrenching concerns. The group of British scientists included more than its fair share, as one Bureau memo put it, of "big names." Many of them émigrés from Nazi Germany, they had studied atomic theory with Max Born in Edinburgh (which was like studying gravity with Newton) and in the process had helped to reinvent physics. After their time in New York, several of them had also been recruited to work in key positions at the secret compound in Los Alamos, New Mexico, where the atomic weapon had been constructed. They were all precisely the sort of well–placed, knowledgeable agents the enemy would want to recruit.

It was such a ghastly possibility that Bob's mind rebelled against it. He did not want to believe that any of these British scientists, no doubt vetted first by MI5 and then by the Manhattan Project authorities, had all along been working for the Russians. But then Meredith called. In his usual tentative, almost self-effacing way, the code breaker told Bob that he had something "you might want to see if you're not too busy."

Bob accepted the latest decrypt from his friend, a cable sent to KGB headquarters from the New York *rezidentura* nearly five years ago, in February 1944. He quickly scanned the words until he came to the sentence Meredith had underlined. He read aloud:

"Rest arrived in the Country . . ." Bob stopped, and Meredith explained that "Country" was Moscow Center's cover name for America.

He continued reading: ". . . as a member of the Island . . ." Another pause, and once again Meredith dutifully filled it: "Island" was KGB-speak for England. Then Bob went on to finish the sentence: ". . . mission to Enormoz."

There was no need to explain what "Enormoz" stood for.

Bob read the entire decrypted cable again. When he spoke, his words were directed to his friend, but he might just as well have been speaking to himself.

There's no longer any doubt that Rest was part of the British scientific delegation, he said.

None, Meredith agreed.

At last resigned to the distasteful task, Bob hurried back to headquarters, determined to find the traitor.

IN THE HUNT FOR A spy, the standard counterintelligence strategy is to pursue opportunity and motive. There were fifteen names on Bob's list, and after just a glance he saw that the question of which of them had the opportunity to steal America's atomic secrets could be answered in a flash—depressingly, they all did. Therefore, Bob decided he'd make better use of his time by concentrating on which of the scientists possessed a motive. Once again, he did some quick elimination. Money, sex, blackmail—none of these usual motivations for betrayal, Bob's instincts told him, were in play in this case. All his experiences on the SE desk suggested this was a political operation. The spy had gone to work for Moscow Center out of an allegiance to the Soviet cause. It was a crime driven by ideology, not passion or greed.

Yet even as Bob took this investigative tack, he pursued it with a measure of distaste. He had been raised by a famously (at least in the mines and saloons of Mullan) contrarian father, a man who liked to lecture that people have a right to think and talk as suited them. That was what America was all about, Joe Lamphere was fond of saying. And Bob was his father's son. While there were many passionate cold warriors on the Bureau's fifth floor (including, he knew, the director) who could work themselves up into quite a lather about the Red Menace, Bob never could muster their knee-jerk outrage. Spying was one thing, but being "a little bit pink," as he'd put it, was another thing entirely. In fact, despite all the recent headlines Senator Joseph McCarthy had been making, Bob couldn't help feeling (and the instinct would, with hindsight, build over the years into an angry conviction) that McCarthy's "approach and tactics hurt the anti-Communist activities in the United States." Bob was totally committed to battling the KGB's operations in America, but at same time he believed "McCarthy's star chamber proceedings, his lies and overstatements, hurt our counter-intelligence efforts." Tar and feathering people based on little more than contrivance and innuendo—that had no place in Bob's kind of patriotism.

Still, when his burrowers now dug deeper, four names on the list came back to him with distinct ties to Communist organizations. And Bob understood that this alignment of potential motive as well as certain opportunity made each of the four scientists a prime suspect. Each fit the profile of a sympathizer who had volunteered his services to Moscow Center, or had been targeted for recruitment.

After a more intensive search, Bob quickly winnowed down his list. Two of the scientists, he discovered, had only a youthful infatuation with communism. He could find none of the incriminating signs—Party membership cards, presence at demonstrations, signatures on petitions, or finger-pointing reports from the legions of FBI informants who had pervasively infiltrated both the Party and the aligned front organizations—that suggested any ongoing sympathy with Moscow. Perilously aware that the spy could still be actively working for the Center, that Rest could be passing secrets about the ongoing manufacture of the hydrogen bomb, Bob decided to move

forward. He concentrated his attention on the two names that remained.

His first target was the leader of the British mission, Rudolf
Peierls. After just scratching the surface, Bob was convinced he'd
found gold. The scientist's biography could've served as a casebook
history of a Soviet mole. A German émigré who had continued his
studies in England, Peierls had met his wife, a Russian physicist,
on a visit to Odessa. But what set off alarm bells clanging in Bob's
mind was that following their marriage—in Leningrad, in 1931—no
obstacles had been placed on Eugenia Peierls's emigration, or on her
acquiring German citizenship. The spiteful Russians were rarely so
accommodating in such circumstances, and certainly would have
been even more resolute when the immigrant was an acclaimed
physicist doing sensitive work. Why had they so complacently cut
her loose? The answer to this question became even more perplexing when Bob probed her family tree. Her sister was a biologist, and
her widowed mother had remarried a writer. This was the sort of
intellectual family that Stalin would be more likely to ship off to
Siberia than allow, seemingly without the slightest restrictions, to
leave the Motherland. Adding more kindling to Bob's fire of suspicion, Peierls's brother was an expert on electric condensers who had
also married a Russian, a member of the Soviet Trade Delegation in
Berlin. They were a family with such improbable biographies that
Bob was convinced that their histories could only be a collection of
cover stories written for long-term penetration agents working for
Moscow Center.

Confident he had found his man, Bob nevertheless went ahead
and dutifully did his due diligence on the final suspect on his list.
Klaus Fuchs, also known as Karl, was the "K. Fuchs" who had written the gaseous diffusion report that wound up on a desk in the Lubyanka. Fuchs had impressive academic credentials—he had studied
under two of the high priests of theoretical physics, first in Leipzig
with Werner Heisenberg (who would become a principal scientist on
the Nazi nuclear weapon project) and then, after escaping to England,

with Max Born at the University of Edinburgh. His family background seemed equally admirable. His father, a Lutheran pastor, had converted to Quakerism and held a chair in theology at the Educational Academy in Kiel. When the Gestapo targeted the Quakers, Fuchs, who had apparently inherited his father's pacifist streak, was one step ahead of the storm troopers, escaping first to France, and then making his way to England, where he was taken in by a Quaker family. After working with the British scientists in New York, he spent the next two years as part of the theoretical division team at the Los Alamos laboratory. There was, Bob decided after making his way through the background file the AEC had provided, nothing here to raise suspicions. All his tracking through Fuchs's life, Bob was certain, had only served to eliminate him as a suspect. Besides, he already had his man: Rudolf Peierls was Rest.

Or was he? For just as Bob decided he was ready to write his report for the fifth floor, his buddy Ernie Van Loon pulled him aside. Following up on Bob's order, Van Loon had been digging through the Bureau's own files, and he had found not one but two items that he felt the man running the show had to see. At once.

The first was a Gestapo document, part of the Nazi records trove the Allies had gotten their hands on after the war, and which Military Intelligence had recently passed on to the FBI. This file identified Klaus Fuchs not as a Quaker but as a militant Communist who had been fighting the Brown Shirts in the streets of Kiel. There were orders for his arrest on sight.

Bob read the document, but he was not yet willing to accept it. Instead, he tried to persuade himself that "Klaus Fuchs" was a common name. How many young men must have shared that name in Kiel? he wondered. It was a good-sized city, after all.

So Van Loon offered up his second find—an address book. After the defection of Igor Gouzenko, the Soviet embassy cipher clerk, the Canadian authorities had used the leads he'd provided to round up Russian agents. In the apartment of Israel Halperin, a mathematician who was also an agent of the GRU, the Russian military intelligence organization, they found an address book with Fuchs's name. It seemed a stretch, Van Loon pointedly argued, that a Soviet agent who had been poking around the Canadian uranium production facility would be in touch with a Los Alamos scientist simply to talk about the weather.

But Bob remained unconvinced. Enormoz was a KGB operation. In his experience there was about as much crossover between the GRU and the KGB as, well, between the FBI and the CIA. Before Van Loon started treating this thin evidence as counts in an indictment, a lot more had to be established. Stubbornly, Bob held on to his belief that Peierls was Rest.

Then Meredith called.

MEREDITH WAS IN A STATE of high excitement. Bob recognized the now familiar telltale signs—the beaming, proud smile, the uncharacteristically rapid speech, the gesturing with his hands—as soon as he entered his friend's office. And as Bob listened to Meredith's briefing, he, too, grew excited. A flurry of recent decryptions had added more flesh to the previous bare-bones description of Rest.

A cable from the Center, sent in February 1945, had asked about Rest's postwar activities: "Advise forthwith . . . the object of his trip to Chicago and whom he met there. . . ."

In addition, an earlier cable—dated November 16, 1944—from the New York *rezidentura* informed the spymasters in Moscow that Rest "is at Camp No. 2"—the KGB's cover name for Los Alamos. "He . . . telephoned his sister . . . and promised to come on leave for Christmas."

Bob closely followed his friend's discoveries, and all the time his investigator's mind was making the evidentiary connections. When he left that afternoon he took with him three new clues: Rest had been to Chicago after the war; he'd worked at Los Alamos; and he had a sister. He was optimistic that it wouldn't take him long to draw direct lines between each of these items and Rudolf Peierls.

As he'd expected, it didn't take Bob long to find the matches for which he'd been looking. Only, he had been wrong about where they'd lead.

Four of the fifteen British scientists on the original list, including both Peierls and Fuchs, had worked at Los Alamos. But only one had been to Chicago in the winter of 1945. And only one had a sister who lived in America.

These revelations shattered Bob's previous certainty. And now, when realigned, the scattered parts fit together seamlessly. He had been wrong, but at last he'd gotten it right. The mystery was solved. Klaus Fuchs was Rest.

26

W HEN BOB HAD BEEN TAKING law classes at night in Washington, one of his professors had shared a much quoted wisdom: "If you have the law on your side, hammer the law. If you have the facts, hammer the facts. If you have neither, hammer the table." But that advice, Bob wanted to moan, came up empty when he had *both* the facts *and* the law on his side yet was restrained from using them. In this complex situation, all that pounding the table would get him would be bruised fists.

That was the frustrating dilemma Bob confronted as he tried to plot a strategy for dealing with his unmasking of Klaus Fuchs. The strongest evidence he had that the scientist was a Soviet spy code-named Rest was not only inadmissible in court, it couldn't even be whispered to anyone but the handful of people who had been cleared for Venona, as the Arlington Hall decryptions were now known among the initiates. All the confirming facts about Fuchs's Communist background were black marks against his veracity and would jeopardize the scientist's security clearance, but they were not proof of any crime. And, not the least of the many factors making prosecution a murky possibility, Fuchs was no longer in America. He was a well-respected naturalized British citizen. The likelihood of the British extraditing him to stand trial—and for what? the decrypted cables were capital that could never be tapped—hovered near nonexistent. For all practical as well as legal purposes, Fuchs was beyond the reach of the decidedly foreshortened arm of American law.

A victim of these circumstances, Bob, with a gloomy resignation, did the best he could. First, he opened a formal criminal investigation into Fuchs; Foocase was the Bureau's code name. And for good measure, he sent the industrious Ernie Van Loon to dig up all he could on Fuchs's sister, Kristel, and her husband, Robert Heineman, who were living in Cambridge, Massachusetts. Next, he wrote a carefully guarded memo—no mention of the Venona decryptions; only the thin charade of a "reliable informant" as his source—that nevertheless laid out a persuasively incriminating case against Fuchs. On his orders, the memo was hand-delivered to the representative of His Majesty's secret intelligence service at the embassy in Washington; or the STOTT, as this intelligence liaison officer was known in Bureau-speak. And then he waited impatiently for the British reaction, all the time harboring the unnerving knowledge that a Russian spy was well entrenched in a top-secret nuclear research facility.

Three maddening weeks passed before British intelligence replied to Bob's memo. And the official response was no less maddening. MI5 "felt bound to advise the appropriate authorities in England that the continued employment of Fuchs in the Atomic Research Station at Harwell, England, represented a grave risk to security and that Fuchs should be consequently removed." Yet despite the lip-service acknowledgment of "grave risk," the British had so far taken no action. In fact, as they pondered how to proceed, their interim strategy was to make sure Fuchs had no reason to suspect he was under scrutiny. He was given a promotion, a salary increase, and, as a further mind-boggling reward, residency in one of the highly prized detached houses at Harwell.

Bob exploded. While he had previously restrained himself, now all his irritation bubbled over. He had reached the state where he just might follow his professor's advice and give his desk one hell of a hammering. It seemed evident that there would be no reckoning. Fuchs could only be convicted by his own admission, and Bob was convinced there was no chance that a sly spy like Rest would ever betray himself.

———

YET REST WOULD BE SLOWLY nudged toward a confession—and the initial shove would come from a most unlikely quarter.

There was a Russian spy in the British embassy in Washington. Meredith had ferreted him out months ago, decrypting cables that revealed that a busy agent code-named Homer had been regularly scooping up piles of classified message traffic that passed through the embassy and forwarding copies to the Soviets. Cable after lengthy cable sent to Moscow Center began with the heading "Materials from Homer." Bob had alerted the STOTT officer that "a fairly high placed person in the British embassy" was a mole, but, as best Bob could determine, MI5 was either unconvinced or infuriatingly complacent. Whenever he inquired, the response was a weary shrug followed by a terse "nothing new." It would be two more years before the British got around to unmasking Homer as Donald Maclean (and by then the British foreign service officer, one prescient step ahead of the authorities, would have hightailed it to Moscow). But in the autumn of 1949, Homer, still the diligent spy, had passed on to the spymasters in the Lubyanka the news that the Americans had alerted the British about Fuchs.

Moscow swiftly let Sasha know that his agent "could be placed under surveillance by MI5 at any moment." And the shaken handler couldn't help noting that "this memo was written in the somewhat alarmist terms that were atypical of the Center." Still, the KGB directorate, their eyes firmly fixed on the prize, refused to put Rest "in hibernation," as the jargon would have it. "Fuchs," Sasha would write in an attempt to justify his boss's callous operational pragmatism, "was giving us immensely valuable information and every month counted."

Still, an increased level of caution was required, and so the news was shared with Fuchs. And it left him spooked. The interior world of any traitor is always in mayhem, always poised for one slowly festering nightmare to rise up suddenly and wreak havoc. The Center's agitated warning pushed Fuchs closer to this breaking point. Informed that the Americans and the British were breathing down his neck, Fuchs began to look for a way out of the madness that had become his life.

A letter Fuchs had received from his father became the opening move in his rapidly improvised game; and such was Fuchs's anarchic mood that even as he played along, he had no idea where it would end, or even how he hoped it would end. The letter had announced that the elder Fuchs was planning to take a chair in theology at the University of Leipzig, behind the Iron Curtain that had cut off East Germany. Dutifully, the son went to Henry Arnold, the Harwell chief security officer, and shared this development. He offered it up accompanied by the sullen acknowledgment that it would undoubtedly affect his security clearance; it was bad business for the East Germans to have potential leverage on a scientist doing extremely sensitive research.

Arnold, who had already been briefed on Bob's memo, told Fuchs he'd pass this on to the Harwell managers. They would decide what, if any, action to take, he deadpanned. But when Arnold informed the authorities, he couldn't help adding that it seemed as if Fuchs *wanted* to be stripped of his clearance. The scientist, he judged, was suffering through "a full-blown psychological crisis."

YET FUCHS CONTINUED TO SPY, reconciling the warring sides of his life by what he'd call "a controlled schizophrenia." With a brush pass down the block from the Spotted Horse pub in Putney, he gave Sasha a packet of documents that included a diagram of the next generation of hydrogen bomb. Accompanying the schematic of the Super, as the weapon was nicknamed by the boastful scientists bringing it to life, was the official estimation of its destructive power:

"Blast—100 square miles. Flash burn to horizon or 10,000 square miles if detonated high up. Radioactive poison, produced by absorption of neutrons in suitable material, could be lethal over 100,000 square miles."

The Russians read this report with a shudder. The new weapon could destroy a city the size of Moscow.

In response, the Soviet Council of Ministers established a new thermonuclear research team to be based at a secret facility 400 miles east of Moscow called Arzamas-16. Its urgent mission: to manufacture a Russian hydrogen bomb.

IN ENGLAND, MEANWHILE, MI5 HAD come around to deciding that it was time to apply pressure to Fuchs. Perhaps a little heat might thaw him from his seemingly frozen state, they reasoned. The job was assigned to William Skardon, an intelligence officer who had shrewdly coaxed confessions from Nazi collaborators during the war. Using the excuse Fuchs had conveniently provided, Skardon went to Harwell to question the scientist ostensibly about the elder Fuchs's appointment to an academic post in East Germany.

They sat down cordially in Fuchs's office on December 21, 1949, and the interrogation was the opening act in what would become a long-running play whose dialogue lurched back and forth between friendly concern and outright hostility. Yet all the while Skardon was deliberately hurling his questions, one moment a lob, the next launched like a missile, at Fuchs's self-exposed vulnerability.

This first session ambled along, Fuchs chattering happily about his time in America during the war. Then Skardon, as if the thought had just come to him, challenged: "Were you in touch with a Soviet official or a Soviet representative while you were in New York?"

Fuchs did not answer.

And Skardon did not press. But finally: "And did you pass on information to that person about your work?"

"I don't think so," Fuchs tried half-heartedly. But in the next moment he recovered sufficiently to assume a defiant stance: "I never did such a thing."

But Skardon's question hung in the air. Both men could feel its presence crowding the room as they broke for lunch.

After lunch, Skardon came out swinging, but Fuchs remained on his feet. Nevertheless, Skardon returned to London that evening convinced that the Americans' suspicions were accurate. It would not be long before Fuchs, who had already adopted the fatalistic look of a man staring from his cell at the gallows, put his own head in the noose.

Two more meetings occurred, Fuchs alternating his strident demands "to tell me what the evidence is" with ponderous soliloquies about his "contributions to science." Finally, something inside Fuchs broke and one morning he called Arnold, the Harwell security chief. He asked to see Skardon.

On January 24, 1950, seated across from Skardon in his office at Harwell, Fuchs confessed. The words spilled out in a flood, as if he were glad to be at last sharing his secret life. There was no written statement at the time. Only later would he dictate his confession, an account of his descending deeper and deeper into the circles of hell that became his life:

"At first I thought all I would do would be to inform the Russian authorities that work on the atomic bomb was going on. I concentrated . . . mainly on the product of my own work, but in particular at Los Alamos, I did what I consider the worst I have done, namely to give information about the principle of the plutonium bomb."

Yet the session ended with its own sort of lunacy. Fuchs, with a valiant incomprehension, resisted conceding that he had done anything criminal. He hoped, he told Skardon, that his admission would not prevent his still attending the scheduled Anglo-American conference on the declassification of nuclear research as Britain's representative. And Skardon, a victim of his own wild logic, concluded the interview by simply walking off; MI5 officers were prohibited from making arrests.

Three long weeks would pass before the inspector for the State Commission for Atomic Energy, an old acquaintance of Fuchs's, called to suggest the scientist come to his office in London to "clear up some of the details." When Fuchs got off the train at Paddington Station, teams of police converged around him. "You're under arrest!" a Scotland Yard inspector announced. Burly men grabbed Fuchs's arms and led him off, the scientist staring into the distance, his eyes fixed in disbelief.

MOSCOW RULES—THE TERM REFERS TO the careful procedures used by spies throughout the Cold War when working in enemy territory—dictate that the handler always provide his joe with a fall-back date. If the agent for any reason—the flu, a nagging spouse, an error of memory—fails to appear for the scheduled meet, he knows when the next rendezvous, and even the one after that, is scheduled. Just show up and all will be forgiven.

In the nearly two months between Skardon's first conversation with Fuchs and the scientist's arrest, Sasha waited for Rest on each of the designated fallback dates. He'd return to the Spotted Horse, near the Kew Gardens underground, order his beer, and try to find that consoling mixture of wishful thinking and grand purpose that allows a spy to sustain his covert life.

"Deep down I knew something had happened to Klaus Fuchs," he'd plaintively concede, "but waiting there I hoped a miracle might happen: in one minute the door would open and a very cool Klaus, just another respectable gentleman, would be smiling at me."

On February 3, 1950, Sasha read the banner headline in the morning paper—"Spy Arrested for Atomic Treason." It was only then that he realized he would never see "a very cool Klaus" smiling at him again.

WHILE THE BRITISH HAD SEEMED in no hurry to arrest Fuchs, they were suddenly in a great rush to conclude the legal proceedings. Such high-level treason was an embarrassment to His Majesty's government. And another reason for haste, the public didn't know about the facility at Harwell or, for that sensitive matter, the independent

British atomic weapons project—and the authorities wanted to keep things that way.

Fuchs came to trial on March 1 at the Old Bailey courthouse, and the carefully orchestrated show was over in less than ninety minutes. The British attorney general ruled that Fuchs could not be prosecuted for espionage since, other than his rambling confession, there was no independent evidence to corroborate his treason. He was charged with four deliberately vague violations of the Official Secrets Acts. The only witness was Skardon. Fuchs did not testify.

The scientist sat stoically in the defendant's cage. He assumed the judge would decree that he should be hanged by the neck until dead. Instead he received the maximum possible sentence for the crime of conveying secrets to a wartime ally: a fourteen-year jail term. When his fate was announced, it was as if his imploding world suddenly came back into focus. "I felt what someone who is on death row must feel when he's told, 'You will not be executed; you're going to live,'" he'd reflect years later, still amazed to have escaped the hangman.

As his agent began his jail sentence, Sasha planned his own escape. The Center had instructed him to get out of London in a hurry, but he had convinced the spymasters that if he suddenly rushed to the airport, MI5 would realize his role in the case. Why should we assist the opposition? he argued. After all, in the course of his interrogation, Rest had not revealed his handler.

"How old is he?" Skardon had asked.

"He's neither young nor old. Let's say thirty-five," Fuchs parried.

"Is he tall?"

"Well, yes, rather tall."

"How well does he speak English?"

"Very well. He's very fluent and has an excellent vocabulary."

"But does he have an accent?"

"Oh yes! He does have an accent."

"A Russian accent? Or Slavic?"

"I wouldn't know. Possibly Slavic."

MI5 deduced that Rest's London case officer was an "illegal," as nondiplomatic assets are known. Probably, they decided, a Czech or a Pole who had been living in London for some time, and most likely had become a naturalized citizen.

Sasha continued as second secretary at the embassy for two months after the trial, making a point to live his cover. He laid flowers on Marx's grave in Highgate Cemetery and went to a screening of *The Battleship Potemkin* the Young Socialists held at Oxford. When he was recalled to Moscow in April 1950, none of the MI5 watchers thought it was anything other than a routine diplomatic reposting.

But the case was far from closed. For the FBI spy hunters, there remained one lingering mystery. During the course of his interrogation by Skardon, Fuchs had revealed he had an American contact to whom he had passed the stolen atomic secrets.

He had offered few identifying details. Perhaps this was the cornered agent's stubborn refusal to share all he knew with the opposition; or, quite possibly he'd never paid much attention. As best Fuchs could recall, the contact was around forty, about five feet ten inches tall, with a "broad build and round face." He knew him only as "Raymond."

When Hoover read the transcript of the interrogation, he quickly realized it was imperative to locate this Raymond. The courier, after all, might still be active, he still could be serving as a go-between for the spies in the field and their KGB handlers. The hunt would be, the director said, "one of the most difficult and important quests ever undertaken by the FBI." Nevertheless, "there would be no excuses for not finding him," he decreed.

He chose Supervisor Lamphere to go to London to interview

Fuchs and get the information that would lead the Bureau to Raymond.

On the thirteen-hour flight, first stop Labrador, and then on across the Atlantic to London, the weather was calm, but a tempest raged in Bob's mind. He knew he could confront Fuchs with an advantage that Skardon never possessed, yet he wondered if it would be sufficient. He wistfully hoped that the information Meredith had uncovered—the catalogue of Venona secrets that could only be hinted at, never revealed—might succeed in prodding Fuchs's feeble memory, even perhaps loosen the restraints on his defenses. Yet never once in the course of his long, restless journey did he contemplate the other mysteries that would unravel after he pulled this thread.

Part III

Dominoes

27

His plane landed under a gunmetal-gray London sky in the early morning, and Bob felt not just jet-lagged, but also in danger of coming completely unglued. From his throne on the fifth floor, the director had pointed his scepter straight at Bob: it was Supervisor Lamphere's responsibility to get Fuchs to put an actual name to Raymond. "The whole pressures of the world," Bob would grumble, his nerves stretched taut, "were on my shoulders to get that thing wrapped up." And as if that weren't burden enough, the weeks leading up to his departure had only added to the pile of woes weighing on his broad shoulders.

There had been a whirlwind of preparations—an intense session locked away with Meredith to review one final time all the references to Rest in the KGB cables; a visit to the State Department, where an officious junior staffer shuttled him about with a flattering deference as his diplomatic passport was issued; a mind-numbing lecture delivered by a Bureau lab man who had done some work with the AEC and who now attempted to pass on the rudimentary principles of constructing an atom bomb so that Bob would be able to speak knowledgeably with Fuchs, brandishing an authoritative vocabulary that included such previously unknown phrases as "implosion trigger," "critical mass," and "plutonium core"; and, not least in his complex and ticklish world, a heart-to-heart with Sarah suggesting that some time apart might do them both some good. And then, late on a Friday afternoon just thirty-six hours before his scheduled departure, Bob received the phone call.

It was from "Trout Mouth," as the rank-and-file agents called the Bureau's assistant director, Hugh Clegg. The nickname was a tribute to his habit of pursing his lips when he talked, a mannerism that, to hear the headquarters' catty gossip, left him always ready to bestow a sycophantic kiss on the director's broad posterior. But it wasn't just Clegg's doglike obedience or stream of unctuous praise for Hoover that had gotten under Bob's and the other agents' skin. Clegg headed the dreaded Inspection Division, and therefore he sat in stern and constant judgment over supervisors like Bob who were in the trenches doing, they felt with haughty pride, the actual work to catch the bad guys. Clegg wasn't an investigator; he investigated the investigators, and was, danger of dangers, an empowered critic who had Hoover's ear. And now Clegg was calling to ask Bob to send him the Fuchs file.

Bob's first thought was malicious: this guy is so isolated from the field that he has no idea that the Foocase already ran to nearly forty volumes. Perhaps, Bob tactfully suggested, rather than wade through the entire file, you'd prefer to read the summary brief? Clegg agreed that would be better, and at the same time somehow managed, Bob couldn't help feeling, to imply that it was his idea.

It was only after Bob hung up the phone that a panicked question jumped up in his mind: Why the hell does Clegg want the Fuchs file?

He ran to Al Belmont, the assistant director of domestic intelligence.

Belmont gave it to him straight: "He's going to London with you."

"Jesus Christ, no!" Bob erupted.

But it was the director's order and hence could not be challenged. The most Belmont could do was offer a consoling summary of what had led to this last-minute decree. It seemed someone on Capitol Hill had whispered into Hoover's ear that a Bureau official with genuine stature, perhaps Associate Director Clyde Tolson, should accompany Supervisor Lamphere to London; the snooty Brits, after all, were sticklers for protocol, and Lamphere was too far down on the Bureau totem pole to impress them. The director, eager to keep the powers on the Hill in his corner, swiftly agreed. Only, he wasn't prepared to send his number-two man (and, if the rumors had it right, his significant other) out of Washington for what might stretch into weeks on end. So he decided that Clegg could do the job; he was high enough in the pecking order to assuage the British sense of propriety; also, his absence from the fifth floor for an indeterminate period was a loss that Hoover could endure.

A still simmering Bob and a distant Clegg, unreconciled partners in a shotgun marriage, left Washington on Monday, taking the train to New York where they'd catch the flight to London. But no sooner had their train pulled out of Union Station than the first crisis occurred. Clegg broke his eyeglasses; Bob silently predicted this was just a small harbinger of what was in store now that a lifelong deskman had been sent out into the field.

Finding his G-man voice and stare, Bob had to convince the conductor to hold the train in Baltimore while a rattled Clegg telephoned his wife with instructions to contact his ophthalmologist and get his prescription phoned in to the supervisor of the New York field office. Then Clegg called New York and, after making sure that it was understood he was on a *special mission ordered by Director Hoover*, arranged to have a new pair of glasses waiting for him at the airport when he checked in. Throughout the entire comical episode Bob did his best to hold his tongue. "Anything other than the respect due his position," as Bob later recalled, "would have been a sure way to earn his displeasure."

But Bob's discipline was put to further test on the interminable plane ride across the Atlantic. Clegg had absently inquired if Bob was Protestant. Yes, Bob confessed, just making conversation. Yet once Clegg heard that, he launched into a tirade, one Protestant to another, about "how the Bureau was suffering from an overabundance of Catholic influence in the hierarchy." This talk of a Papist conspiracy at headquarters left Bob, who had a live-and-let-live attitude toward religion as he did to most personal predilections, "saddened and infuriated."

And that wasn't all that was giving Bob second—or was it by now third?—thoughts about what he'd gotten himself into. While Clegg's streak of prejudice was appalling, a more immediate concern to Bob was his "lack of knowledge about espionage and counter-intelligence operations." Clegg had the Foocase summary open on his lap for the entire flight and every few minutes he'd turn to Bob demanding an explanation of one term or another. How was Clegg going to interrogate a long-running KGB spy like Fuchs if he didn't understand the fundamental rules of tradecraft by which a covert life is lived? Bob fumed.

Clegg, to his credit, must've been asking himself the same question. Because after struggling through the case summary—the references to dead drops, brush passes, and handlers were as intim-idating to him as was the nuclear physics that had been dished out to Bob—Clegg threw up his hands in surrender. He'd be present at the interviews, but, he announced, it would be Bob who handled the actual questioning of Fuchs. His job, as he presently defined it, would be to spread good cheer among his brother MI5 officers, to let them see that their American cousins appreciated the courtesy they were extending in letting the Bureau sit down with a British prisoner.

Bob felt he'd won a small victory. But after Clegg had dozed off and he sat wide-awake in the darkness with his racing thoughts for company, Bob began to wonder if he'd been outsmarted. If there were any disasters, if Fuchs refused to speak, if Raymond could not be identified, there'd need to be a scapegoat. And the head of the Inspection Division, who'd have a ringside seat to the disaster, would place the blame squarely on Supervisor Lamphere.

ADDING TO ALL BOB'S MOUNTING concerns, and making his mission even more consequential, was the somber fact that as he headed off to London, the Bureau had not been able to make significant progress in its search for Raymond. The director had made it clear that none of the Bureau's resources would be withheld; neither cost nor manpower would be an issue. Yet so far, Bob conceded with as much stoicism as he could muster while staring defeat in the face, "we were getting nowhere fast."

Meredith was the ace hidden up Bob's sleeve, and in the frenzied weeks after Fuchs's arrest and circumspect confession, he had done his best to play the Venona card. The two friends sat together in Meredith's gloomy office much like they'd done when they were first starting out on their hunt; only now, as they were gratified to acknowledge, their once quixotic collaboration had already bagged a Soviet agent-in-place at a British atomic center. With one scalp nailed to the wall, they had the confidence it would be short work to get the next. "The Big Picture," as Bob hopefully called it, would come into focus.

Meredith went back over the cables that had been sent between 1943 and 1945 and now when he stitched them together it became clear that Raymond's presence had been lurking in them all along. Only the KGB, guided by a very cautious tradecraft, had added one more concealing layer of word code to protect their cutout's identity. In the cables, Raymond had been rechristened as Gus. Or was it Goose? Meredith couldn't be sure of the precise translation. But there was no doubt that Raymond and Gus/Goose were the same man.

Bob was a rapt audience as Meredith trotted out example after example to prove his point. On February 9, 1944, a cable sent from the New York station noted: ". . . a meeting took place between Goose and Rest." Another cable: "When he checked out Rest's apartment, Goose was informed that Rest had left. . . ." And still another: ". . . Rest did not appear at the meeting and Goose missed the next meeting."

Bob quickly conceded that Meredith was correct: Goose and Raymond were one and the same. Yet, he impatiently challenged, where does this get us? One impenetrable code name had simply been replaced by another. One mystery had given way to a new one. And he might just as well have felt like shouting, *How does your deduction stop Hoover from breathing down my neck?*

Locked in his doldrums, Bob returned the next day to backtracking over the transcript the British had sent of Skardon's interrogation of Fuchs. According to his annoyingly superficial confession, Fuchs had met Raymond five times in New York, and, when the scientist had been working at Los Alamos, twice in Santa Fe, New Mexico. Bob rolled that about in his mind, looking for something to exploit. And little by little, he began to think that maybe he had something. The New York meetings would've gone unnoticed; there were countless ways to hide in a big city. But by the same logic, it was a lot easier to attract attention in a southwest cowboy town like Santa Fe. A tweedy scientist with a pronounced German accent and a Soviet courier might stick out. The locals might remember these two strangers sitting in a restaurant or talking in a hotel lobby. It was, Bob had no doubt, a "real long shot." But with all "the nagging questions" he "continually received from the Bureau higher-ups," he decided he'd better try something.

He instructed the New Mexico field office to dispatch agents to bus stations and airports across the state to see if anyone remembered an "unusual" visitor in the summer of 1945. In response, a flood of nearly five hundred sighting reports piled up quickly on his desk; "unusual" offered the locals room for a good deal of subjective leeway. Bob dove in, but in the end he found no needle hidden in this haystack.

It was necessary, he realized, to refine his search, to give the agents in the field something more specific to sink their teeth into. But what? As he pondered this problem, he found his thoughts circling back to Meredith's discovery.

What if, it suddenly struck him, Gus or Goose was not a code name? What if it were Raymond's *real* name? It would be another long shot, arguably even more improbable than his previous theory, but the fifth floor's constant badgering had brought him to this desperate state. He sent a flash alert to the New Mexico field office ordering a check on hotel registers during that same crucial summer for a guest named either Gus, Goose, or a close enough proximity of the two. He let it be known the inquiry involved the Foocase, but he once more cloaked his source under the veil of a "reliable informant." Then he sat back and prayed.

And lo and behold, his prayers were answered. A registration card for La Fonda Hotel in Santa Fe, filled out in June 1945, had been signed by a Gerson Gusdorf. It was, he wanted to believe, too similar to be a coincidence. On his orders, agents began scouring the southwest for Gusdorf, the Soviet courier.

The manhunt lasted two breathless weeks. And when the dogged agents finally located Gerson Gusdorf, they found a seventy-year-old proprietor of a Taos curio shop. The closest Gusdorf had ever come to any contact with the KGB, the Bureau discovered after a vigorous interrogation, was that he once, maybe twice, he eventually conceded, had downed a shot of Russian vodka.

And with that fiasco, "we went back to square one," Bob acknowledged in complete and utter defeat.

28

YET LEAVE IT TO MEREDITH to find something fresh to gnaw on. Despite Bob's petulant outburst at their last encounter, Meredith had not walked away from the hunt for Raymond. And returning to the cables, not surrendering until he could unlock the final recalcitrant block of code, Meredith had made a fresh discovery. Previously he'd determined that Rest had a sister. But now when he went back over this ground, his study isolated a fact that had been overlooked: the courier might very well have met with the sister.

He shared the significant cables, all sent from the KGB's New York station in 1944 and 1945, with Bob: ". . . I sent Goose to Rest's sister. . . ." "Goose will travel to Rest's sister on 26th September." "On Arno's"—Goose's cover name had been changed in one of the Center's periodic bursts of routine housekeeping, Meredith explained—"last visit to Charles's sister"—Rest, too, had a new name—"it became known . . ." And on and confirmingly on.

Bob instantly grasped the significance of this new intelligence: someone else had possibly seen Raymond. Fuchs's sketchy description of the courier might be amended with new eyewitness details.

Two agents from the Boston field office were sent to interview Kristel and Robert Heineman, Fuchs's sister and her husband, in Cambridge, Massachusetts. On Bob's orders they were instructed to tread carefully; Kristel, who suffered from schizophrenia, had been in and out of mental hospitals. His concern, though, was more pragmatic than humane: he feared that if Fuchs's sister felt threatened, a potentially promising lead would be shut down.

The agents were all tact, and quickly they reaped the rewards. Both husband and wife had seen Raymond on two occasions, once when he came to meet Fuchs, and also when he knocked on their door without warning trying to find the scientist. He'd introduced himself simply as Raymond, and they had no reason, they said, to press for a last name. But they could describe him: white male, age forty to forty-five, five feet eight inches tall, dark brown hair, broad build, and a round face. Bob now had no doubts they'd met with Raymond; the description tallied with the one Fuchs had shared. Only, he also acknowledged with a renewed frustration, it "could fit any one of several million Americans." At that low moment, Bob felt like putting down the interview summary and just walking away from his desk.

But he read on. And there it was! As the agents were leaving, Robert Heineman had accompanied them to the street and, away from his wife, grew more talkative. He revealed that in his own conversation with Raymond the visitor had shared a little of his life's story. He was a chemist, or maybe he was an engineer; Heineman couldn't be certain. But Raymond had said he'd worked at a firm developing pesticides as well as an aerosol container. His efforts, however, had not amounted to much, Raymond bitterly complained. A partner had cheated him out of his share of the business. Or maybe the culprit was simply a colleague, Heineman had also suggested; his memory of the conversation was shaky.

Armed with these new leads, Bob, working hand-in-hand with the dogged Van Loon, went back to work. The Bureau's files offered several hundred names of left-leaning chemists or engineers who could fit Raymond's general description. But Bob, with the wrath of the fifth floor growing hotter each day, wanted to believe he had found his man. Joseph Arnold Robbins was a heavyset, Brooklyn-born chemical engineer—Heineman's memory was better than he'd realized, Bob felt like telling him—with a Bureau dossier crammed with left-wing affiliations. The finishing touch on the incriminating portrait, in Bob's mind at least, was that Robbins had graduated from City College in 1941, the breeding ground of Liberal's network.

A photo of Robbins was delivered by special messenger to London, and the next day it was waved in front of Fuchs. Was this Raymond? he was asked. Fuchs studied it intently. "It might be the man," he agreed at last. Are you sure? the British pressed. Fuchs, as if back in his old life, once again a scientist weighing the validity of a new hypothesis, announced he had "very fair certainty."

That was good enough for Bob. Full-time surveillance was placed on Robbins; perhaps, Bob hoped, they could catch him making a pickup from another of the spies in his network. And at the same time the two tactful Boston agents had been dispatched once again to Cambridge. They were to persuade Robert Heineman to travel to New York, where, after observing Robbins from a discreet distance, he could confirm that the target was Raymond.

The trap was nearly ready to be sprung. Bob notified the fifth floor that an arrest was imminent. But just as he was poised to set things in motion, Van Loon came rushing in. The latest background check on Robbins had unearthed new intelligence: Robbins had been in New York throughout the entire summer of 1945. He had not left the East Coast for a single day, let alone the time it would have taken him to travel to New Mexico and meet with Fuchs in either June or September. And the Bureau was also certain he'd never been to Cambridge, never met the Heinemans.

Which meant, Bob understood with a fresh surge of desperation, that Robbins was not Raymond. And he had no other suspect to take his place.

IN 1945, ABOUT 75,000 LICENSE permits had been issued to chemical manufacturing firms in New York City. Just looking at the long list gave Bob a migraine, but he'd resigned himself to the task of going down it one company at a time in the dogged belief that Raymond had to have a connection to one of them. Yet as he was rolling up his sleeves, preparing to go through the mechanical process, Van Loon suggested a shortcut.

He was a newcomer to counterintelligence, not an old hand like Bob, and so when he'd first come to headquarters he realized he had to give himself an education. Conscientiously, he'd worked his way through the files documenting Soviet covert operations in America and while doing so he had read up on the Red Queen, Elizabeth Bentley. In her lengthy confession to the FBI she had disclosed her role as courier making pickups from a chemist, a man who ran the Chemurgy Design Corporation in Philadelphia—Abe Brothman.

Bob completed Van Loon's thought: So you think Brothman could be Raymond?

Perhaps, his friend concurred. And he had more—another suspect. The grand jury that followed up on Bentley's accusations had brought Brothman in to testify. The chemist got on the stand and, as Van Loon judged his story, "lied through his teeth." He claimed he'd only given Bentley and her control, Jacob Golos, information that was "harmless," industrial processes that were public knowledge. He had no idea either Bentley or Golos was working for the KGB. In fact, they came to his company with sterling recommendations; Harry Gold, a chemist and one of his valued associates, had made the introduction. When Gold appeared in front of the grand jury, he, too, pleaded ignorance. He'd believed Golos was a legitimate businessman and now was shocked to learn differently.

It had been Brothman's and Gold's sworn testimony against that of an admitted Communist spy whose reputation was further sullied by her characterization in the leering press as a loose woman. The grand jury decided to believe the two chemists, and the FBI washed its hands of the whole matter.

But as Bob listened to Van Loon resurrect all this recent history, he came around to thinking there might be something there. And, not for the first time, he had a premonition that the loose ends of his past investigations were reaching into his present inquiry.

With resolve, as well as considerable trepidation, he wrote up a memo for the fifth floor. With so much at stake, he posited, the Bureau must throw aside restraint—as well as the law. He wanted the hierarchy to authorize a black bag job. The target—Brothman's Chemurgy Design Corporation.

Hoover agreed.

The burglars were in and out without attracting attention. And when their booty was examined, it was clear that they'd brought back a prize: a typewritten document "which referred to the industrial application of a process of thermal diffusion."

Bob read the pages, and when he was done he was convinced he had just been studying a KGB courier's summary of the classified paper Rest had provided on gaseous diffusion.

Either Brothman or Gold, he felt satisfied, was Raymond. But as the Philadelphia office began its digging into the two chemists and their local company, the full glare of their suspicions quickly shone on Gold. "Many of the details the agents were able to obtain about Gold's life and travels fit in with the nuggets about Raymond gleaned from Fuchs's confession," Bob crowed, ready to open a celebratory bottle of champagne.

What clinched the match was that Gold looked the part. The shortish, balding chemist with a body shaped like a bowling pin was nearly the spitting image of the descriptions offered by both Fuchs and the Heinemans. He *had* to be Raymond.

With great expectations, Gold's photo was presented to Fuchs.

The scientist looked at it quizzically. Then he shook his head dismissively. "This is not the man," he snapped.

THIS WAS THE BAGGAGE, a heavy load of frustrations, dead ends, and anxieties, that Bob carried with him as he walked off the plane in London on that May morning. John Cimperman, the Bureau's man based at the American embassy, was there to escort Bob and Clegg to MI5 headquarters. As the embassy car drove through the surprisingly cold and dreary city, Bob looked out into the streets and was shocked by what he saw. It was five years since the war had ended, but the effects of the German air raids remained. The rows of smashed buildings lining the pavement like cadavers, the rubble scattered about the street—it all left him feeling as if the war were still on.

With that disheartening thought, his whole mood began to be transformed. It brought him around to reminding himself that a war, in fact, still raged, but in this Cold War the spies and the spy hunters were the soldiers. And now, closer to his prey, he shrugged off all that had been weighing on him. With a renewed commitment to his mission, he continued on through the city. He remained silent, pretending to sleep, but it was the quiet of resolve. Bob now looked forward to the challenge. He considered the opportunity to interrogate Klaus Fuchs "one of the great opportunities of my life."

29

FLANKING THE STURDY FRONT GATE of Wormwood Scrubs prison in Hammersmith, on the outskirts of London, were two dark towers that tapered as they rose, evoking bishops on a chessboard. Each was decorated with a relief depicting a Victorian-era prison reformer, and when Bob was informed of this curious fact he could not help but think the tribute was all irony. "Abandon all hope, ye who enter here," he could almost hear the guards solemnly intoning each time the gates swung open and he passed beyond the tall prison walls and into the dank fortress.

He had first arrived at the prison—"dreary, bare, and cold," was his initial and most lasting impression—on May 20, 1950, unceremoniously huddled with Clegg and Skardon in the back of a darkened police van. Clegg, fearing that the British newshounds would churn out disparaging stories about how the FBI had come to "beat the truth out of Fuchs" (and, worse, that the clippings would make their way back to the director), had insisted on this covert transport in his opening meeting with the British spymasters. MI5 thought such subterfuge excessive, but ultimately, in the interest of keeping the Atlantic partnership floating tranquilly along, acquiesced. So Clegg fired his next shot, and once more British eyebrows were swiftly raised. He announced the interrogation would proceed "right away—tomorrow." The deputy director of MI5 gingerly explained that wouldn't be possible; the next morning was a Saturday, as well as the start of the Whitsun holiday weekend. Once again, Clegg remained adamant. He was used to getting his way, unless of course the conversation was with Hoover or Tolson.

Early Saturday morning the police van drove through one, then another of the prison's huge gates, came to a sudden halt, and the trio climbed out. They were escorted by the warden to a room near the entrance—the "solicitors' room," he explained. And from the earnest way the warden spoke the words, Bob had the impression he was being led to a history-steeped wood-paneled chamber, a clubby retreat for the well-spoken, frock-coated British lawyers who inhabited his imagination.

The room was not much bigger than a prison cell, and just as grim. There were two narrow windows, little more than slits, that looked out on the sunless exercise yard, and a small glass panel in the door that offered a view of an officer on constant guard. The walls had once been gray, but the ancient paint had faded to the color of a lingering fog. A round table, surrounded by a circle of metal chairs, dominated the room. And it was cold; nearly the end of May, but Bob felt chilled to the bone.

Then Fuchs was brought in. Like an affable host, Skardon made the introductions, and as he did Bob took measure of his adversary. Fuchs looked, he'd say, as he'd expected from the photographs he'd studied— "thin-faced, intelligent, and colorless." He was thirty-nine, only seven years older than Bob, but the FBI man felt there could be decades, no, centuries, separating him from the stoop-shouldered, sallow-faced, balding figure he faced. Imprisonment had aged the scientist and left him, Bob judged, vulnerable. But Bob sensed something else in Fuchs's hard stare—a determination to disguise the fears that raced inside him. Fuchs was well aware he had already lost, but he would refuse to surrender. In defeat, his last resort would be defiance.

They sat around the table, like players settling in for a game of cards. Clegg had a pen in his hand and a pad in front of him. Skardon fussily loaded his pipe. And Fuchs had his hands folded like a man in prayer.

They waited for Bob to begin.

FUCHS, THOUGH, HAD THE FIRST words. He had clearly spent some time in his cell preparing his small speech, and it was made with precision, each word bristling with hostility. He *did not*, he said emphatically, have a legal obligation to answer any questions from the FBI. Therefore, he wanted some guarantees before *he*—again the forceful emphasis—decided whether or not to be interviewed. He wanted assurances that nothing would happen to any of the people with whom he'd been associated in the United States.

Fuchs kept his scowling gaze fixed on the two FBI men, but Bob pretended to be unaware of this. And rather than push back, Bob chose to tread lightly. I'm afraid you don't understand the function of the FBI, he explained in his most reasonable voice. The Bureau simply conducts investigations, not prosecutions. "Only a judge or an attorney general could make a promise not to bring a suspect to trial," he said, hoping to put an end to the matter.

Fuchs ignored this disclaimer, and his voice once again rose in indignant anger. A vein that angled up from his eyebrow to his temple throbbed as he spoke. This time he was more direct, revealing what was provoking his hard-line stance: he was concerned about the safety of his sister. He wanted assurances that Kristel Heineman would not be prosecuted.

Bob listened, and as he did, Fuchs's "unspoken words were coming through as loudly as the spoken ones." Fuchs, he now grasped, was racked with guilt. Bob was not naïve enough to think that the scientist, a true believer, had any regrets about his treason; the West, in his acid assessment, remained bloated, vulgar, and bellicose. Yet locked away in his dismal cell, the prisoner had lived each day and every long night with a torturous fear: that his beloved sister, already sickly, would be punished for his crimes.

From Fuchs's perspective, Bob imagined in a sudden burst of empathy, it would be logical to assume the FBI must be cut from the same authoritarian cloth as the Gestapo or the Soviet secret police. Fuchs's tormented mind would have no trouble conjuring up images of jackbooted FBI agents carting a screaming, straitjacketed Kristel off without trial to a detention facility for reeducation, or worse.

After Fuchs had made his demand, a ponderous silence settled in. He cast a questionable glance toward Bob, waiting for him to respond, but Bob refused to acknowledge it. Time, Bob knew, was on his side. He wanted Fuchs to feel the mounting pressure.

Everything, the success or failure of the entire interrogation, Bob intuited, depended on his next move. He could trek up the high road, explain to Fuchs in his considerate, calm government-servant's voice that America was not Nazi Germany. Innocent people were not carted off. Sisters do not pay for a brother's sins. Or, he could exploit Fuchs's fears.

In the end, Bob decided that since Fuchs had offered him the stick, he would use it. "I was not above letting Fuchs conclude that if we were the bastards he posited us to be, Kristel would continue to be in jeopardy," he recalled, still unrepentant years later. "We knew where Kristel was and would continue to keep tabs on her," Bob recalled warning Fuchs.

But after the stick, came the carrot. He had "no reason to believe," Bob went on, "that Kristel had any involvement with Fuchs's espionage in the United States other than the fact she had been contacted by Raymond. . . . I do not regard this contact as significant," Bob said.

Yet his implication was clear: the meetings between Kristel and Raymond could become "significant" if Fuchs refused to cooperate.

With the tacit bargain dangling in the air, time was no longer on Bob's side. He needed Fuchs to make up his mind before the scientist could begin to speculate on whether the FBI's implied threat was a bluff. He wanted Fuchs to commit *now*.

Moving quickly, Bob laid out a dozen photos across the table. Some were head shots of men previously suspected to be Raymond. Others were old photos of Gold from the Bureau's files. And three were recent snaps of Gold. On Bob's train ride from Washington to New York, two Bureau agents had boarded in Philadelphia with a surveillance movie of Gold shot through the window of a parked car; the photos had been made from the film.

"Do you recognize Raymond?" Bob asked.

In every interrogation there is a moment when all the bets have been placed and the wheel starts spinning. When the decision is made to cooperate, or to refuse. A bolt of anticipation shot through Bob's chest as he waited to see what Fuchs would do.

With a swipe of his long, thin fingers, Fuchs pushed one of the photographs dismissively aside; and Bob nearly let out a sigh of relief. One after another, he dismissed all the other stills except for the three recent surveillance images of Gold.

Fuchs studied them with concentration. "I cannot reject them," he told Bob finally. Which, Bob silently rejoiced, was an improvement, however guarded, over the scientist's definitive rejection of the photograph of Gold the British had shared with him. Nevertheless, the photos were not clear enough for him to state unequivocally that they were of the man he knew as Raymond.

BUT BOB NOW HAD FUCHS talking. And in time, as Bob searched the spy's memory in the hope of supplementing the hazy portrait the Bureau had of Raymond, Fuchs shared the operational history of his meets with the KGB courier.

January 15, 1944, four p.m.—with numbers Fuchs was always precise. A winter's Saturday on a street on the Lower East Side of Manhattan as a concealing twilight settled over the city. Fuchs stood in front of the entrance to the Henry Street Settlement House. As instructed by his handler before he'd left London with the contingent of British physicists, he had a green book in one hand, a tennis ball grasped in the other. He waited for a man wearing gloves, yet who would also be holding an additional, solitary glove.

Raymond, a glove in his gloved hand, approached. Keeping to the prearranged word code, he asked directions to Chinatown.

"I think Chinatown closes at five p.m.," Fuchs replied, reciting his line of the script.

Raymond hailed a cab and they took it north to Manny Wolf's, a restaurant in the East Fifties. They did not speak much during the meal, the spy and the handler apparently sizing each other up.

Afterward, they walked toward the East River. It was cold and dark, and the sidewalks were nearly empty. Fuchs explained that he was working on the construction of an atomic device for the U.S. Army. He said it would be the most powerful weapon ever made. It would change history. He would bring reports on his work at their next meet. In two weeks, Raymond suggested.

That was how it all began.

On Monday, though, Bob was back in the present, and the Wormwood Scrubs solicitors' room had been transformed into a screening room. Blackout curtains covered the narrow windows that faced the yard, and another piece of dark cloth had been stretched across the door's glass panel. A boxy screen had been placed at one end of the room, and just beyond the table, John Cimperman, the embassy liaison, stood by a projector. On Bob's command, the film started rolling.

It was the watchers' film that had been shot only days before in Philadelphia. There was little action and even less plot. Just Gold, a short, dumpy, stooped figure, walking down a city street in his desultory, shambling way; then suddenly coming to an abrupt halt, as if he'd remembered something until, apparently satisfied, continuing on with his journey.

"I cannot be absolutely positive," Fuchs announced as the lights came back on. "But I think it is very likely him. There are certain mannerisms I seem to recognize."

But after having spoken, Fuchs amended his initial impression.

There was something about the man in the film that didn't seem to fit with his memories of Raymond. You must understand, he added as if making a small apology for his indecision, it had been five years since he'd seen his American contact.

"Run it again," Bob ordered.

When it was over, Fuchs decided he knew what was holding him back from providing a firm identification. There was something about the man's manner that wasn't quite right. In the film he was "serious." The Raymond he had known was jovial, "bombastic . . . as if pleased with the importance of his assignment."

"Run it again," Bob ordered, doing his best to rein in his building impatience. This time, though, he had Cimperman position the projector near the rear wall, increasing the distance from the screen and thus enlarging the image.

As the movie rolled, Bob focused his attention on Fuchs. The physicist was an impassive audience. His face revealed nothing.

When the lights came back on, Fuchs hesitated. Then he offered his judgment. "Very likely," he decreed.

Which Bob, his stomach sinking, knew was very likely not good enough to get an arrest warrant issued for Harry Gold. Nor very likely to be sufficient to appease the director.

STYMIED IN THE PRESENT, BOB once again explored the past with Fuchs.

February 16, 1945. Winter in Massachusetts, piles of snow on the ground, when Raymond arrived at the Heineman home. The courier had purchased a book he thought Kristel would enjoy, a novel about the relationship that develops between a black and a white family. For the Heineman children, he brought candy. As a father of twins, a boy and a girl, he told the Heinemans, he knew what they'd like. But this was more cover. Raymond had no children, nor was he married to the department-store-model wife he bragged about.

Fuchs was waiting for him in the living room. Kristel soon left to pick up the children from school, and the spy and his guest went upstairs to talk in private. They sat in a room facing a snowy street, a weak wintry sun shining through a window flanked by parted curtains. The scientist had recently returned from Los Alamos, and he had brought with him what he described as "a quite considerable packet of information." It was a primer for building a plutonium bomb.

The two men agreed to see each other again in early June, this time in New Mexico, near the top-secret nuclear research compound. Fuchs gave Raymond a folded map. At the top of one side were the words "Santa Fe—The Capital City in the Land of Enchantment." The scientist opened the map, spread it out on the bed, and pointed to where he wanted to meet. Four o'clock on the first Saturday in June, Raymond agreed.

Without warning, one of the Heineman children poked his head into the room; they had just returned from school. Raymond said he'd better go, folding the map quickly as he talked, and then putting it into his pocket.

But after Kristel came upstairs and shooed the curious boy from the room, Raymond was no longer in a rush. He announced there was something else. He had a Christmas present for Fuchs, a gift from Moscow Center. It was a wallet, very thin, the sort that might be used on an occasion that called for formal dress. Fuchs accepted it, looking at it with more bewilderment than gratitude. Raymond said that the Center had also provided something to go along with the wallet. The courier handed his agent an envelope containing $1,500, a munificent sum.

Fuchs's face distorted as if he had just experienced an unpleasant smell. Insulted, he returned the envelope to Raymond. He was not assisting the Soviet Union for his own personal gain, he said with a stony contempt.

Raymond was suddenly in a hurry to leave.

———

LEAVING THE PRISON AFTER THAT second long day, Bob and Clegg went directly to Cimperman's office in the embassy. Each night they had to cable the results of the day's session to Bureau headquarters—attention, the director. First they would write their report, and then they would use a one-time pad to encipher it. As they worked, Bob couldn't help remembering that it was the failure to employ a one-time pad correctly, as well as Meredith's genius, that had allowed him to bring the entire operation this far—to the threshold of uncovering the identity of the courier for a Soviet atomic spy. But at the same time, he knew that the length of the operational road he had traveled would not be any consolation to the unforgiving Hoover. Fuchs had not definitively identified Raymond; and Bob therefore had not accomplished his mission. Bob handed the encoded cable to the clerk in the embassy code room for priority dispatch to Washington, feeling that with its transmission his career, as well as his opportunity to bring about the downfall of a ring of spies, was doomed.

30

STILL, IT WAS A WAR fought on several fronts, so even while Bob's spirits sank in London, across the Atlantic, in Philadelphia, the Bureau's troops moved forward. Shortly after eight a.m., Philadelphia time, on the same Monday as the inconclusive screening at Wormwood Scrubs, two agents knocked on the front door of Harry Gold's home.

The appointment had been amicably arranged days earlier. On May 17, the two agents—Scotty Miller, who by chance was Bob's happy-go-lucky buddy from their days together on the SE squad in New York, and Richard Brennan, a hulking, saturnine veteran; their teaming in line with the classic good cop/bad cop tandem the Bureau relished—spent an exhaustive nine hours interviewing Gold. Throughout that marathon session in the Philadelphia field office, both the interrogators and their subject had done their best to project a genial goodwill toward one another. The FBI men conveyed that they were embarrassed by their assignment, just underlings going through the motions to appease their bosses in what they knew would ultimately prove to be a pointless fishing expedition. Gold was magnanimous and composed. A man of the world, he knew too well about wrongheaded bosses, his helpful demeanor suggested. Ask whatever you like; he had nothing to hide. And, no, he didn't need a lawyer. Only guilty people need lawyers.

Yet it had all been an act. As the lengthy interview ground on and on, all the players had been determined to give the performances of their lives. The FBI agents were treading lightly because they had nothing substantive to throw at Gold. Their fear was that if they followed their every instinct and attacked, then the chemist would lawyer up and they'd never get the chance to wangle an incriminating admission out of him. As for Gold, whose heart was thumping violently the whole tense time, he wanted to believe that his cooperation, supplemented by his silent prayers, would result in all of the Bureau's suspicions fading away. But he didn't trust them, and he knew they didn't trust him.

Gold, however, was trapped. The chemist felt as if he had no choice but to take everything the two smiling agents said at face value. So, when they asked for handwriting samples, he cordially wrote out page after page. When they asked if he'd mind if they shot some motion picture footage, he said why not, and found the calm to make a joke about how this screen test could land him a whole new career. And when they asked if they could search his house, he didn't make some snarky comment, like "Sure, if you have a warrant." Instead, he suggested they come by the following Monday, when he knew his father and brother, with whom he lived, would not be home. Absolutely, no point in inconveniencing them, the agents concurred brightly. See you at eight.

Gold had planned to spend the weekend gathering up any hints of his clandestine activities that he might've carelessly left lying about. But he never got around to it. He told himself that he didn't want to explain an unprecedented flurry of housekeeping to his brother and father; they'd only grow anxious. But on some deeper, unarticulated level, Gold understood that his procrastination was illogical, perhaps even a wishful attempt to deny the existence of the sword poised above his exposed neck.

At five a.m. on Monday, May 22, however, Gold rose from his bed after a restless night and realized he'd better do something. He started looking about for incriminating traces of his secret life and was quickly, he'd later say, "horrified." The enormity of his mistake became apparent. Everywhere he looked, or so it suddenly seemed in the mad panic that swept over him in the first bright light of the spring dawn, another clue was revealed. The stub of a plane ticket from Albuquerque to Kansas City. The draft of a report on a meeting with Rest in Cambridge. A street map of Dayton, Ohio. Instructions from his control. There was so much material. What had he been thinking? But calling upon the self-protectiveness that every spy learns if he is to survive in his dangerous life, he understood this was not the time for self-recriminations. With manic energy, he hurled himself about, racing from room to room, gathering handful after handful of incriminating papers. He ripped them into pieces, shredded the pieces with his determined hands, and then watched them swirl away as he flushed the traces down the toilet.

"Yes, I had taken care of everything," he recalled, rejoicing. And when the knock came promptly at eight, as promised, he had regained all his prior ease. He opened the door, flashed the agents an ingratiating smile, and showed them in as hospitably as if they'd merely stopped by for a morning's cup of coffee.

But Miller and Brennan were acting from a different script than the one they had followed the previous week. Before leaving the field office earlier that morning, they had been informed of Supervisor Lamphere's failure to get Fuchs to confirm definitively that Gold was the agent code-named Raymond. That meant, they had also been advised, the success of the investigation could very well depend on them. And with that knowledge, both agents also felt the sharp edge of a warning. When the two men headed out, they agreed that their pretense of affability had run its course. They would conduct their search with a strict and brisk professionalism.

They cut off Gold's cheery questions about their weekend, ignored his offer of breakfast, and proceeded to his bedroom. Rows of books lined the shelves of a tall bookcase—chemical manuals, math and physics textbooks, stray volumes that had been acquired in a lifetime of reading. They attacked them all, riffling through one book after another with a meticulousness that left Gold appalled, and suddenly very frightened.

"What is this?" challenged Brennan. He had a paperback copy of

Microbe Hunters and was pointing to a small tag on the inside cover: "Shibey Curr and Lindsay."

"Oh, I don't know," Gold answered. "I must have picked it up on a used book counter somewhere." While in the same instant his memory sharply brought it all back into focus: an impetuous purchase at a Rochester, New York, store as he killed time before making his way to a meet.

Then Miller spoke up. He held a 1945 train schedule: Washington–Philadelphia–New York–Boston–Montreal. "How about this?" the agent asked.

"Goodness knows," said Gold. A pensive beat, and then he added as if its significance had just become clear: "I probably got it when I went to New York to see Brothman." But he had known the moment Miller had waved it about. He had consulted the schedule on one of his trips to see the Heinemans.

The agents continued their search, and as one hour passed, and then another, Gold's confidence returned. He had fielded their questions. They had found nothing he couldn't explain away. And they would soon be done. He was going to survive. He would not be exposed.

Brennan had a heavy textbook in his hand, *The Principles of Chemical Engineering*, and he was going methodically through it, when he noticed something stuck between the pages. It was a folded street map for the city of Santa Fe. The agent removed the map and began to study it with considerable attention.

How had I missed that? Gold asked himself in silent reproach. He had been looking specifically for this map earlier that morning, but when he couldn't find it, he'd decided it must have been discarded long ago.

"You forgot you had this, didn't you, Harry?" Brennan said. The taunt of triumph in his voice was unmistakable.

"My God, where did that come from?" Gold tried.

But for the first time the agents saw the chemist's alarm. They waited as a heavy silence filled the room.

"I don't know how that thing got in there," Gold said at last. But of course he did.

RAYMOND WAS EARLY. THE MEET had been scheduled for four on this Saturday afternoon, June 2, 1945, and the bus had pulled into Santa Fe hours earlier. He did not think surveillance would be a problem, but being a conscientious professional, he kept to his cover and, like any tourist, went to the city's historical museum. He tried to show interest in the exhibits, only his nerves were all over the place; he got that way before every rendezvous. At the gift shop he picked up a map, and it was identical to the one Fuchs had given him in Cambridge, a giveaway issued by the Chamber of Commerce. With the map as his guide, he arrived at the appointed spot precisely on time.

The Castillo Street Bridge arched over the Santa Fe River like a small frown. It was a lonely, isolated spot, and the longer Raymond waited the more he grew convinced that Fuchs's tradecraft was faulty. He felt very exposed standing on the bridge; there was no logical reason for him to be there if he were questioned. He kept looking at his watch, wondering if Fuchs would show, if he should abort the mission.

Fuchs at last drove up in his gray Buick, rolled down the window, and told the courier to get in. They drove across the bridge and continued on for a short while. Fuchs parked in a flat, sandy spot; desert and cactus stretched out toward the horizon.

They talked for about thirty minutes. The physicist reported that everyone at Los Alamos was "working hard, almost night and day." The bomb, he said, would be completed soon enough to be used against the Japanese.

Fuchs handed the courier a thick package, and at the same time emphasized the importance of this delivery. It contained "a sketch of the atomic bomb itself." It was a diagram of the device that would be tested within weeks at Alamogordo, in the New Mexico desert.

The weapon's dimensions, components, core, and initiator were all precisely indicated. With the information in this package, Fuchs believed, Russian scientists would be able to manufacture their own bomb.

The momentous package held tightly in his hand, Raymond left the car. He began the long, dusty walk back to town, hoping he could find his way in time to catch the next bus to Albuquerque.

"I THOUGHT YOU SAID YOU'D never been out West," Miller objected.

"Give me a minute," Gold said. Miller rose from the chair where he'd been sitting, and absently Gold took his place. He sank down into it, diminished. He asked for a cigarette, although he didn't like to smoke. He just wanted to do something other than answer the question.

All the while, Gold's thoughts were churning rapidly. The map of Santa Fe, he told himself, wasn't in itself too incriminating. He could talk his way out of this. But what if Fuchs identified him? And the Heinemans? And Brothman revealed all he knew? He had piled lie upon lie, and as soon as the FBI knocked one loose, the entire structure would come tumbling down. At that unsteady moment, as Brennan stood across from him with the map in his hand, Gold finally grasped the inevitability of his exposure.

"Yes, I am the man to whom Klaus Fuchs gave the information on atomic energy," Gold said, the words a soft, doleful surrender.

RAYMOND HAD BEEN FOUND, BUT Hoover was still not satisfied. He had sent Lamphere over to London not just to get Fuchs to identify the courier, but also to demonstrate that the Bureau, his vaunted creation, could accomplish what the British, what any other law enforcement agency, for that matter, could not. Only the FBI could get a Moscow Center spy to crack. And if events had moved too swiftly to allow that prideful point to be made to the world, Hoover was determined to manipulate history until it unfolded to his liking.

Gold had confessed at 10:15 on Monday morning, but his arraignment was deliberately postponed for two days. Hoover hoped it would be enough time for reality to catch up to his version of the truth.

While a forlorn Gold sat in custody in Philadelphia, Al Belmont scurried about headquarters, making sure that new still photos and motion pictures of the chemist were shot and sent by special air courier to London. And he sent a flash cable to Bob and Clegg. Along with sharing the still secret news that Gold had signed a written confession, he ordered them to keep their next session going "as long as possible without interruption." The implicit message was clear: it was now more important than ever to get Fuchs to identify Gold.

Bob went into the session on May 23 with the resolve of a man who knew he would be making a last stand. He had not told Fuchs about Gold's confession, just as he had not previously revealed that the chemist was the Bureau's primary suspect. His only operational advantage was the newly arrived still photographs and the motion picture footage. The photos were not surveillance shots, but clear, crisp images taken under good lighting; they reminded Bob of the portraits from his high school yearbook. He wanted very much to believe they would resolve Fuchs's small but lingering doubts.

As the blackout curtains were being draped over the windows and the film was being threaded into the projector, Bob took an impetuous gamble. He laid the new photographs on the table in a neat row.

Fuchs needed only a quick look. "Yes," he said, "that is my American contact."

Clegg hurried out of the room, eager to get a cable off to the Bureau. The next day, May 24, when Fuchs's arraignment was reported in the *New York Times*, the headline spread across the front page announced, "Philadelphian Seized As Spy on the Basis of Data from Fuchs." Hoover could at last enjoy his triumph.

Bob, too, was lifted out of the doldrums. "The Director had charged us to find Fuchs's American contact, and we had fulfilled that assignment," he recalled, still relishing his accomplishment. Two days later he passed the still photographs of Harry Gold to Fuchs, along with a pen. He watched as the man he had once known only as Rest turned the photos over and began writing on the back, on one photo after another: "I identify this photograph as the likeness of the man whom I knew under the name of Raymond—Klaus Fuchs, 26th May 1950."

At that moment, Bob would say, without embarrassment, "an unbelievably great weight seemed to lift from my shoulders."

31

THE SIX-STORY WHITE-BRICK BUILDING ON Pestschanaya Street in Moscow had been built by German prisoners of war, and so it was still nearly new when Sasha and his wife and young daughter moved in shortly after his return from London in April 1950. They shared rooms in a communal apartment, but it was with only one other family. The space felt luxurious. During his postings to New York and London, the family's belongings had been scattered among many relatives for safekeeping. Back, at last, in Moscow, it was a comfort to be able to gather all their possessions in their own home.

The Center assigned him to the British section, part of the KGB's First Chief Directorate for foreign intelligence. The spymasters were grooming Sasha for bigger things and they wanted to keep an eye on him, curious to see if as a deskman he would live up to the promise he'd shown in the field. His old friend Yatskov had also returned to Moscow, still part of the Tenth Department, science and technology. They would meet from time to time for a drink; after the intensity of their long days at the Center orchestrating complex and fitful covert plots around the world, the two friends needed to unwind before returning home to their families.

One evening a few days after Victory Day (May 10, 1950), Sasha peered into Yatskov's office, hoping to suggest a drink.

His friend looked, he'd remember, "drawn," his eyes "lifeless."

"Do you have a minute?" Yatskov asked.

Sasha took a seat, but rather than start right in, Yatskov pulled himself up from his desk and closed the door. The unusual precaution took Sasha by surprise, and he had a sudden sense of dread.

"We have a traitor in our American networks," Yatskov said after he had returned to his desk.

Sasha waited to hear more, but the sickness in his stomach had already started.

"It's Gold, that strange bird," he announced. The words were a small attempt at gallows humor. The Russian word for goose—*gus'*—was Gold's code name. Neither of the friends, though, could manage a laugh.

The Americans were still looking for Raymond, but Yatskov, full of a gloomy certainty, explained that he had no doubt that with Fuchs in custody they would eventually find the courier. And when pressure was applied to Gold, he was sure to break. He'd reveal all he knew about the American networks.

They left for their drink, telling each other that it was still possible the enemy would never find Raymond. But that night, a beautiful May evening, both men got very drunk. Two weeks later, on May 24, when the ominous news spread through the Center that the FBI had arrested Harry Gold, Sasha had to admit to himself that his friend's prediction would come true. "Disaster," he acknowledged, is "now at hand."

The next day there was, Sasha heard, a series of quickly convened meetings where one spymaster after another spoke up, each saying something had to be done to save our agents in America. But all the sessions ended with the same head-hanging realization: there was little that could be done. At this point, it was too late to make the complicated arrangements that would be necessary to get them out of the country. And if the Center's escape plans failed, if the FBI caught the fleeing agents as they were furtively attempting to make their way behind the Iron Curtain, it would immediately establish their guilt and reinforce the validity of the enemy's accusations. Worse, it would compound the KGB's visible failures. It was agreed: all the Kremlin would do was offer vehement, outraged denials if the Americans charged their agents with espionage.

In the days that followed, the mood in the Center grew more upbeat. Any fatalistic thinking, the spymasters confidently insisted, was precipitous, even unwarranted. The FBI was a collection of clumsy farmhands. They would never succeed in breaking our networks.

Yet Sasha was not so reassured. He foresaw the future with a woeful prescience. "When dominoes are lined up," he knew, "the first one to fall draws all the others with it."

32

A S BOB, DETERMINED TO BE the courteous American guest, made his farewells in London—a mischievous gift of nylons to the MI5 linkman's pretty wife; a pipe purchased on Regent Street for the helpful Skardon—the Bureau in these first days of June was already on full battle footing. The once sleepy SE squads, agents formerly resigned to tracking Soviet officials from a discreet distance, had become headhunters. The bagging of a Soviet atomic spy and his courier had left the men in the field excited by the prospect of what might lie ahead. They all wanted a piece of the looming counterintelligence prize.

Yet despite these high hopes, the dampening reality was that in the two weeks that followed Gold's arrest, his interrogations had yielded a thin product, its promise more tantalizing than its operational value. In weepy soliloquies to his court-appointed attorneys, the chemist remained determined not to "turn rat," to be a "squealer." There were boundaries he refused to cross.

In response, the Bureau ratcheted up the pressure. From his desk at headquarters, Al Belmont issued stern instructions. He cabled the interrogators in Philadelphia that Gold was to be "exhaustively interviewed for all the information in his possession." Belmont had his heart set on the pot of gold that he knew was waiting at the end of the rainbow—the "descriptions of his contacts in the espionage field." Bring me, he ordered, the names of "other persons engaged in espionage at Los Alamos or at any other locations." The Bureau had finally come around to Bob's way of looking at the world: it was riddled with active Soviet spies.

After two weeks of being subjected to almost daily interrogations, Gold's obstinacy proved no match for the agents' persistence. As the Bureau's inquisitors kept flaying away at him with sharp questions, his resolve staggered. He realized there was no choice but to accept the harsh terms of his unalterable fate. Yet still trying to cling to a small measure of honor, Gold broke not with a bang but with a series of whimpers. He doled out his betrayals of the networks he'd served one laconic revelation at a time. As Scotty Miller, who had led the team trolling for his secrets, complained, "Interviewing Gold was like squeezing a lemon—there was always a drop or two left."

Nevertheless, when Bob returned to headquarters in early June he found a bounty of gifts welcoming him home. "Cases developed from the confession of Harry Gold were breaking everywhere— dozens of them every day," he recalled. And with this sudden frenzy of activity—the constant flurry of priority teletypes from the field offices as they pursued one lead after another, normal business hours and five-day weeks replaced by a nearly round-the-clock commitment—Bob at last had the enemy's secret armies arrayed in his line of fire. Over the past year he had rambled on to Meredith in a largely abstract way about "the Big Picture," his code for the enemy's master plan, but this would be his long-anticipated opportunity to shove the KGB's picture out of focus. "We would continue to race ahead to the point where we would be able to arrest whole KGB networks." And making his return home even sweeter, the fifth floor, formalizing what had long been the reality, christened him administrative director of the whole operation. Bob was in command.

Gold only had to offer up a name and Bob's troops fanned out to take the enemy agent down. The chemist, for example, had started out in his hedging way referring to an agent he had serviced code-named

Martin. Seven meets over a series of years, in locations from Rochester, New York, to Oak Ridge, Tennessee. The yield was a wealth of industrial secrets; the best material involved the manufacture of explosives. But now Gold's hesitancy slipped away and he added an identity to that KGB code name—Alfred Dean Slack. Soon enough Slack was in custody, telling the Bureau all he knew, and providing more fruitful leads in the process.

Next, Gold turned on an old friend, Thomas Black, identifying him as the Soviet asset who had recruited him for the KGB back in 1936. And now that they had Gold talking, the Bureau, still bitter about the lies that had allowed Abe Brothman to walk away unscathed, sicced the chemist on his old business associate. Gold spilled all he knew, and the Bureau now had the goods to make a perjury case against both Brothman and his longtime girlfriend, Miriam Moscowitz.

The dominoes, as Sasha had dolefully predicted, were indeed starting to fall.

BUT AS HE SENT HIS agents scurrying off in all directions, Bob's mind was elsewhere. A small piece of intelligence Gold had revealed to the interrogators kept bothering him, the proverbial pebble in the shoe that made its presence felt with each new step. On its surface, the courier's account of his meet in Los Alamos jibed with what Fuchs had told him in their sessions in Wormwood Scrubs; even the date matched. Nevertheless, there was something that left him troubled, something that didn't seem quite right about Gold's version of the June rendezvous with the physicist on the Castillo Street Bridge. Only Bob couldn't quite put his finger on it. Mystified, he picked up the interrogation transcript and began to reread the relevant section:

"I traveled to Albuquerque on this first meeting via train to Chicago, then by train to Albuquerque, and finally by bus to Santa Fe. My meeting with Dr. Fuchs was on Saturday afternoon. Then I returned from Santa Fe to Albuquerque by bus that same day. As I re-call, I slept in the hallway of a rooming house where those who were unable to obtain local hotel accommodations were bedded."

Bob went over the section one more time, still suspicious, yet still baffled. And then all of a sudden he was shouting at his clerks, telling them to bring him bus and train schedules. He wanted to see if there was a more direct route from Chicago to Santa Fe, one that wouldn't have required the courier to pass through Albuquerque.

It did not take Bob long to establish that there was a train that went straight to Santa Fe. There was no apparent reason to stop at Albuquerque. With that clear in his mind, when Bob went back to Gold's statement still one more time, the connection was made: The courier had not only traveled through Albuquerque, but he'd stayed the night. Gold couldn't get a hotel room, yet he still had spent a night in Albuquerque. Why?

Bob thought he knew, but he needed Gold to say it.

When the interrogators put the question to Gold, he understood at once that they were on to him. Cornered, he swiftly conceded de-feat. He shared what he had been holding back: yes, he'd had a meet in Albuquerque.

Gold told the story haltingly, and with few specifics, but he in-sisted it was his memory's fault; he was trying to cooperate. As he was preparing for his meet with Fuchs in Santa Fe he'd been summoned to New York by his Soviet control. There he was given an additional assignment: he was to make a second pickup on his trip out West. His control gave Gold a piece of cardboard torn from a Jell-O box; the agent would have the matching piece. If the fragments fit together, he was to proceed with the pickup.

In Albuquerque, Gold went to a private house, and the recog-nition signal was exchanged. He couldn't remember the address, or the agent's name. The best he could offer was that the agent was a "U.S. Army man," noncommissioned, married, the wife's name "may have been Ruth," and they both had New York ac-cents. The soldier gave him some handwritten pages and a sketch;

they concerned the atomic bomb. He suspected the soldier was a
technician, someone with a scientific background. They talked
of a future meeting in New York where the soldier would deliver more material. Gold handed him $500, which the soldier
accepted, and then Gold left.

Bob read the interrogator's thin report, and he knew with a reinforced certainty what he had known all along. Meredith had been
right: *a possible link between Enormoz and wartime nuclear fission research*. There was another Soviet spy at Los Alamos. Just as Meredith
had also told him.

FEBRUARY 1950. A GRAY AND chilly winter's day in Washington—
Bob's memory, unlike Gold's, remained clear. A quick mental transposition, and Bob found himself back in that heady, fast-moving
time. Meredith, working brutal hours, was making discoveries almost
daily. And nearly as rapidly, his previous theories were being revised
as the more recent decodings dictated. The search for truth, Meredith
repeatedly lectured his friend with dogmatic pedantry, was a constant
search for better hypotheses. And now, once again, that frigid day
summoned up in his thoughts, Bob was making the bone-chilling
walk across the base's campus, and there was Meredith pouncing on
him before he had a chance to make his way to the office's rattling
radiator to thaw out.

Meredith wanted to talk about the second Soviet spy at Los Alamos.
It was an argument he had been stitching together for a few weeks, sharing with Bob from time to time provocative fragments from the cables
he'd been deciphering; and now he was ready to make a preliminary
finding. He laid the results out as a prosecutor might, exhibit after exhibit. Bob followed along with only brief interruptions, judge, jury, and,
in the event of a guilty verdict, avenging angel.

Exhibit One was, on its surface, as incriminating as any KGB
transmission Meredith had ever decoded. The November 1944 cable
from the New York station to Moscow Center read:

"Bek"—Meredith explained: Sergei Kurnakov, Soviet agent working under journalistic cover in New York for the *Russian Voice*— "visited Theodore Hall, 19 years old, the son of a furrier. He is a graduate of Harvard University. At present time Hall is in charge of a group at Camp-2—"

Now Bob chimed in; this was not the first time they had gone over this cable. Camp No. 2 is the atomic research facility at Los Alamos, he clarified, making sure his friend knew he had his attention. Meredith agreed, and then resumed reading from where he'd left off.

"He handed over to Bek a report about the Camp and named the key personnel employed on Enormoz. He decided to do this on the advice of his colleague Saville Sax, a Gymnast"—i.e., Young Communist League member, Meredith offered—"living in Tyre"—which, as we know, said Meredith, is code for New York City. "We consider it expedient to maintain liaison with Hall through Sax."

Okay, Meredith said. When we first grappled with this, we'd focused on the fact that both Hall's and Sax's names had been sent *en clair*. No code names had been used. That meant they weren't KGB agents.

No crime, no foul, agreed Bob. We had nothing on them, unless we were willing to go to a U.S. attorney and reveal the existence of Venona. Besides, by the time you deciphered this, Hall had been long gone from Los Alamos and government work. Our hands were pretty much tied.

Meredith didn't disagree. He simply moved on to his Exhibit Two, a cable from New York to Moscow, sent in May 1945. He read:

"Mlad's material contains (a) a list of places where work on Enormoz is being carried out. . . ." That is, a list of the Manhattan Project research centers, he explained; and then he resumed reading: "(b) a brief description of four methods of production of 25—the diffusion, thermal diffusion, electromagnetic and spectrographic methods."

When Meredith came to the end of the cable, he put on his professor's voice and offered up a brief lecture to his class of one. "Mlad" is short for the Old Slavonic adjective *mladoi*, which means young. A code name that might very well be appropriate for the nineteen-year-old Hall. And as further confirmation of that assumption, Meredith went on confidently, Mlad often appeared in the cable traffic in conjunction with his cutout, Star. Which, Meredith explained, was the short form of the adjective *starii*, or old.

Bob completed the theory: Which would mean that Hall, now Mlad, had become an active Soviet agent during the war. And maybe he was still spying, still using Sax as a cutout. Young and old—a team of spies.

But before Bob could take that disquieting thought any further, Meredith rolled out his third, and final, exhibit. He read a November 1944 cable:

"Wasp has agreed to cooperate with us in drawing in Bumblebee (henceforth Kalibre) . . . with a view to Enormoz. On summons from Kalibre she is leaving on 22 November for the Camp-2 area. Kalibre will have a week's leave. Before Wasp's departure Liberal will carry out two briefing meetings."

But even as Bob began to process this new information, Meredith offered more. It was a cable sent from the New York *rezidentura* to the Center on January 8, 1945:

"Kalibre has arrived in Tyre on leave. He has confirmed the agreement to help us. . . ."

Bob needed a few moments to gather his thoughts. When he was done, the findings left him stunned. One: there was a female (courier? sweetheart? wife?) code-named Wasp who had gone to Los Alamos in 1944 for a week. Two: she was part of Liberal's network. And three: there was another Soviet spy at Los Alamos—code-named Kalibre. And Kalibre (a soldier? a scientist assigned to the facility?) had gone on leave in January 1945, coming to New York.

All of which confirmed, Bob believed with increasing alarm,

that there were three Soviet spies at Los Alamos—Rest, Mlad, and Kalibre.

But Meredith wasn't so sure. He suggested another theory, a very tentative one, he conceded. What if, he threw out, Kalibre was Hall's new code name? Had the Soviets, as part of their frequent security housekeeping, rechristened Mlad as Kalibre?

Bob did his best to follow Meredith's rambling logic, a path that took him down a maze of code names and possibilities. But in the end, with a lawman's fondness for facts, he decided to focus simply on the operational intelligence: there was a Soviet spy code-named Kalibre who had a furlough in January 1945. And just two months earlier, Kalibre's female friend had spent a week with him in the Los Alamos area. These were solid clues he could exploit.

In the weeks that followed Bob's meeting with Meredith, the FBI field agents pursuing "unsub Kalibre" had scrutinized the leave records of more than 2,600 soldiers and civilian scientists stationed in Los Alamos. When they were done, Bob received a list of sixty-two names, all men, whose furloughs roughly coincided with Kalibre's.

One of the sixty-two names, Bob was convinced, was a Soviet spy. It was only a matter of finding the right one.

The Albuquerque field office attacked this list, and before long had winnowed it down to a series of candidates. One possibility was William Spindel, a young soldier from Brooklyn working in the Army's Special Engineering Detachment at Los Alamos, whose furloughs seemed to match Kalibre's. But since the Russians were after classified research about the bomb, the field agents grew convinced that Kalibre was a scientist. They paid some attention to Stanislaw Ulam and Victor Weisskopf, scientists whose leaves, if the dates on their records were stretched enough, occurred around the time Kalibre returned to New York. But the "most logical suspect for the Soviet agent," according to Percy Wyly, the head of the Albuquerque office, was Edward Teller, who had returned to Los Alamos with the title of assistant director of weapons development to work on the hydrogen bomb. Not only did Teller have relatives in Communist Hungary, but he had traveled to New York in January 1945—same as Kalibre. No less damning, according to the cocksure Wyly, Teller "made frequent trips away from the Los Alamos Project and could have furnished information to the Russians on a regular basis."

But Bob wasn't so sure. He had genuine reservations about the Albuquerque office's deductions; and, to his relief, Teller was soon cleared. And then, as was often the case when the fifth floor became involved, the identification of Kalibre became overwhelmed by a rush of new priorities. First there was the search for Rest, and then the all-out quest for Raymond. Next, Bob was off in London, and the hunt for Kalibre, for another spy at Los Alamos, had been put on the back burner.

BACK IN THE PRESENT, RECALLING these events from his desk at headquarters in the summer of 1950, with the transcript of Gold's latest interrogation in front of him, Bob saw things from a fresh perspective. He focused on Gold's description of the young soldier who had passed him information about the atomic project, and now the spy's identity became apparent. The agent Gold had met in Albuquerque was Kalibre. And Kalibre, as Meredith had suspected, was Hall.

A memo signed by Mickey Ladd, who as the chief of domestic intelligence communicated directly to the fifth floor, informed the director that the identity of Gold's contact was close to being solved. "Theodore Hall, subject to an espionage case, who was at one time in Los Alamos, might be identical with this individual."

33

THE BUREAU'S WATCHERS CALLED IT a "hatbox operation": you box the target in and then follow his every move with a posse of lurking G-men in fedoras. The surveillance on Ted Hall and Saville Sax had been, on Bob's orders, hatbox all the way, four teams of three, men in cars and on the street maintaining morning-to-night coverage of each of the targets. And for good measure, the post office ran "mail covers"—all incoming and outgoing mail was inventoried, the information passed on to the Bureau.

The two men had been tracked in the spring of 1950 to Chicago, and when Bob had sent out his request for surveillance two months later he'd tagged it "Espionage R." The teams knew they would be trying to catch a pair of Russian spies in the act. But Bob had not confided all he knew; the watchers weren't cleared for Venona material. He couldn't share with them that Hall and Sax had been identified as Mlad and Star. Or how Hall fit into the burgeoning investigation to find "unsub Kalibre."

Nevertheless, the watchers had been told enough to know they needed to be diligent. Hall, his wife, Joan, and their newborn daughter lived in a ramshackle three-room apartment on East Fifty-Sixth; it was just a coincidence that their home was a short walk from Stagg Field, where the first artificial nuclear reactor had been built, though that had given the Bureau something to think about at first. Hall was studying for his Ph.D. in physics at the University of Chicago, and they clocked him going to classes, returning home for lunch, working in the lab, spending long evenings in the library. The surveillance teams could find nothing out of the ordinary in his daily patterns, in his walks around campus or the college neighborhood. If graduate school was cover for his espionage activities, then, the exasperated watchers complained, he sure was living it. Or maybe he just was what he seemed to be—a grad student. And Hall's political memberships also had them scratching their heads. Both husband and wife were active in two do-gooder liberal groups—the Progressive Party and the Chicago Tenants Action Council. Yet standard KGB tradecraft insisted that all political affiliations were prohibited. Spies don't attract attention by joining organizations that could, in the enemy's narrow minds, be categorized as Communist fronts.

The Bureau's coverage of Sax was also drawing blanks. He was, at least according to the watchers' sneering talk, a weird sort—a Harvard dropout who ran a mimeograph business out of his apartment on Minerva Avenue, when he wasn't sending off lofty essays about beauty and truth to magazines that returned them promptly with terse rejection notes. But if he was still a Soviet courier, they couldn't find the evidence, or even a hint of a suspicious rendezvous. He did subscribe to *The Worker*, the Communist Party paper, but that, too, only reinforced their assessment that Sax was clean. Covert KGB agents made sure to keep their distance from anything that could point to their secret lives.

After keeping close tabs on the two men for several weeks, the Chicago field office decided that Washington's suspicions were unfounded. The report that wound up on Bob's desk concluded: "it appears likely that neither Hall nor Sax is presently engaged in surreptitious espionage work."

As things would turn out, "presently" was the operative word. The Bureau had shown up too late.

———

THE MEET HAD BEEN ARRANGED via a simple book code. Walt Whitman's *Leaves of Grass* was the key; a reference in a letter to a line and verse number in a poem would reveal the month and date for the face-to-face.

In the fall of 1944, Ted Hall, assigned to the Experimental Physics Division at Los Alamos, sent Saville Sax, his former Harvard roommate, a longish letter. He wrote about how he'd enjoyed the time they'd spent together in New York during his October furlough, and, in passing, he shared how moved he'd been when recently reading one of Whitman's verses. The letter had to pass through the scrutiny of the Los Alamos censors; Hall, a genuine wunderkind, worked with the teams designing both the uranium and plutonium bombs. The censors found no cause for concern.

Before Christmas, Sax left New York on a bus to New Mexico. In case anyone asked, he had a cover story ready. He was on his way to Albuquerque to visit the University of New Mexico; he was considering enrolling in the university's field anthropology program. And in his shoe he had a thin sheet of carefully folded paper. It was a list of questions for his friend that had been typed by a Soviet intelligence operative.

Sax checked into an Albuquerque hotel. Hall already had a room in a hotel near the train station. When the time for the meet grew near, both men went on foot to the prearranged spot. They were an odd pair of spies. Hall had barely started shaving. Sax had a habit of talking to himself, often gesturing emphatically with his hands as he conducted these conversations with unseen entities. And their tradecraft was atrocious. They approached from the same direction and then pretended, in case anyone was watching, their bumping into each other was pure coincidence.

But their meet went undetected. Hall answered the technical questions on Sax's typewritten list. Then he passed on to his friend a handwritten page or two. It contained the key principles necessary for the creation of the plutonium bomb.

The two men spent the evening together, walking about the town, having dinner, before returning to their separate hotels. In the morning, Hall headed north to Los Alamos. And his courier began the trip back to his Soviet control in New York, the plans for the plutonium bomb folded between the layers of clothes in his suitcase.

BOB HAD NO PRECISE KNOWLEDGE of how the meet between Mlad and Star had gone down. All he had driving his suspicions were Meredith's decrypts. The story the cables told was short on details, but the intel left no doubt in his mind. And so when the evaluation came in from the Chicago office clearing the two men, he decided he wouldn't accept it. Maybe Hall was no longer active, but that didn't mean he hadn't passed secrets to Gold. Hall was the "unknown soldier." Hall, Bob was certain, was Kalibre. Bob wired Chicago asking for their surveillance photos of Hall and Sax.

The inmate wings of Philadelphia's Holmesburg Prison radiate out from the warden's office like the vertices in a star. One late June morning in 1950, Harry Gold was led from his cell down the long cellblock corridor to the interrogation room adjacent to the warden's office. The FBI had been pumping him day after day for all sorts of information—"squeezing the lemon," as Scotty Miller had said—but that day the interrogators had only a single question.

Gold took his seat, and on the table a line of photos was placed in front of him. They were shots of two men, both with thinning dark hair, both young, one boyishly thin, the other more fleshy. The photographs had been taken from a distance, nothing posed, all apparently taken without the subjects' knowledge. By now Gold recognized surveillance photos when he saw them.

Do you know either of these men? he was asked.

Gold took his time. He studied the photograph of the rail-thin man. Then he turned his attention to the shot of the darker, heavier one.

"I've never seen either of them," he answered truthfully.

While Gold was being led back down the corridor to his cell in the Philadelphia prison, an agent placed a call to Supervisor Lamphere in Washington.

Bob didn't want to believe the news. But he knew it must be true. Gold had no reason to protect either Hall or Sax; with his trial scheduled, he was eager to cooperate. But if Hall wasn't Kalibre, then who was? Trying his best to shake off the deep sense of defeat that had suddenly enveloped him, Bob could only wonder if he would ever find him.

34

A S IT HAPPENED, THE BUREAU had already found Kalibre, only neither Bob nor anyone else had realized it.

It was on a morning nearly five months earlier—the unusually warm last week of January 1950, a balmy seventy degrees in the middle of a New York winter—when Kalibre had received the call at his apartment on Rivington Street. Special Agent Lawrence Spillane wanted to come by that afternoon to talk. Kalibre listened and felt suddenly sick, and he knew it was fear. He had been dreading this day, and now it had finally, inevitably, come. He had to be at work at four, he tried. But Spillane would not be put off. I'll be there at two. It won't take long, he promised.

Just long enough to snap a pair of handcuffs on a Soviet spy, Kalibre thought as he hung up the phone. Then he quickly threw on his clothes and hurried off to inform his handler.

It was a short walk across Lower Manhattan to Pitt Machine Products, where he found Liberal. Liberal listened, and when he finally responded, it was with the sort of reasonable good sense doctors use to reassure anxious patients as they're wheeled into surgery. There's nothing to worry about, he said. There's no way they could have anything on you. Kalibre had difficulty believing him.

When Spillane arrived punctually at two, Kalibre, along with his pregnant wife—the woman code-named Wasp—sat with him at the kitchen table. If this was the end, the young couple wanted to confront it together.

The agent had come to discuss Kalibre's time at Los Alamos during the war, but, to their surprise, his concern was thievery, not espionage. Some of the engineers at the tube alloy machine shop, Spillane explained, had walked off with souvenirs. Those hollowed-out golf balls of uranium-238 that had been lying about after the scientists had finished cutting them up, well, you soldiers got the clever idea to use them as ashtrays. You might've thought you were bringing home a conversation piece, but what you were doing was stealing government property. The government wants its property back, Spillane concluded with force.

Kalibre had stolen a detonator cap and a Lucite disk that were integral components of the bomb and had passed them on to Liberal, but the only thing the vaunted FBI had come to hound him about was an ashtray. He couldn't believe his luck. Or the government's stupidity. A sense of order returned to his world for the first time since he'd picked up the phone that morning.

Afraid I can't help you, he told Spillane. I never took anything.

The next morning, Kalibre found the khaki army sock in the bottom of his bedroom closet that held the uranium-238 souvenir ashtray. He shoved it into his pocket and then walked the six short blocks to the East River. When he hurled the sock into the swift moving water, he felt as if he were casting off all his secrets, sinking them to the bottom of a deep gray sea.

But precisely a week later, David Greenglass was jolted from his sleep by a persistent knocking. He rose from his bed, abruptly aware that good news was never delivered at daybreak by someone drumming on the front door. An all too familiar sickening feeling swiftly rose from his stomach. He opened the door to find his control—his brother-in-law, Julius Rosenberg.

It wasn't tradecraft that led to their decision to talk outdoors. They had no reason to suspect the apartment was bugged. It was just that neither of them wanted Ruth, David's wife and Liberal's sister-in-law, to overhear their conversation.

They headed up Sheriff Street toward Hamilton Fish Park. Rosenberg asked if his agent had seen the story in yesterday's newspaper about the arrest in London of Klaus Fuchs.

Kalibre nodded, but he remained puzzled. The enemy's success was a loss for the cause, but how did this specifically affect his world? Why the early-morning urgency?

"This guy Fuchs," Rosenberg explained, all his usual steadiness gone, "is the man who was contacted in this country by Dave."

Now Greenglass understood. Dave was the code name the courier, Harry Gold, had used when he had made the pickup from him in Albuquerque. Greenglass's equilibrium started to teeter. He could see his future unfolding: Fuchs leading the FBI to Gold, and Gold leading the agents straight to him.

"Now you will have to leave," Liberal ordered.

FROM THE SOLITUDE OF HIS lonely desk in the British Section in the Center, Sasha knew it was time not just for Kalibre to run, but for the entire network to escape. He wanted to reach out to them, to send the message that they must save themselves, but he no longer had the authority. A professional, he remained bound by the inflexible hierarchy of his trade. All he could do was hope *his* American agents, the network *he* had run, understood there would be no shame in their flight, just as he had not been dishonored by his own departure from London. For those who had crossed into the secret world, survival meant always staying one shrewd step ahead of the opposition.

But what a network it had been, he recalled with a proprietary flush of pride. Even his boss in New York, the severe Kvasnikov, had been unable to conceal his excitement, literally jumping to his feet, after Sasha had announced that Liberal had a soldier brother-in-law who had been deployed to Los Alamos. It was the sort of stroke of luck, he had said, that confirmed the rightness of all they were doing in America. Unless it was, Kvasnikov worried with his next breath, too good to be true.

But Liberal had vouched for this new recruit. "I'll give my right hand to be chopped off if he lets us down," he'd vowed. And his imprimatur carried the confirming authority of his own large operational successes. Just weeks earlier, two days before Christmas, 1944, at a Horn & Hardart cafeteria on West Thirty-Eighth Street, Liberal had brought a big carton for Sasha. "Your present," the spy told his handler. "Careful, it's pretty heavy."

The Christmas present must have weighed fifteen pounds, so Sasha had taken a cab back to the consulate. He waited until he was upstairs, behind the locked steel *rezidentura* door, before undoing the tightly tied string. The contents, he'd recall, left him "totally flabbergasted." The Center had designated information about the Americans' proximity fuse a high priority. This was the device that initiated an explosion when a surface-to-air missile approached its target; a direct hit was no longer required to destroy a plane. Liberal had delivered not a schematic but the actual device, brand-new and in working order. He had managed, Liberal later explained, to smuggle it out of the electronics factory where he worked in the back of a security van whose driver believed he was giving him a lift home with his groceries. After the fuse had made its way by diplomatic pouch to the Center, the Council of Ministers had been so impressed that they'd issued an emergency decree establishing a factory to mass-produce Russia's own version of the device. With this unprecedented accomplishment in his file, Liberal was granted wide-ranging operational leeway, and the Center's suspicions about the serendipity of Kalibre's arrival into the ring were assuaged.

There had been, however, one problem. Liberal couldn't effectively run Kalibre as he did the other operatives in his ring. On his furlough to New York in January 1945, Kalibre had delivered hand-drawn sketches of a high-explosive lens, a complex and specialized device that was an integral component of an implosion bomb. Neither Liberal nor his handler knew enough physics to begin to understand the explosive device's significance, or even to ask Kalibre the pertinent questions. "It's very important that David be able to talk to one of your specialists," Rosenberg told Sasha. "Is that possible?"

On the evening of January 10, Sasha introduced his agent to Yatskov, only he called the Russian John, appending another cover name to the lengthy list of aliases the two friends had used over the years. John, he said, was an expert on scientific matters, which was a bit of a stretch, but he certainly was more knowledgeable than Sasha. From now on, John would run Kalibre.

Rosenberg telephoned his brother-in-law and told him there was someone he wanted him to meet. The snap to his voice signaled that it was not a family matter but a summons to their secret life; only by now, of course, both men realized that the disparate strands of their relationship were fatally intertwined.

Greenglass borrowed his father-in-law's Oldsmobile and, as instructed, drove to an address on First Avenue near Forty-Second Street. Rosenberg came out of a bar, checked the surroundings, and then went back in and emerged with John. The three men got into the Oldsmobile, and as Greenglass drove through the nighttime New York traffic, the Russian sitting next to him asked questions about the plutonium-core implosion bomb, the secret weapon that would destroy the city of Nagasaki.

But now, five years later, Sasha understood that those heroics were as distant to the events of today as was the glorious upheaval that had dethroned the tsars. The time had come for his spies to run.

The Center knew this, too. They understood what was in store if Gold led the FBI to Kalibre. Sasha's hopes soared when in a cable to the New York *rezidentura* the Center warned: "The competitors in the end will force them [Greenglass and his wife] to testify, with all the consequences proceeding from this for King [Rosenberg's new code name], his group, and all our work in the country."

But despite this somber prediction, to Sasha's bewilderment, the spymasters took surprisingly little concrete action. It couldn't be simple indifference, he thought despondently. Perhaps, he finally concluded, they had come to believe the FBI would never connect the links in the chain.

35

OB, IF HE HAD BEEN privy to the Russians' disparaging thoughts, might very well have confirmed them. He, too, had begun to lose confidence in the Bureau's ability to iden-tify Kalibre. Now that Gold had been apparently squeezed dry, only one investigative tool remained—the Los Alamos furlough records. Meredith had already provided the dates when the spy had traveled to Albuquerque and New York. If he returned to the files, backtracked once again, Bob wanted to believe that this go-round he'd find the incriminating match.

But when Bob sent a request to the Bureau's St. Louis field of-fice asking them to dig deeper into the Army records at the nearby National Personnel Records Center, the responses he received left him ready to scream. First they notified him that the records had been "messed up." When he shot back that they'd better unmess them, the agents came up with another excuse: apparently the rec-ords "had been routinely destroyed." And in the aftermath of this disastrous run of institutional incompetence, when some ambitious fieldman in the Boston office sent him a flash teletype with the totally improbable deduction that Fuchs must also be Kalibre, Bob had to do all he could to avoid sending off a response that read "No repeat no you nitwit."

At the end of the day, feeling no wiser than the clueless Boston agent, he channeled his festering anger into a strongly worded memo that went out to all the field offices across the nation. He warned them "to get into high gear on the case—instantly."

He didn't say what the consequences for failure would be. Let them sweat, he thought. Just as he was sweating each day that Kalibre, a Russian atomic spy, remained on the loose.

IN NEW YORK, MEANWHILE, ANY plans the Greenglasses might have made for escape had gone up, literally, in flames. As Ruth, six months pregnant, leaned over the bed to wake her husband, the hem of her flannel nightgown fell against the open gas heater that had been warming their small apartment. Fire engulfed her. Her frantic husband managed to extinguish with his bare hands the shooting flames, but not before Ruth had been severely burned from head to toe.

Rushed to the nearby Gouverneur Hospital, she lay for days in critical condition, delirious with fever. She spent a painful, difficult month in the hospital, yet the fetus, miraculously, survived.

Ruth gave birth in May to a healthy daughter, their second child. On the day she returned with the baby from the hospital, Rosenberg came by the apartment. But it was not a visit from a brother-in-law welcoming a new addition to the family. He came as their control, to issue a warning.

Rather than flowers, he brought a copy of that day's *New York Herald Tribune*. A front-page headline announced: "U.S. Arrests Go-Between for Soviets in Fuchs Case." And there was a photograph of Harry Gold.

The new parents recognized the courier who had made the pickup at their apartment in Albuquerque.

They stared dumbfounded at the photograph as Rosenberg raged, panic driving his anger. Don't you see you must run? he challenged. Take the children, take whatever you need, but go! His agitated mood finally settling, he revealed an escape plan the Soviets had concocted.

The Greenglasses were to travel to Mexico; passports wouldn't be necessary, just routine tourist visas. After they arrived in Mexico

City, they must write a letter to the Soviet embassy there. A line of word code was to be included, a mention of the United Nations. Then his brother-in-law was to wait in a plaza where there was a statue of Christopher Columbus. He was to arrive at five p.m., his thumb in a Mexico City guidebook, and wait for the courier to arrive. "Have you ever seen such a statue before?" the courier would ask. Greenglass must reply, "No. I have lived in Oklahoma all my life." The identities confirmed, the Soviet cutout would hand over American passports for the entire Greenglass family. He would also provide expense money, and instructions for their travel to Stockholm. Once in Sweden, they would be met and given the itinerary that would take them to Prague. As soon as they arrived, they were to announce their presence to the Soviet ambassador. Moscow was only a short flight away.

David Greenglass listened to this fantastic scheme with feigned interest, first accepting $1,000 and days later another $4,000 from Rosenberg to finance their escape. But he had no intention of leaving the country. In his ambivalent way he could spy against America, but he could not bear the thought of abandoning it. "If I go, I'll never read 'Li'l Abner' again," he would remember despairing.

A new child, his wife's condition still uncertain—concerns about his family, their future, hung heavily on Greenglass. He knew he needed to protect them. Plans were explored, decisions made, and then just as quickly abandoned. Yet all the time spent trying to come up with a solution proved dangerous. He began to suspect that what he really wanted to escape from was his life, from the corner he'd boxed himself into. With each terrible day, the anxieties mounted. The grievous realization that there would be no way out tightened around him.

AT HOLMESBURG PRISON, AS ROSENBERG feared, the inquisitors kept chipping away at Harry Gold. And so it was that one of the agents, doggedly looking for a new angle of attack, threw out a suggestion to the prisoner. Try to imagine, he proposed as though it were a game, the walk to your contact's house in Albuquerque.

Gold willingly played along, talking out loud to his attentive audience as he made the mental journey. There he was going up the street, past the Santa Fe Railroad tracks, continuing on for maybe five blocks, no, eight—yes, eight, he corrected. Then he turned left. And here the street was shaded; he remembered a much welcomed canopy of trees offering protection from the broiling New Mexico sun.

Encouraged, the Philadelphia agents went to work. They swiftly contacted the Albuquerque office and requested maps as well as photographs of the streets he'd described. They hoped they could use these visual aids to pry open further Gold's memory.

In New Mexico, the agents got busy. It didn't take the local officers long to retrace Gold's journey. It led them down a shady street to a recently renovated apartment building. Yet even as the photographs were being sent to Philadelphia, they began combing their own files. They quickly hit pay dirt. The building's address had appeared on the list of sixty-two names of Los Alamos personnel whose furloughs coincided with the dates previously forwarded by Supervisor Lamphere; for unknown reasons, no one had paid much attention to it at the time. In fact, the soldier who had lived at this address five years ago had also been a suspect in the theft of uranium-238 souvenirs.

Just before six p.m. at headquarters, a clerk handed Bob a copy of a telex that had also been sent to Philadelphia by the Albuquerque field office. He ran his eyes across it, assuming it would be one of the dozens of inconsequential bureaucratic updates on the unsub Kalibre investigation he received in the course of each long day.

"Investigation in area suggested by tel. reflects house located two naught nine North High. Situated geographically to somewhat resemble premises described by Gold as site of contact with unsub."

An address! They got an address, Bob realized. His interest rapidly rising, he read on.

"Landlord advises that this two-story house in nineteen forty-five consisted of several apartments, one of which occupied by landlord and wife and another occupied by individual David Greenglass."

Have we finally found Kalibre? Bob wondered with a sudden, yet still cautious, excitement.

FOR GREENGLASS, THE DAYS HAD taken on their own sort of escalating hysteria. He spotted a van parked outside his apartment building, and he immediately suspected its real purpose. The advertisement painted on its side read: Acme Construction Company, 1400 First Avenue, Manhattan. But when he checked the telephone directory, there was no such listing. And now he was certain that it wasn't his imagination fueling his fears. It had become something very real.

He should run, he lectured himself once again. Take the family and head to Mexico as Julius had instructed. This time he made up his mind to do it. Yet no sooner had he firmed up that decision than another replaced it. He would go to the Catskills, rent a bungalow, lie low with the family, and this would all pass over like a bad dream. But on the six-hour bus trip to Ellenville, New York, he grew convinced the bus was being followed by a dark sedan with two men in the front seat in fedoras. He arrived, only to turn around and return home at once. The logic made perfect sense to him at the skittish time.

Adding to his troubles, Ruth's burns had become infected. Now he asked himself: Was this the final reason he'd needed for running? What sort of medical attention would she get in jail? Or was it a further rationale for staying in place? How could the family flee New York when his wife was ill? He couldn't make up his mind, his constant internal arguments flying about in all directions. And so he did nothing.

Then, on the afternoon of June 15 there was a pounding on the apartment door. It was the sound of the insistent tattoo that had echoed through his nightmares all these years.

THE TWO AGENTS FROM THE New York office, Leo Frutkin and John Lewis, didn't have a search warrant. Nor did they have an arrest warrant. But these formalities proved unnecessary. They confronted a man at the end of his tether and that was all that would matter.

The agents began by saying that they were following up on the souvenir uranium thefts. But Greenglass just ignored that pretense, and so they quickly dropped it and got down to business. Without much discussion, Greenglass signed a consent form authorizing the agents to search the four-room apartment. It also gave them the authority to take any papers or photographs they wanted. Greenglass wanted to believe he could win them over with his cooperation. It was as if he refused to acknowledge, even to himself, the enormity of his crimes.

It didn't take the agents long to discover one of the items the Bureau had been struggling to get their hands on for weeks—several photos of the Greenglasses taken in Albuquerque in 1945. With the snapshots grasped in his hand, Frutkin dashed downstairs and, like a runner in a relay, handed them off to Agent William Norton, who had been stationed by the building's entrance. Norton took them, and started off on the next lap—a sprint by speeding car to Harry Gold in Philadelphia.

Inside the apartment, the agents kept hurling questions at Greenglass. He did his best to deflect them, claiming he just couldn't remember. After three hours of this fruitless back-and-forth, they politely asked if he'd like to continue the conversation downtown. It'd be easier without the children around. He could have refused, but they seemed nice enough. He could talk his way out of this thing, he told himself.

They led him to a conference room on the twenty-ninth floor of the U.S. District Courthouse on Foley Square in Lower Manhattan, the building where the Bureau's field office was located. The questions continued, but he remained vague. It was five years ago, Greenglass complained with lighthearted exasperation. The agents realized they were getting nowhere. And the prospect of knowing he was guilty but having to release him left the agents increasingly on edge.

How about we break for dinner? Frutkin suggested, more to give his own jangled nerves a break than anything else.

As Greenglass finished off one, then another hamburger, in Philadelphia Gold studied the photographs that had been taken from the apartment on Rivington Street. One held his attention. It showed the smiling young couple on the steps of 209 North High Street, Albuquerque. The camera shop had stamped a date on the back of the print—November 8, 1945.

The agents stood silently, their anticipation growing, as Gold picked up a pen and started writing on the back of the photo in a cramped longhand.

"This is the man I contacted in Albuquerque, N.M., in June 1945 on instructions from my Soviet Espionage Superior, 'JOHN.' The man in the picture gave me information relative to his work at Los Alamos, New Mexico, which information I later gave to JOHN."

Now all the pent-up emotions in the room spilled out. Applause erupted. One agent flung his arm around his buddy's shoulders in a spontaneous outburst of joy. And agent Norman Cornelius grabbed the phone to call New York.

In the courthouse conference room, the agents returned from the dinner break with a new authority. All their previous friendliness had vanished. They stood erect and their voices were firm. And they began with the one question Greenglass had been hoping they would never ask.

Tell us about the visit to your apartment in Albuquerque from a Soviet courier in June 1945, one of the agents demanded.

Greenglass didn't answer. He tried to think of a way out of this, a response that would suggest he was still cooperating.

Then the interrogator played his next card. He announced that Harry Gold had minutes ago positively identified him. David Greenglass was Kalibre.

The truth now lay exposed between them. All Greenglass had to do was reach out and grasp it. But he was frozen. The silence stretched on and on until it felt like it had to break.

And in this long moment of dread Greenglass came to see that nothing he could do or say would change things. His only choice was to accept his fate. Besides, after seven hours with the agents, Greenglass had run out of stories, as well as the will to invent new ones. He no longer had any desire to resist. He just wanted it to be over.

It was 9:25 p.m. when, as a stenographer hurried in to take notes, he started to confess.

36

I T WAS THE TIME IN Bob's life when he would lie awake in
bed, taking inventory of his failures. The discomforting list
stretched from his inability to find Kalibre, to his powerlessness
to dismantle Liberal's network, to, invariably, his final late-night destination, his shaky marriage. And so he would tell people he was not
quite asleep, drifting along with his unhappy thoughts in the darkness, when the ringing phone on his bedside table jolted him wide-
awake as if it were a scream.

It was just after two a.m., and headquarters was on the line. Dick
Whelan, the head of the New York office, had called Washington
minutes ago to read the confession Greenglass had signed that morning. Now an agent shared it with Supervisor Lamphere.

"On or about November 29, 1944," Bob followed along, his
ear glued to the receiver, "my wife, Ruth, arrived in New Mexico from New York City and told me that Julius Rosenberg, my
brother-in-law, had asked if I would give information on the Atom
Bomb. . . ."

Another new name, Bob realized with a start. Who is this Rosenberg? Where does he fit into the Soviets' operations? But he pushed
those questions aside for the time being, as the disembodied voice
continued reading.

"About February 1945, my wife moved to Albuquerque, New
Mexico, from New York City. . . . Approximately a month after that
time, a man came to the place where Ruth was living, 209 North
High Street, Albuquerque, New Mexico. I did not know this man's

name at the time but recently recognized his pictures in various news-
papers as being Harry Gold. . . ."

We've nailed Kalibre! Bob rejoiced. We've finally got him! And
all the time, oblivious to Bob's leaping heart, the matter-of-fact
reading of the confession continued. Snippets intruded, battling for
his attention with the plans that were already starting to take shape
in his operational mind: ". . . a torn or cut piece of paper card which
fitted a torn piece of paper card furnished me as a means of identifying this man. . . . Gold gave me an envelope containing $500. . . .
I furnished him with information concerning the Los Alamos Project. . . ."

Then the confession shifted in tone, and Greenglass's earnest rationale for his treason held Bob's full consideration: "I felt it was gross
negligence on the part of the United States not to give Russia the
information about the Atom Bomb because she was an ally."

Therefore, Bob thought with utter contempt, you took it upon
yourself to betray your country, and in the reckless process change
the course of history. Not for the first time he wondered how much
of what was done in life, good and bad, was a result of self-delusion.
Or was it merely a quest for self-importance, to be an actor strutting
across the world stage rather than a member of the audience stuck in
the back row?

But Bob understood there would be time later for those sorts of
musings. Bob swiftly put aside all his personal animosity, all his unforgiving speculations about the motives for treason, and instead focused on the tasks ahead. Sleep was no longer possible. Instead he
bolted out of bed and swiftly began getting dressed. He hurried to his
car, and drove, he would recall, "like a crazy man" to headquarters.
He needed to ensure that orders were sent immediately to the New
York office. Greenglass must be detained overnight. He could not be
released to warn Rosenberg or anyone else in the network. And Bob
had another sudden, but rapidly developing fear—Rosenberg must not
be allowed to flee.

It was still hours before dawn, and as Bob arrived at the Justice

Department Building, he saw that it was ablaze with lights. He wasn't the only one who had concerns about what the day ahead would bring. Al Belmont, an assistant director, and his boss Mickey Ladd, who ran the Domestic Intelligence Division, were already at their desks, and Belmont handed him a sheet of paper. It was the initial cable that had come from New York reporting the results of the Greenglass interrogation. On it was a penciled note, written in a familiar schoolboy cursive, the first letter in each word capitalized for emphasis. "We Must Move Promptly," the director had written.

Bob drafted the teletype that was sent straight off to New York. They were to confront Rosenberg at his apartment at eight a.m.; it was presumed he'd be home at that hour. "Question him concerning his knowledge of Greenglass, and if appropriate, work into questioning him on his own activities," Bob ordered.

He needed to know where Rosenberg fit into the case. In his head he was already trying to forge a link to the network of spies and code names Meredith had uncovered. And, wish of wishes, to Liberal, their ringleader. At that speculative predawn moment, his nerves taut as he anticipated the days ahead, he wanted to believe he was getting closer, moving in on them. He tried to convince himself that the first tentative steps he'd taken two years ago in Meredith's office had been leading him to this moment. But thinking of Meredith and the valuable lessons in his friend's deliberateness, he also had to concede that his own impetuosity had often betrayed him in the past, and might well be pointing him in the wrong direction this strained morning.

ROSENBERG HAD BEEN SHAVING, AND he was still shirtless when he opened the door to the two agents, William Norton and John Harrington, at eight that morning. Your brother-in-law has been picked up for questioning in connection with charges arising out of his wartime work in Los Alamos, the agents explained with a deliberate vagueness. Then they waited to see how he would react. Rosenberg was unruffled. Perhaps, the agents silently wondered, he assumed the Bureau had once again been hounding Greenglass about the stolen U-238 ashtray souvenirs. Or maybe he did realize this was the catastrophe he'd been anticipating for years but had long ago girded himself with a soldier's battlefield resignation. Then again, the agents also had to concede, there was always the chance he was an innocent man. The two FBI men considered all these possibilities as they weighed the suspect's calm, collected reaction to their early-morning appearance at his door. But they could draw no conclusion.

Rosenberg at last told them to take a seat; he needed to finish shaving and dressing. And when he returned and they asked permission to search the apartment, he flatly refused. Not without a warrant, he said evenly. It was only when they suggested he might prefer to continue the conversation at their offices that he softened and acquiesced.

At Foley Square, the questioning dragged on for six hours, growing increasingly barbed and reproachful. Had he known about his brother-in-law's secret work at Los Alamos? Had he spoken to Ruth Greenglass about approaching her husband to pass on secret material to the Soviets? Had he arranged for a Soviet courier to contact Greenglass? Had he introduced Greenglass to the Russian agent who'd hurled questions about detonation lenses during an evening's drive around Manhattan? Rosenberg's responses were a snapped drumroll of no, no, no, and more nos.

Agent Harrington, frustrated, fearing the interrogation would soon come to an end without any conclusive results, decided to shake Rosenberg out of his complacency. "What would you say if we told you your brother-in-law said you asked him to supply information to the Russians?" he pointedly challenged.

"Bring him here," Rosenberg shot back without skipping a beat. "I'll call him a liar to his face."

Greenglass was just down the hall, but the FBI was not ready to have the two men face each other. The outcome was too unpredictable. They had Greenglass's signed confession, but how would he respond when staring into his brother-in-law's stony, unforgiving face?

After that, things began to fall apart. The FBI had tried to shake Rosenberg, but he had not budged. He would not admit to anything. Sensing their loss of confidence, Rosenberg finally asked to call a lawyer.

"Ask the FBI if you are under arrest," the lawyer instructed.

Rosenberg put the question to his interrogators, and they conceded he was not.

"Then pick yourself up and come down to our office," the lawyer advised.

Rosenberg rose from his chair and, after giving the agents a bow whose formality was nothing but mocking, turned on his heels and left. He undoubtedly felt he'd handled himself well. He had taken all their shots, rebuffed all their questions, and he had not revealed anything.

But in the course of questioning, Rosenberg had absently mentioned his wife's name, and this small disclosure would come back to haunt him even before the day was over.

THEY SAT SIDE BY SIDE around a conference table that was very much like the one in Foley Square, only this one was in the Justice Department Building in Washington. Jim McInerney, a shrewd former FBI man who now headed the Justice Department's Criminal Division, presided, and Bob, along with Belmont and Ladd, were the Bureau's representatives. Experience had taught Bob that these discussions were too often tugs-of-war between the FBI and the Justice lawyers over whether the Bureau had built a sturdy enough case against a suspect to prosecute, and over the years Bob had come out on the losing end of these arguments more times than he liked to recall. This morning, his nerves jangling from too little sleep and too much coffee, he'd entered the arena with his mind set to put up an epic fight. He knew that at the same time in New York both Greenglass and Rosenberg were being interrogated and he was going to do all he could to make sure they weren't turned loose.

The chance that either of them might flee before he had a chance to prove whether they were operatives in the network he and Meredith had been pursuing made him reckless. His temper was famous, and even though he was the lowest-ranking man in the room, he was ready to let it fly. He took measure of the government lawyers, and all he could see were newcomers, and not very knowledgeable ones at that, to what had for so long been his own personal mission.

But no sooner had Bob settled into his seat and the latest summaries of the talkative Greenglass's post-breakfast revelations had been passed around than it became apparent that everyone was of the same mind, at least regarding one of the suspects. Greenglass had revealed that Rosenberg had introduced him to a Soviet agent who had "asked me questions about a high-explosive lens which was being experimented with at the Los Alamos Bomb Project." Justice was all onboard with charging the former soldier with conspiracy to convey to another country information vital to the national defense of the United States. As Bob listened, the call was made to the U.S. attorney in Manhattan requesting that Greenglass be taken into custody.

With that done, the discussion moved on to Ruth Greenglass and Julius Rosenberg. Greenglass had implicated both of them, but McInerney argued that without additional supporting evidence there was no case against the couple. Ruth, he pointed out, hadn't even been questioned. And as for Rosenberg, the agents in New York reported he was holding strong, not admitting to anything.

Bob, as if on cue, erupted. We can't let him run. There's too much at stake, he insisted, more emphatically than he knew was appropriate.

Perhaps, then, it was simply to give his friend a moment to pull himself together that Mickey Ladd spoke up. He patiently made the case that it was unlikely Rosenberg would try to escape. He had a family. Two children. And his wife was David Greenglass's sister. Ethel, he added, after consulting one of the pages in front of him.

The discussion continued, but Bob no longer had any awareness of the debate. In his mind he was transported back to Meredith's office.

And there was the code breaker in his soft, yet confident, voice sharing his latest "Special Study." *Intelligence on Liberal's wife. Surname that of her husband. Christian name Ethel. 29 years old.*

Bob knew he had at last found Liberal.

At that instant he knew he would break the ring.

And with that sudden heartening understanding, with his thoughts focused on the investigations he'd need to launch, Bob's anger seeped away. He sat there mutely, the conversation swirling around him. All his thoughts were centered on the attack he'd lead, on the KGB cables filled with code names he hoped to soon untangle. When the meeting concluded, and the decision had been made that "process should not be issued at this time" against Ruth Greenglass and Julius Rosenberg, his reaction was restrained. Then he hurried back to his desk, eager to share what he had just learned with his friend at Arlington Hall.

"Discreet surveillance?" BOB BELLOWED INCREDULOUSLY to Al Belmont. The Bureau's lackadaisical policy made no sense, he argued, his temper once again ignited.

A month had passed since Greenglass's initial confession, and while Bob had begun to make progress in identifying other members of the ring, he had also grown increasingly concerned that Liberal would slip away before he finished the job. Yet the Bureau was only maintaining a half-hearted watch on Rosenberg. Worse, Bob knew from reading the New York agents' reports that the Knickerbocker Village housing project where Rosenberg lived was a surveillance nightmare. The buildings were connected by a maze of underground passageways; an army of watchers would be put to the test if Rosenberg took it into his head to flee. A few agents, most of them working straight nine-to-five shifts, could never get the job done. Bob came to work every morning, he confided to Belmont, waiting to hear the news that Rosenberg had fled, vanished into thin air.

But Belmont said his hands were tied. The fifth floor was working with Justice on this. And the official position, frustrating as it might be to Bob, was that there wasn't sufficient evidence to move against Rosenberg. Greenglass's initial confessions were not enough. And apparently on the advice of his attorney, who was busy trying to work out a plea deal, he'd stopped talking.

Bob shuffled off in disgust. He had the evidence to convict Rosenberg. It was there in the cables that Meredith had decoded. The incriminating words screaming at him. Only the government wouldn't allow the decrypted messages to be introduced as evidence in court. It could not be revealed that Arlington Hall had cracked the Soviets' code. Hell, even the president had not been told about Venona. The intelligence brass would rather the ringleader of a KGB spy network escape than let the Russians know we had read their mail. It was sheer madness. To be this close and yet unable to claim his rightful victory left Bob deeply demoralized.

Then on July 17, even though a plea deal had not yet been fully negotiated, both of the Greenglasses started talking once again. The husband's statement ran for seven typed, single-spaced pages, and for the first time he portrayed Rosenberg as the linchpin in a network of Soviet spies. He claimed his brother-in-law had contacts with scientists and engineers—his "boys," Rosenberg had proudly called them—and made regular deliveries of microfilmed documents to Russian couriers. He had even stolen a highly classified proximity fuse from his job at Emerson Radio. And Rosenberg had repeatedly urged him to run, giving him money as well as sharing an escape plan the Soviets had devised.

Ruth Greenglass's statement was, in its own bitter way, no less damning of her brother-in-law, but, more significant, it also for the first time made accusations against Ethel Rosenberg. She said that her sister-in-law had been present when Rosenberg had asked her to persuade David to "make scientific information available to the Russians." In fact, she claimed, Ethel "told me I should at least ask" her husband to spy.

Bob read these statements as soon as they came in over the

teletype. After only his quick initial read, he was certain that he had just been handed the evidence he needed. But just in case, he read them again. Finally satisfied, he confronted Al Belmont, gave him a quick summary of the smoking guns he was holding, and asked Belmont to accompany him; the sticklers at Justice would pay a lot more attention to an assistant director than to a supervisor.

The two of them confronted Jim McInerney in his office. McInerney had grown up on the streets of New York, a tough Irish kid who had made it, against all odds, to Fordham Law School, and he still had a lot of fight left in him. If the two Bureau men thought they were going to steamroll him to reverse his original decision not to prosecute Rosenberg, they were in for a battle. But after he read the new statements, he was a convert. He told them to have the New York field office issue a complaint and an arrest warrant for Julius Rosenberg.

There was not, however, sufficient evidence to charge Ethel Rosenberg. "So far," as McInerney saw the case, "it appears there would be just one witness against Ethel to show her complicity, which witness would be Ruth. . . ."

And that, Bob thought to himself, was how he saw things, too. He still remembered the deciphered cable: *Christian name Ethel. In view of her delicate health she does not work.*

At six forty-five in the evening of that same day, seven agents marched into the Knickerbocker Village apartment and arrested Julius Rosenberg. His eight-year-old son, Michael, had been listening to *The Lone Ranger* on the radio. One of the agents abruptly turned the set off; it was a small, petty gesture, but he apparently felt it was nevertheless a necessary one.

The boy, his father's son, turned the radio back on.

BOB RECEIVED THE NEWS ON August 7 that Ethel Rosenberg would be summoned before a grand jury. The government's evidence against her, he knew better than anyone, consisted of only Ruth Greenglass's assertions; and he still remembered enough of his law school classes to know that hearsay was inadmissible. So he'd been surprised that she'd been subpoenaed, and then further taken aback to learn that she had invoked the Fifth Amendment rather than testify.

Four days later, Ethel Rosenberg was summoned again. This time she was told if she would not answer questions, she would be charged with conspiracy. She refused, and was arrested.

Sitting at his desk in Washington, Bob thought about the Justice Department's strategy. Perhaps her indictment was a way to ramp up the pressure, to get her to talk. After all, she must have known about her husband's activities. A case for conspiracy, Bob had to admit, could reasonably be made. But at the same time, he recalled something Meredith had pointed out: Moscow Center had not considered her significant enough to have a code name. *Christian name Ethel. Does not work.* Yet, Ruth Greenglass's complicity had been obvious to the Russians. The KGB had given her the code name Wasp—and she was not facing any charges. Bob told himself nothing would come of Ethel Rosenberg's indictment.

Only later, he'd say, would he remember another moment that happened just days after this indictment. His eyes had strayed to a newspaper on an adjacent desk at headquarters. The headline was about the fighting in Korea. The conflict was less than two months old and going badly for the UN Command led by over 100,000 U.S. troops. Nearly every day American soldiers were dying in a war that many believed would not have come about if an emboldened Russia had not had its own atomic weapon to brandish. And by the time that memory rose up in his mind, Bob had lost all his previous certainty about Ethel Rosenberg's fate. Instead he found himself grappling with the sickening notion that this nation, feeling threatened, might prove to be as ruthless and vindictive as its enemies.

37

I N THE INCREDIBLY HECTIC WEEKS that followed the Green-glass confession and the Rosenberg arrest, Bob had the grati-fying sense that his life had come full circle. The perplexing mysteries from his past, once shoved aside in frustration, had now returned, but with a new clarity. He had believed all along that the clues Meredith had assembled from the cables would lead straight into the clandestine heart of Soviet operations in America, but he'd been unable to make sense of them. "Now," he would recall, "many things we had struggled for several years to understand in the deciphered KGB messages became clear." With this new hard-won knowledge, he at last had the keys to unlock the doors that protected a covert kingdom, and he went to work.

Moving forward, it quickly became evident that one dormant clue was intertwined with another. And with Bob's first firm shove, the long-running network began to topple. *Antenna was sent by the firm to work in Carthage. There he visited his school friend Max Elitcher, who works in the Bureau of Standards.* Now Bob understood "it was Julius Rosenberg who had contacted Max Elitcher in Washington and tried to recruit him." Two years ago, Bob had futilely tried to mine this faint clue with the ineffective tools of background checks and surveillance. This time, however, when FBI agents, armed with a lot more than shadowy suspicions, brought Elitcher down to Foley Square for questioning in the days after Rosenberg's arrest, he began to open up.

On the first day of questioning, Elitcher confirmed that he had

"six to eight" conversations with Rosenberg about "giving information concerning secret material and developments to the Russians."
Elitcher maintained he had simply found his old school friend's offers
"flattering." He had never cooperated. But Bob didn't buy it. Would
Rosenberg, clearly a careful operative, keep trying to recruit Elitcher,
would he continue to put himself and the entire network at risk, only
to be rebuffed time after time? That sort of recklessness went against
everything Bob knew about Soviet tradecraft. Keep pressing, Bob
ordered.

When the agents confronted Elitcher the next day, he still refused to incriminate himself, but he quickly gave up his friend
Morton Sobell. Rosenberg, he said, had told him that Sobell had
already been supplying information. Which, Bob noted as he sifted
through the transcript of the interview, was precisely what he had
suspected years earlier; only back then making a case against Sobell
had been beyond his grasp. Now, seeing all his labors finally beginning to bear fruit, he "experienced," he'd remember, "a sense of
closure and completeness."

But in the next moment a new thought supplanted all the others,
and his satisfaction was abruptly undermined. "If we had gone ahead
and picked up Elitcher and questioned closely after our surveillance in
1948," he chastised himself, the entire ring might have been broken
so much earlier. It had been a squandered opportunity, and Bob felt
he was to blame.

The self-recriminations persisted. When Bob gave the order to
bring Sobell in for questioning, the agents couldn't find him. He
wasn't at work. Neither he nor his family was at home. Sobell, Bob
suddenly suspected with a terrible sense of foreboding, "had flown the
coop." Once again, Bob fixed ample blame on himself for not having
anticipated this turn of events. After all, he berated himself, hadn't
Greenglass disclosed that the Russians had been trying to get him to
Moscow by a complicated escape route that originated in Mexico?
And no sooner had Bob's thoughts returned to that discarded intelligence morsel than he decided, more in an act of desperation than

even a hunch, that he had stumbled on a plan of attack. At least it was worth a try, he told himself.

A check of airline offices revealed that Sobell, along with his wife and two children, had purchased tickets to Mexico City on July 22, five days after Rosenberg's arrest. Bob received that news and immediately suffered another pang of guilt: by now the Sobells must be on their way to Moscow. The task of finding them would be, he realistically conceded, "almost impossible." Nevertheless, with a perfunctory diligence, he sent instructions to the Bureau liaison officer in Mexico City to be on the lookout for Sobell.

And they found him. Sobell was subsequently spotted leaving the Soviet embassy in Mexico City. He had not informed the New York *rezidentura* of his plans to run, and so he'd been frantically hustling about Mexico, trying to book passage on a freighter, while also checking in from time to time at the Soviet embassy to see if they'd received word from Moscow Center confirming that he was the secret operative he'd claimed to be. He was having a late supper in his rented apartment on Calle Octava de Cordoba when three Spanish-speaking men, waving pistols menacingly, took him into custody for "robbing a bank in Acapulco." He was hurled into the back seat of a waiting car, his wife and children forced into another vehicle, and the caravan sped nonstop the entire 800 miles to the Texas border. Sobell was promptly transferred into the custody of a waiting squad of FBI agents and charged with "five overt acts" of "having conspired with Julius Rosenberg and others" to violate the espionage statute.

When Bob picked up his phone in Washington to hear the jubilant agent in Laredo announce the arrest, he understood at once just how improbable this victory had been. What were the chances that Sobell hadn't already made his furtive way deep behind the Iron Curtain? What were the odds that a longtime spy, without disguise or any attempt at subterfuge, would walk straight out the front door of the Soviet embassy? Nevertheless, the arrest went a long way toward soothing the corrosive guilt that had been eating into him since he'd come to realize he should have pursued the Elitcher connection with more operational vigor years earlier.

IN THIS FIRMER MOOD, HE continued his attack on the ring. *"Gnome deserves remuneration for material no less valuable than that given by the rest of the members of the Liberal group who were given bonus by you. Please agree to paying him 500 dollars."* That message, sent from the New York KGB station on September 14, 1944, had left both Bob and Meredith puzzled since it had first been partially decrypted in 1948. Who was "Gnome"? And what—this a more unnerving question—had he delivered to Liberal that the parsimonious spymasters at Moscow Center deemed worthy of a $500 bonus? The only clue that Meredith had been able to claw out of the cables was that Gnome did not live in New York. But now, when Bob returned to this mystery, he did so fortified by the certainty that Gnome and all the operatives in the ring "were interrelated, and that the linchpin had been Julius Rosenberg."

Once again, Bob went back over ground that he had trodden years ago. But from his new perspective, the evidence took on a more incriminating shape. William Perl, an authority on the design of supersonic aircraft, lived and worked in Cleveland, and had gone to school with Julius Rosenberg. He had sublet an apartment from Alfred Sarant, and was friends with Joel Barr—two other suspects Bob had chased without success. And, Bob was now convinced, Perl was Gnome, a spy on Moscow Center's payroll.

Yet when questioned by the FBI, Perl wouldn't break. He was innocent, he protested, snarling with indignation through several rounds of interrogation. Bob read the interviews, and was near to admitting defeat. How can I win, he asked himself, if I must be restrained by such stringent rules? If he couldn't reveal the existence of the Arlington Hall decrypts, he doubted he'd be able to make a solid espionage case against Perl. But Perl saved Bob the trouble of having to continue his chase. In sworn testimony before a grand jury on August 18, 1950, Perl denied knowing either Julius Rosenberg or Morton Sobell. *Gotcha!* Bob told himself with a genuine satisfaction. He immediately went to work building a perjury case—a crime punishable by five years' imprisonment for each count—against Gnome.

WHICH LEFT BOB WITH THE two "good friends" he'd tried without success to identify years ago—code names Hughes and Meter, mentioned in a November 1944 cable. *"Liberal has safely carried through the contracting of Hughes. Hughes is a good friend of Meter. We propose to pair them off and get them to photograph their own materials. . . ."* Now when Bob did his sums he realized that his earlier suspicions had been pointing him in the right direction. He had been on their trail, although he hadn't fully comprehended their significance at the time. At this moment, though, like someone who has finally adjusted the lens of his telescope, he saw it all clearly. Joel Barr was Meter. Alfred Sarant was Hughes. But now when Bob made the connections that directly tied the two friends to Julius Rosenberg and his ring, it was too late.

When Bob had last tried to locate Barr, he'd discovered Barr was abroad, perhaps living in Finland, and he'd routinely passed the inquiry into the electrical engineer's whereabouts on to the CIA. But then Bob had become caught up in the tempest of activity that surrounded the Fuchs and Gold investigations. All concerns about Barr were, quite reasonably, or so it had seemed at that naïve time, superseded by other priorities. Now Barr was once again in Bob's crosshairs. He traced him in the summer of 1950 to a rented villa in Neuilly, outside Paris. An urgent cable was dispatched to the Bureau liaison officer in the American embassy in Paris, and he rushed out to Neuilly—only to find Barr was gone. From Washington, Bob sent cable after frantic cable demanding that the agent pursue all leads, dig into every clue; in the wishful part of his mind, Bob wanted to believe that, as in the Sobell case, he'd get lucky. But it was already too late. In the days after Greenglass's arrest, the KGB had swiftly guided Barr to Switzerland, and then put him on a train that carried him deep behind the Iron Curtain, into the safety of Prague.

Bob resigned himself to settle for Sarant. He'd build an espionage case against the engineer. But once again he found his efforts hampered because the Arlington Hall decrypts—unimpeachable evidence!—could not be revealed. His hope was that when pressure was applied, Sarant would either confess or incriminate himself. Therefore, on July 18, 1950, he sent agents from the Albany Bureau office to Sarant's home in Ithaca, New York, with the explicit orders to turn the screws.

They worked away at him with increasing success. At first Sarant insisted he barely knew Rosenberg. By the end of the interview, however, he wearily conceded that perhaps he had been "sounded out" about working for the Soviets by Rosenberg. "But," he told the agents haughtily, "I did not bite."

Bob read the transcript of this interview and grew encouraged. It would not be long before Sarant broke, he predicted. Sarant undoubtedly reached a similar conclusion. A week after the FBI had shown up at his house, he made his escape. Leaving his own wife behind, he and his neighbor's wife drove by a circuitous route into Mexico. Shrewdly, he made no attempt to contact the Soviet embassy in Mexico City; he expected it would be carefully watched. Instead he reached out to the Polish embassy. Under their protection, the couple hid out in Mexico for six tense months. A Moscow Center–designed escape route at last led them to Guatemala, then on to Spain, and finally to Russia. Bob knew none of this, however. All he knew was that the agent code-named Hughes had somehow managed to disappear, and the loss stung.

BUT THERE WERE STILL TWO provocative leads lingering from Meredith's handiwork—the agents code-named Mlad and Star. With absolute certainty Bob knew that Ted Hall and Saville Sax were guilty. The Venona decrypts had established their espionage. But once more, even as he outwardly appeared to be moving forward, he felt the strong pull of the restraints that continued to hold him back. Meredith's discoveries could not be revealed. The government had decreed that the continued secrecy of the covert work at Arlington Hall was still a higher priority for the nation's security than any of the secrets it had uncovered. Hall and Sax would be allowed to live out their lives without paying penalty for their treason.

And Bob, despite all his years of striving to stem the flow of evil, would have to live with an awareness of his inability to fulfill his mission. In his struggle to defeat the nation's enemies, he was beginning to suspect that there would always be unfinished business.

"I WAS BOTH A BIT frustrated and quite pleased"—that was how Bob summed up his continually seesawing state of mind as he made his final push against Soviet operations in America. There was, however, one action that he took in these variable days that gave him no qualms.

As the conspiracy trial of the Rosenbergs, Sobell, and David Greenglass moved closer, Bob made a trip to Arlington Hall. He made his way across the campus to Meredith's office, and it is easy to imagine that on this auspicious day his thoughts traveled back to his first visits, to his unproductive, almost hostile encounters with the reticent code breaker. Yet despite only the flimsiest of shared motives, they had managed to find a way to work in tandem, each growing to appreciate the other's judgment and cunning. Against all odds, or even logic, they had conspired together to do the impossible, day after day. They had succeeded in running a dangerous, consequential network of the enemy's spies to ground. And in the process, paying whatever price was demanded, making whatever sacrifice was required, they had also discovered the rewards of a sustaining friendship.

As if to mark the end of their common quest, Bob arrived carrying a gift. In the past, it was Meredith who had produced the "Special Studies." Now Bob, wanting to reciprocate, had written one for his friend. It was addressed "Lamphere to Gardner" and titled "Study of Code Names in KGB Communications."

He handed it to the code breaker, and Meredith began to read:

"[I]t has been determined that one JULIUS ROSENBERG is probably identical with the individual described as ANTENNA and LIBERAL. . . . It is also believed now that DAVID GREENGLASS is identical with the individual described as KALIBRE, and that RUTH PRINZ GREENGLASS is identical with the individual known under the code name OSA. . . .

"More complete details concerning these individuals will be furnished to you at a later date."

When Meredith completed his reading, he had little to say. His silence was testimony to the momentousness of the occasion, and a tribute to the mysteries that had been finally solved.

Full of purpose, he went to his filing cabinet and removed his large pile of decrypted messages and placed them on his desk. Sorting through the stack, he found a relevant cable. He inserted it in his typewriter.

A line of dashes was typed across the bottom of the page. Then he typed "Comments." Next, he began to annotate the message to reflect this new information. He added the first footnote. "Osa: i.e. Wasp. Ruth Greenglass." Then he moved on to the next, and with each typed revision, their long journey proceeded to its final destination.

And all the while as he typed, Bob looked on with a keen concentration, proud and, in truth, overwhelmed, as their mutual accomplishment made its way onto the page, and into history.

38

THEN THERE WAS THE TRIAL. Julius and Ethel Rosenberg and Morton Sobell were charged with conspiracy to commit espionage. David Greenglass had already pleaded guilty and was awaiting sentencing; his wife was never charged.

It began on a gray, bleak morning, March 6, 1951, in Room 107 in the U.S. Courthouse in Manhattan. Bob, from his desk at headquarters in Washington, followed the events closely. Sasha, on his morning subway ride to Moscow Center, would read the daily accounts Tass, the Soviet news agency, had prepared for the Russian press.

As the proceedings played out, both men—the FBI counterintelligence agent who, after learning about the existence of Liberal's network in a decoded Soviet cable, had led the hunt for the spies, and the KGB handler who had run the network—began to wish for the same conclusion. Both hoped Julius and Ethel Rosenberg would confess.

Bob wanted the Rosenbergs to tell the Bureau everything they knew. He wanted to get on with his job, to chase down the operatives who had eluded him. He believed that with the Rosenbergs' cooperation, he could return to the cables, ferret out more clues, and at the end of this renewed chase he'd be able, he confidently predicted, "to arrest ten or fifteen more people."

Sasha, from his isolation a world away in the corridors of the Lubyanka, found himself reduced to imagining heartfelt conversations with his "dear old Libi and Ethel." What harm would a confession do? he would plead. The Americans can't touch us. Yatskov, myself—we're safe, beyond the enemy's clutches.

Both men, as they watched the trial move forward toward its inevitable conclusion, wanted the Rosenbergs to save themselves. The penalty for conspiracy to commit espionage could be death.

The trial was short, just three weeks. Only three witnesses were called to testify against the Rosenbergs—David and Ruth Greenglass, and Harry Gold.

Neither Julius nor Ethel Rosenberg would confess.

At eleven a.m. on March 29, 1951, after a single night's deliberation, the foreman read the unanimous verdict: Julius and Ethel Rosenberg and Morton Sobell were guilty as charged.

Judge Irving Kaufman announced that the sentencing would take place on April 5.

"THOSE EIGHT DAYS WERE AMONG the most difficult in my life," Sasha would recall.

Meredith was stunned. "I never wanted to get anyone in trouble," he would tell people, his voice nearly breaking with despair. He had consciously chosen a life of the mind, a world of cerebral puzzles and intellectual pleasures. But now he was caught up in something very real and very troubling, and he blamed his own vanity for goading him on. He did not want the spoils, the praise, not at this cost.

Bob, in his practical way, did what he felt he could by drafting a memo that Hoover would pass on to Judge Irving Kaufman. A death sentence for Julius Rosenberg "might be correct," but only if it was accompanied by the judge's announcing that it would be reduced if Rosenberg cooperated fully with the FBI. "No purpose," he argued, "would be achieved by sentencing Ethel Rosenberg to death."

On the morning of the sentencing, Judge Kaufman looked sternly down from his seat on the bench at the defendants, and then spoke.

"I believe your conduct in putting into the hands of the Russians the A-bomb, years before our best scientists predicted Russia would perfect the bomb, has already caused, in my opinion, the Communist aggression in Korea, with the resultant casualties exceeding fifty thousand, and who knows but what millions more innocent people may pay for the price of your treason? Indeed, by the cause of your betrayal, you undoubtedly have altered the course of history to the disadvantage of our country."

Morton Sobell received a thirty-year prison term.

Julius and Ethel Rosenberg were both condemned to die in the electric chair.

And both Bob and Meredith knew beyond any doubt the wrongness of Ethel Rosenberg's death sentence. *Christian name Ethel. Does not work.* They had seen the incontestable proof with their own eyes, the source unimpeachable. Only they had been ordered to keep this knowledge secret. If they were to betray what they knew, write a revealing letter to the judge, perhaps the president, or even slip an informed hint to a reporter, they would be committing treason. Their dilemma, in its broad challenges, they came to appreciate with a ghastly sense of recognition, was not unlike the one that Julius Rosenberg and the other operatives in the ring had faced when they had decided to work for the Soviet cause. Either they could throw everything over to follow a grand moral principle, care nothing about compromise, the opinion of others, reduce their lives to the one thing that mattered, or they could do nothing.

In the weeks, then months, that followed, as the appeals worked their tedious way through the courts, both Bob and Meredith tried to believe that the Rosenbergs would confess. They would save their own lives and in the process spare the two men who had so avidly hunted them. Neither of the men had any misgivings about rooting out traitors. Justice, they felt with a patriotic certainty, demanded that the Rosenbergs and the members of their ring be punished. But vengeance was something else entirely. And now the two friends were left grappling with a sophism that struck at the core of their own lives. They had embarked on their shared quest, determined to stop the progress of evil. But if they did nothing when they possessed the truth, if they allowed a woman, a mother of two young sons, to die, they would be reinforcing all that they knew was wrong. And with their inaction they would be condemning themselves to another sort of death sentence.

A Toast

AT EIGHT P.M. ON A warm June evening in 1953, Julius Rosenberg was strapped into the oak-paneled electric chair in the Sing Sing prison death chamber. One electrode was fastened to his leg, another covered the shaved crown of his head. The switch was thrown at 8:04. Two minutes later, he was pronounced dead.

A guard mopped up the urine that had collected under the seat. He used an ammonia solution, but its sharp smell was not sufficient to cloak the lingering odor of burning flesh.

Ethel Rosenberg was brought into the death chamber minutes later and strapped into the chair. At 8:11, 2,000 volts of electricity jolted her body, three times in rapid succession. But her heart remained beating, and so two additional surges were administered. At 8:16, she was finally dead.

Both died without making any confessions.

SASHA, BEREFT, BLAMED THE KGB. The spymasters should have taken the necessary steps to have helped the Rosenbergs escape. But if that had been too difficult to organize in time, then his country could have intervened at the trial. "The U.S.S.R. should have openly declared that Julius Rosenberg and Morton Sobell had passed on electronic secrets that were used in the struggle against Nazi Germany," he complained to his friend Anatoly after he had heard the horrible news. It would have told the Americans the truth: they were not atomic spies. And it would have sent a message to Libi, letting him know he was freed from any obligation to keep silent. His agent, his friend, could have confessed and saved his own life. As well as his wife's.

Bob heard the news in Mickey Ladd's office, where a direct line to Sing Sing had been installed. From his vantage point by the window, his eyes darted from the silent phone to the darkening sky closing in on the courtyard five floors below. He had lost all hope by the time the news arrived, but nevertheless it came as a shock.

As he was walking out of the office, one of the agents made a joke, something crude and grisly about burning flesh. Bob whirled on him, fist clenched. But then he realized there was no longer any point. And nothing he could do, no punch he could throw, would lessen the immense sense of guilt he felt. He turned and left without a word, suddenly feeling very alone.

Meredith could not sleep after he heard the news. He was sitting in his armchair in the living room, reading, when his wife, after realizing he wasn't in bed, had discovered him just before dawn. Blanche knew better than to ask why he was awake. She simply picked up her own book, sat in her armchair, and, pretending to read, kept her husband company as the light of the new day began to spread across the sky.

IT TOOK TWO YEARS, AND Bob put the blame on a series of bureaucratic indignities when he quit the Bureau in July 1955. The truth was, however, as he'd later acknowledge, that in the aftermath of the Rosenbergs' execution, his heart was no longer in his playing spy catcher. That was why, rather than head to the CIA, which had offered him a top-level position when the news of his departure from the Bureau had begun circulating around the intelligence community, he decided to take a job at the Veterans Administration. He had had enough of the heavy responsibilities that went hand-in-hand with the secret life.

As for Meredith, he, too, needed to get away. The memories of what he had done at Arlington Hall, and its unforeseen consequences, were too raw. In his private notebooks, home to a madcap scattering of thoughts big and small, one jotting stood out with an eerie prominence. "I hope the Rosenberg sons won't get on my trail and come around with a gun," he had written. Anyway, he made sure he was soon beyond their reach. When the chance came to work abroad, breaking codes at the Cheltenham facility in England, he took it without hesitation. He was eager to leave, to put a physical distance between himself and all the reminders of his complicitous silence.

Sasha, still the professional, his role as the handler of the Rosenberg ring still a secret from the opposition, returned to America just before the 1960 presidential election. He had diplomatic cover, but he was, as he had always been, a spy. In recognition of his work, he had been appointed the Washington, D.C., *rezident*, running operations out of the Soviet embassy on Sixteenth Street. And each day as he set in motion new covert schemes, as he sent his agents off to steal America's secrets, he did so determined to get vengeance for what a barbaric enemy had inflicted on his dear Libi and Ethel.

IN SEPTEMBER 1996, SASHA, NO longer a secret agent, just an old man getting used to his retirement, walked through the gravestones lined in orderly rows in Pinelawn Cemetery on Long Island. It took him a while to find what he was searching for.

It was a squarish gray stone, the name "Rosenberg" boxed with a black border. It bore two laconic inscriptions, carved parallel to each other.

ETHEL	JULIUS
Born: September 25, 1915	*Born: May 12, 1918*
Died: June 19, 1953	*Died: June 19, 1953*

There is a Russian custom to leave some soil taken from one's home on the grave of loved ones buried on distant shores. The gesture is meant to demonstrate that neither the many miles, nor the expanse of oceans, can separate the departed from the strong pull they continue to have on the heart.

In a small bag, Sasha had a handful of soil he had gathered from under an apple tree at his dacha, and he now spread the rich brown earth in front of the gravestone.

Standing at attention, he spoke as one soldier to two others. "Julius and Ethel," he began formally, "here I am at your graves to pay my respect." But his voice broke as he continued. "Forgive us for not having known how to save your lives," he pleaded.

When he was done, he still couldn't bring himself to leave. He stood there, hoping that somehow they had heard him, and somehow across the blackness of time and space they could convey to him that he was forgiven.

IT WAS THAT SAME YEAR when Bob and Meredith, both also in retirement, met up for dinner in a French restaurant in Washington. Bob was living in Arizona, playing a lot of golf, and Meredith, who had his notebooks and the *London Times* crossword puzzle to keep him busy, had moved to a condominium a short drive from the restaurant. Meredith came with Blanche, and Bob brought his fourth wife, Martha, an elegant Southern lady he had married in 1985 (the marriage to his third wife had been, by mutual agreement, a short-lived mistake). It was to be a social occasion, Bob had promised Martha, just two old friends sharing a friendly evening. He had told her not to worry, they wouldn't be going on about the past. But Martha felt her husband must have known they'd get around to it.

They wound up talking about nothing else, and Martha felt very estranged; she was not, as she'd tell people, "Bob's FBI wife." Names were being thrown about that meant nothing to her; she'd never paid too much attention to politics, she explained defensively. Her recollections of the entire evening were vague. Except for one small incident that left her puzzled at the time, and still stuck sharply in her memory years later.

It was toward the end of the meal, and Bob had looked across the table at Meredith and spontaneously raised the glass of scotch he'd been nursing. "A toast to old times," her husband had proposed. "To what we accomplished."

Meredith raised his wineglass as if to clink against Bob's, but abruptly he hesitated. Then he lowered his glass.

Bob slowly placed his back on the table, too.

The two men sat across from each other, staring, gripping their glasses tightly as if in anger, as a leaden silence descended between them.

What, Martha would always wonder, was that all about?

Notes on Sources

On a brisk, late October day in 2005, John F. Fox, the studious Ph.D. who served as the FBI's official historian, stood at the podium at the annual Symposium on Cryptologic History and launched into a riveting presentation. "One man," he began, "was tall, thin, a genius linguist at the NSA who was working on breaking coded telegrams sent from Soviet offices in the U.S. to Moscow. The other was a lawyer and cop, a young FBI supervisor recently transferred to Headquarters. . . ."

Nearly a decade later I received the transcript of this short speech describing the unique working partnership of Bob Lamphere, an FBI counterintelligence agent, and Meredith Gardner, the man who re-created the KGB codebook. It had been sent my way by a friend in the intelligence community who presciently thought "there might be a bigger story here." After my initial reading, I knew he was right. Here was a true-life espionage tale, a story of two very different and very unlikely friends who had teamed up to chase down the most consequential spy ring in American history—the atomic spies. And it was also the story of one of the nation's great, but barely known, intelligence triumphs, the long-running secret operation—hidden away at a former school for well-bred young women in Virginia—that had cracked the "unbreakable" Russian codes.

It was a tale, I quickly realized, I wanted to tell, and I began my own hunt to get at the previously unknown heart of the story and the people who had lived it.

This book is the result of that investigation. It is a narrative non-fiction spy tale. It has no ambitions to be a scholar's buttoned-down, footnoted tome. Still, it is no less a true story. It is no less a history. It is no less buttressed by a firm foundation of facts.

My covenant with the reader is this: When I relate certain events in this drama—whether on the world stage, behind the closed doors of secret intelligence, or in the minds and hearts of my characters—they are products of the historical record and my research. They can be substantiated by official government records, documents, and reports; bookshelves filled with volumes of Cold War histories; memoirs; personal notebooks; contemporaneous newspaper reports; previously transcribed conversations; and, not least, lengthy interviews I conducted with the close relatives of the main actors in this story (Bob Lamphere and Meredith Gardner are deceased).

Therefore, when quotation marks enclose any dialogue in this book, this is an indication that at least one of the principals was the source. Further, when a character reveals what he is thinking or feeling, I will have found this, too, in a memoir, a letter, a notebook, a transcript of a previously published conversation, or an interview.

Here, then, are some of the sources that helped me shape this story. It is a select, certainly not exhaustive, list, merely the key books and interviews that I relied on most often as I crafted this account. They are shared with the hope that any reader who continues to be curious about the tense Cold War spy-versus-spy chess game described in the preceding pages (or how I went about its molding) will find them to be rewarding starting points for further exploration.

At its narrative heart, this is a story about people who made history. Bob Lamphere's candid account, written with Tom Shachtman, of his career at the FBI and his friendship with Meredith Gardner was invaluable (*The FBI-KGB War: A Special Agent's Story*, New York: Random House, 1986). I also relied on his voluminous FBI Field Personnel Files (which Dr. Fox, the FBI historian whose insightful presentation had started my quest, kindly helped me obtain). I interviewed Bob's nephew, Theo Schaad, who wrote the self-published family history "A Lamphere Anthology," and Bob's sister-in-law, Phyllis Lamphere; they also provided several of the photographs reproduced in this book. And I sat in an apartment in Richmond, Virginia, and spoke at length with Bob's gracious and elegant widow, Martha. Further, Richard Rhodes, whose own magisterial histories of the events surrounding the manufacture of both the atomic and the hydrogen bomb were essential sources throughout the writing of this book (*The Making of the Atomic Bomb*, New York: Simon & Schuster Paperbacks, 2012; and *Dark Sun*, New York: Touchstone, 1996), has posted the transcript of the thoughtful, wide-ranging interview he'd conducted in Arizona with a long-retired Bob Lamphere in three parts on the Web, *Voices of the Manhattan Project* (http://www.manhattanprojectoralvoices .org/oral-histories/Robert-lamphere-interview). Bob Lamphere also appeared in an on-screen interview in the PBS program *Secrets, Lies, and Atomic Spies*, which first aired on February 5, 2002 (http://www .pbs.org/wgbh/nova/transcript/2904_venona.html).

Meredith Gardner was too guarded to publish a memoir. However, I met with his son, Arthur, and daughter-in-law, Michele, in their comfortable home in Wisconsin, and they told me many insightful stories about him and Blanche, his wife. They also generously shared letters, postcards, and the truly fascinating gray notebooks Meredith had kept over the years as a sort of diary of his thoughts and widely varied interests; the Gardner family photographs that are reproduced here were graciously provided by them. Other insights into Meredith's work and personality can be found in Peter Wright, *Spy Catcher: The Candid Autobiography of a Senior Intelligence Officer* (New York: Viking, 1987); Robert Louis Benson and Michael Warner, editors, *Venona: Soviet Espionage and the American Response 1939–1957* (Washington, D.C.: National Security Agency and the Central Intelligence Agency, 1996); and several documents the NSA had posted on its website, including

William Crowell's "Remembrances of Venona" (http://www
.theblackvault.com/documents/nsa/venona/venona_remember
.html) and his "Introductory History of Venona" (http://www
.theblackvault.com/documents/nsa/venona/monographs/mono-
graph-1.html), as well as the Agency's untitled official history of
Venona, declassified in 2004 and available on its website. There is
a specific "Meredith Gardner Page" on the NSA website that was
established after his induction into the agency's Hall of Honor in
2004, and its Cryptologic Almanac 50th Anniversary Series in-
cludes "Polyglot: The Meredith Gardner Story," declassified in
2011, and this, too, is available on the website (https:www.nsa
.gov/). Senator Daniel Patrick Moynihan included some perceptive
remarks about Meredith in the *Congressional Record* on July 12, 1999
(*Congressional Record*, Washington, D.C.: U.S. Senate and Government Printing Office). The obituary by David Stout that appeared
in the *New York Times* on August 18, 2002, is an absorbing account
of a life well lived ("Meredith Gardner, 89, Dies; Broke Code in
Rosenberg Case"), as is his wife's in the *Washington Post* on September 3, 2005. And one of the most revelatory articles on the Gardners
was published in the University of Wisconsin Alumni Magazine
(Candice Gaukel Andrews, "The Code-Breaker and the G-Man,"
On Wisconsin, Winter 2002).

I was able to re-create the tradecraft as well as the personal
history of Sasha, the Soviet handler who worked out of the New
York KGB station, in large part due to his chatty, albeit often self-
serving, memoir: Alexander Feklisov, *The Man Behind the Rosenbergs* (New York: Enigma Books, 2001). I was further assisted
in telling the Moscow Center side of this story by the extensive
top-secret material Vasili Mitrokhin smuggled out of the KGB
foreign intelligence archives (Christopher Andrew and Vasili Mitrokhin, *The Sword and the Shield: The Mitrokhin Archives and the
KGB*, New York: Basic Books, 2001). Also valuable were the eight
thick notebooks and loose pages kept by Alexander Vassiliev as
he researched through KGB archival material, indexed and cross-

referenced by the Wilson Center under the direction of John Earl Haynes, and available on the Internet through the Cold War International History Project. Additionally, I made much use of Alexander Weinstein and Alexander Vassiliev, *The Haunted Wood* (New York: Modern Library, 1999); John Earl Haynes, Harvey Klehr, and Alexander Vassiliev, *Spies: The Rise and Fall of the KGB in America* (New Haven: Yale University Press, 2009); and Christopher Andrew and Oleg Gordievsky, *KGB: The Inside Story of Its Operations From Lenin to Gorbachev* (New York: HarperCollins, 1992). The extent of the Soviet penetration of the Manhattan Project was well documented in the formerly classified papers supplied by the KGB to the Russian Institute for History of Science and Technology and published by the Institute in its journal (V. P. Visgin, ed., "At the Source of the Soviet Atomic Project: The Role of Espionage, 1941–1946," in *Problems in the History of Science and Technology*, 1992). And I found the most authoritative as well as comprehensive history of the Soviet efforts to build an atomic weapon to be David Holloway, *Stalin and the Bomb* (New Haven: Yale University Press, 1994).

As for the depiction of the spies in this story who worked with their Russian handlers, there is a small library of books that helped inform my portraits (writing about the Rosenberg case, for example, is a cottage industry for dueling historians). However, I found myself most frequently returning to Sam Roberts's elegantly written and carefully researched *The Brother* (New York: Random House, 2001) and Ronald Radosh and Joyce Milton's definitive *The Rosenberg File* (New Haven: Yale University Press, 1997). Ted Hall's story is told with verve in a groundbreaking investigative account by Joseph Albright and Marcia Kunstel, *Bombshell: The Secret Story of America's Unknown Atomic Spy Conspiracy* (New York: Times Books, 1997); their book also offers a very readable analysis of encoding and code-breaking techniques that greatly influenced my discussions of those topics. As for Klaus Fuchs, I found his story best told in H. Montgomery Hyde, *The Atomic Spies* (New York:

Atheneum, 1989), which also helped to shape my understanding of the Gouzenko defection; Robert Chadwell Williams, *Karl Fuchs, Atomic Spy* (Cambridge, Mass.: Harvard University Press, 1987); and Mike Rossiter, *The Spy Who Changed the World* (London: Headline, 2015). Elizabeth Bentley gives a fascinating, if dubious, account of her life in *Out of Bondage* (New York: Ballantine Books, 1951), while more objective histories are Kathryn S. Olmsted, *Red Spy Queen: A Biography of Elizabeth Bentley* (Chapel Hill: University of North Carolina Press, 2002); and Lauren Kessler, *Clever Girl: Elizabeth Bentley, the Spy Who Ushered in the McCarthy Era* (New York: HarperPerennial, 2003). A good overview of the KGB's activities can be found in Katherine A. S. Sibley, *Red Spies in America: Stolen Secrets and the Dawn of the Cold War* (Lawrence: University Press of Kansas, 2004).

The telling of this story, however, would not have been possible without the declassification of the approximately 2,900 Venona translations, starting in 1995. These cables—as well as perceptive explanatory monographs by Robert Louis Benson—are available on the NSA's official Venona site (https://www.nsa.gov/news-features/declassified-documents/venona/index.shtml). Meredith Gardner's Special Reports are also available at this site. Further, Mercyhurst College's Institute for Intelligence Studies has facilitated analysis of these cables by turning them into fully searchable Microsoft Word documents, available online (https://www.wilsoncenter.org). The CIA has also issued a cogent summary of the key Venona cables, "Selected Venona Messages" (https://www.cia.gov/library/center-for-the-study-of-intelligence). The story of how these cables came to be declassified is told in Daniel Patrick Moynihan's "Report of the Commission on Protecting and Reducing Government Secrecy; Appendix A: The Experience of 'The Bomb,'" available through the U.S. Government Printing Office (1997). There have also been numerous books written on the Venona decrypts and what they reveal. I found the most valuable to be Nigel West's comprehensive *Venona: The Greatest Secret of the Cold War* (London: HarperCollins, 1999);

John Earl Haynes and Harvey Klehr, *Venona: Decoding Soviet Espionage in America* (New Haven: Yale University Press, 2000); Robert L. Benson, *The Venona Story* (Washington, D.C.: CreateSpace Independent Publishing Platform, 2012); and Herbert Romerstein and Eric Breindel, *The Venona Secrets: The Definitive Exposé of Soviet Espionage in America* (Washington, D.C.: Regnery History, 2014).

A basic comprehension of code writing was necessary to understand the accomplishments of Meredith Gardner and the other code breakers working at Arlington Hall. In addition to the numerous NSA documents available online at the agency's website (many of which I have cited above), my admittedly rudimentary knowledge was informed by David Kahn's exhaustive and definitive *The Code-Breakers* (New York: Scribner, 1996); Stephen Budiansky, *Battle of Wits: The Complete Story of Codebreaking in World War II* (New York: Free Press, 2002); Katharine L. Swift, "How the Germans Broke a U.S. Code," declassified by the NSA in 2012 and available online at the NSA website; and Francis Litterio, "Why Are One-Time Pads Perfectly Secure?" found at web.archive.org.

Also, the writing of this book was greatly influenced by the discussions I had with former members of the intelligence community, several of whom knew Meredith Gardner and were also directly aware of the singular importance of Bob Lamphere's contributions. They spoke to me in off-the-record conversations, and their identities remain protected by this agreement. Further, there was another source that, however obliquely, served as a constant influence as I wrote this story. The critic Leslie Fiedler has written with an iconoclastic insight into the fictional characters whose unlikely yet deep friendships have become cornerstones of American literature. This espionage story of two real-life heroes whose bond was defined and yet also reinforced by their differences owes a narrative debt to Fiedler's entertaining and perceptive body of work.

A final thought: When I began work on this book my narrative ambitions were to share a spy drama, a tale of friendship, courage, genius, and regret. Yet as I researched and wrote the book during the presidential election campaign of 2016 and well into the first year of the new presidency, this Cold War history took on an unexpected resonance. And a chilling prescience. "The past," as Faulkner warned, "is never dead; it is not even past."

Following are the principal sources for each chapter of this book.

Sources

Prologue: Robert J. Lamphere and Tom Shachtman, *The FBI-KGB War* [War]; Martha Lamphere interview [ML]; Theo Schaad interview [TS]; Phyllis Lamphere interview [PL]; Robert Lamphere FBI Personnel Records [Personnel]; FBI File 65–58238, Espionage R, Ladd to Director Hoover, 1/8/53 [Ladd]; Sam Roberts, *The Brother* [Roberts]; Ronald Radosh and Joyce Milton, *The Rosenberg File* [RF]; Arthur Gardner interview [AG]; Alexander Feklisov, *The Man Behind the Rosenbergs* [Feklisov]; "Secrets, Lies, and Atomic Spies," PBS transcript [PBS]; Peter Wright, *Spy Catcher* [Wright]; *Voices of the Manhattan Project*, Robert Lamphere's interview [Voices].

Chapter One: War; Personnel; ML; PL; TS; Theo Schaad, "A Lamphere Anthology" [Anthology].

Chapter Two: Personnel; War; ML; TS; PL; http: waspfinalflight.blogspot.com /geri-elder-lamphere-nyman; neddybee.blogspot.com/geri-elder-lamphere -nyman.

Chapter Three: Arthur and Michele Gardner interview [AG]; Wright; Meredith Gardner's *Washington Post* obituary (August 18, 2002); the NSA's "Polyglot: The Meredith Gardner Story" [Polyglot]; NSA declassified untitled history of Venona [History]; Benson and Warner, editors, *Venona: Soviet Espionage and the American Response 1939–1957* [B&W]; University of Texas Archives; Candice Gaukel Andrews, "The Code-Breaker and the G-Man" [Andrews]; University of Wisconsin Archives.

Chapter Four: William Crowell, "Remembrances of Venona" [Remembrances]; Genevieve Feinstein, "Women in Cryptological History," www.nsa.gov /about/cryptologic_heritage/women [Feinstein]; History; B&W; Robert L. Benson, *The Venona Story* [Story]; Nigel West, *Venona* [West]; John Earl Haynes and Harvey Klehr, *Venona: Decoding Soviet Espionage in America* [Decoding]; U.S. Army Intelligence and Security Command History Office, "Arlington Hall from Coeds to Codewords," http://fas.org/irp/agency /inscom/trail/pdf [Coeds]; Stephen Budiansky, *Battle of Wits* [Wits]; Compendia Virginica, "Social Graces and Espionage,"*Virginia Living Magazine,*

April 22, 2011 [Graces]; War; AG; David Kahn, *The Code-Breakers* [Kahn]; Allen Weinstein and Alexander Vassiliev, *The Haunted Wood* [Haunted]; "How the U.S. Cracked Japan's 'Purple Encryption Machine' at the Dawn of World War II," gizmo.com; Joseph Albright and Marcia Kunstel, *Bombshell: The Secret Story of America's Unknown Atomic Spy Conspiracy* [Bombshell]; Andrews.

Chapter Five: History; West; Haunted; Remembrances; B&W; Kahn; Feinstein; Albert L. Weeks, *Russia's Life-Saver: Lend-Lease Aid to the U.S.S.R. in World War II* (Lanham, Md.: Lexington Books, 2010).

Chapter Six: Decoding; West; B&W; Kahn; Bombshell; Haunted; Francis Litterio, "Why Are One-Time Pads Perfectly Secure?" [Secure]; [AG].

Chapter Seven: War; ML; Personnel; B&W; West; Haunted; Bombshell; Decoding; Feklisov; John Earl Haynes, Harvey Klehr, and Alexander Vassiliev, *Spies: The Rise and Fall of the KGB in America* [Rise]; Christopher Andrew and Oleg Gordievsky, *KGB: The Inside Story of Its Operations From Lenin to Gorbachev* [KGB]; A. S. Sibley, *Red Spies in America and the Dawn of the Cold War* [Sibley]; H. Montgomery Hyde, *The Atomic Spies* [Hyde]; Elizabeth Bentley, *Out of Bondage* [Out]; Kathryn S. Olmsted, *Red Spy Queen* [Queen]; Lauren Kessler, *Clever Girl* [Clever].

Chapter Eight: Feklisov; KGB; Rise; Haunted; Christopher Andrew and Vasili Mitrokhin, *The Sword and the Shield: The Mitrokhin Archives and KGB* [Sword]; Sibley; Herbert Romerstein and Eric Breindel, *The Venona Secrets: The Definitive Exposé of Soviet Espionage in America* [Exposé]; Richard Rhodes, *The Atomic Bomb* [Bomb]; Richard Rhodes, *Dark Sun* [Dark]; David Holloway, *Stalin and the Bomb* [Holloway]; "Problems in the History of Science and Technology," *Journal of Russian Institute for History of Sciences and Technology* [Journal]; B&W.

Chapter Nine: Feklisov; Sword; KGB; Bombshell; Exposé; War; Haunted.

Chapter Ten: Feklisov; War; Sword; KGB; B&W; Journal; Holloway; Bomb; Dark.

Chapter Eleven: Polyglot; Story; B&W; West; Decoding; Bombshell; Remembrances; History; Secure; David M. Glantz and Jonathan M. House, *When Titans Clashed: How the Red Army Stopped Hitler* (Lawrence: University Press of Kansas, 1995); War; Out; Queen; Clever; Sword; KGB.

Chapter Twelve: War, Personnel; Anthology; TS; PL; ML; Sword; KGB; Sibley; Haunted; Clever; Queen; West; Voices; Dark.

Chapter Thirteen: West; Story; Polyglot; History; B&W; War; Haunted; Bombshell; Robert Edwards, *White Death: Russia's War on Finland, 1939–40* (London: Weidenfeld & Nicolson, 2006); Wright; Randy Rezabek, "TICOM: The Last Great Secret of World War II," *Intelligence and National Security* (27:4, 2012);

James Bamford, *Body of Secrets: Anatomy of the Ultra-Secret National Security Organization* (New York: Anchor Books, 2002); Secure.

Chapter Fourteen: Katherine L. Swift, "How the Germans Broke a U.S. Code" [Swift]; History; Story; Polyglot; B&W; Bombshell; West; Decoding; War; AG; interviews with intelligence sources [Intel]; Meredith Gardner Special Reports [Reports]; FBI Report 65–43826–3, 10/18/48 [65]; Kahn; Venona decrypted telegrams [Decrypt]; Haunted.

Chapter Fifteen: War; ML; TS; PL; Personnel; West; Bombshell; History; Polyglot; Story.

Chapter Sixteen: War; History; Story; Polyglot; B&W; West; Bombshell; Decoding; Voices; Meredith Gardner NSA page [Page]; Feinstein; Coeds; Graces; AG; Dark; Feklisov; Journal; Holloway.

Chapter Seventeen: War; AG; West; History; Story; Polyglot; B&W; Decoding; Exposé; Reports; Decrypt; Dark; Holloway.

Chapter Eighteen: War; Personnel; Reports; Decrypt; Sword; KGB; Feklisov; Haunted; Bombshell; Sibley; RF; Roberts; West; Journal.

Chapter Nineteen: Feklisov; RF; Roberts; Sword; KGB; Haunted; Journal; Dark; War.

Chapter Twenty: War; Voices; Personnel; ML; TS; West; Haunted; Decoding; KGB; Sword; B&W; Feklisov; RF; Roberts; Sibley.

Chapter Twenty-One: AG; War; History; Story; Polyglot; Dark; Personnel; West; Sibley; RF; Roberts; Decrypt; Reports; Feklisov; KGB; Sword.

Chapter Twenty-Two: Reports; Decrypt; War; West; Haunted; Exposé; History; Story; Polyglot; AG; Decoding; RF; Dark; Feklisov.

Chapter Twenty-Three: Dark; War; Bomb; Haunted; Sibley; Personnel; Holloway; Decrypt; Bombshell; Sword; KGB; Journal; West.

Chapter Twenty-Four: Feklisov; Dark; Haunted; Hyde; Robert Chadwell Williams, *Karl Fuchs, Atomic Spy* [Williams]; Mike Rossiter, *The Spy Who Changed the World* [World]; West; Decrypt; War; RF; Sword; KGB; Rise; History; Story; Polyglot; B&W.

Chapter Twenty-Five: War; Dark; West; Decrypt; Bomb; George T. Mazuzan and Samuel Walker, *Controlling the Atom: The Beginning of Nuclear Regulation, 1948–1962* (Oakland: University of California Press, 1985); RF; Roberts; Hyde; Williams; World; Haunted; Sibley; Voices; AG; Personnel; ML.

Chapter Twenty-Six: War; ML; TS; Personnel; Hyde; World; Williams; Dark; Bombshell; Haunted; KGB; Sword; B&W; History; Story; Polyglot; Reports; Decrypt; Feklisov; Journal; Holloway; RF; Roberts.

Chapter Twenty-Seven: War; Personnel; Hyde; Dark; Bombshell; KGB; Sword; World; Williams; Haunted; RF; Voices; Decrypt; Reports.

Chapter Twenty-Eight: Decrypt; West; Haunted; Decoding; History; Dark; RF; War; Clever; Queen; Out; Williams; World; Hyde; Voices.

Chapter Twenty-Nine: British Ministry of Justice website, Wormwood Scrubs, https://www.justice.gov.uk/ ... /wormwood; War; Voices; Dark; Hyde; Williams; World; RF; Haunted; Sibley; Feklisov; KGB; Sword; Bombshell.

Chapter Thirty: War; Hyde; Dark; Haunted; Williams; RF; Roberts; Personnel; Bomb; KGB; Sword; Journal.

Chapter Thirty-One: Feklisov; Sword; KGB.

Chapter Thirty-Two: War; Dark; RF; Hyde; Haunted; Personnel; AG; Sibley; West; Decrypt; Reports; B&W; Roberts; Exposé; Decoding.

Chapter Thirty-Three: Intel; Bombshell; War; Personnel; West; Haunted; Dark; RF; Exposé; Allen M. Hornblum, *Acres of Skin: Human Experiments at Holmesburg Prison* (London: Routledge, 1998).

Chapter Thirty-Four: Roberts; RF; War; Dark; Personnel; West; Haunted; Sibley; Feklisov; Journal; KGB; Sword.

Chapter Thirty-Five: War; Dark; RF; Roberts; Bombshell; Sibley; Exposé; Personnel; Decrypt.

Chapter Thirty-Six: War; ML; TS; RF; Roberts; Dark; Personnel; FBI Memo 65–53826–80; Decrypt.

Chapter Thirty-Seven: War; Decrypt; West; Dark; Decoding; Exposé; Bombshell; Haunted; RF; Roberts; B&W; Reports; "Gardner Special Reports," FBI website.

Chapter Thirty-Eight: RF; Roberts; War; AG; Decrypts; Reports.

Epilogue: War; ML; RF; Roberts; Voices; Wright; AG; Feklisov; Gardner Notebook #7, private collection of Gardner family.

Acknowledgments

It would seem that every author whose book takes him out to Los Angeles hears before too long the same hoary bit of wisdom. Writing, the producer—or the studio executive, or the development person— states knowingly, is a solitary endeavor. Making a movie, however, is a communal enterprise.

While they are no doubt correct about what it takes to make a movie, experience has taught me that they're far off the mark when it comes to writing a book. Sure, you sit at your desk by yourself. But bringing a book out into the world is by no means a solitary occupation.

As soon as I got the idea for this book, Lynn Nesbit, my literary agent and friend for the past thirty years, became involved. And I counted on her wisdom and guidance throughout the entire process. It is a genuine blessing to know she is always in my corner. Hannah Davey, Lynn's assistant at Janklow & Nesbit, was also always around to bail me out of the seemingly inevitable publishing crises.

Jonathan Burnham has been the publisher for my last four books at HarperCollins and he's been wonderfully supportive—a wise, well-read, and droll voice. And a friend, to boot. This is my first book with Jonathan Jao as my editor, and his arrival into my literary life has been a blessing. He's thoughtful, conscientious, and he improves all the prose he touches. I owe him a large debt. Sofia Groopman, the assistant editor who worked on this book, was also invaluable in helping it make its way through the process in a timely fashion.

For over three decades Bob Bookman has been my friend and a wise counselor, leading me with kindness and determination through the Hollywood jungle. I'm particularly grateful for his shrewd reading of an early draft of this book. Also in Hollywood, I've counted on my attorney, Alan Hergott, to guide me safely through stormy weather.

I have also benefited from a long relationship with *Vanity Fair*. Graydon Carter and Dana Brown's worldly intelligence and kindness of spirit have been a source of encouragement as I wrote this book, and simultaneously wrote for the magazine.

And at the end of a long day's writing, there are friends I lean on. I'd be lost without my sister, Marcy; she's always there for me. And there's also Susan and David Rich; Irene and Phil Werber; John Leventhal; Bruce Taub; Betsy and Len Rappoport; Sarah and Bill Rauch; Pat, Bob, and Marc Lusthaus; Nick Jarecki; Claudie and Andrew Skonks; Destin Coleman; Daisy Miller; Beth DeWoody; Arline Mann and Bob Katz; Ken Lipper; Elizabeth Bagley; and Sarah Colleton. Sadly, just days after I had written "the end," Bob Mitchell died. He was a brave and tenacious man, as well as a good friend.

My children—Tony, Anna, and Dani—are all grown, young adults on their way into the world from their colleges and grad schools. Their accomplishments fill me with great and sustaining pride.

And, not least, I have to thank Ivana.

Index